# DANIELS' RUNNING FORMULA

## JACK DANIELS, PhD
The State University of New York at Cortland

**Human Kinetics**

To my daughters, Audra Marie and Sarah Tupper, who keep me youthful and zealous about the future, and my loving wife, Nancy Jo, whose presence is a blessing from God.

**Library of Congress Cataloging-in-Publication Data**

Daniels, Jack, 1933-
    Daniels' Running Formula / Jack Daniels.
        p.   cm.
    Includes index.
    ISBN 0-88011-735-4 (pbk.)
    1. Running.   2. Running--Training      I.   Title
    GV1062.D36   1998
    796.42--DC21                                                        98-13356
                                                                        CIP
ISBN: 0-88011-735-4

Photos on pages 11, 128, 156, 163, 188, and 262 by Tom Roberts. Photos on pages 13, 34, 40, 43, 59, 86, 105, 115, 120, 132, 228, 242, and 260 courtesy of the author.

**Acquisitions Editor:** Martin Barnard; **Developmental Editor:** Andrew Smith; **Assistant Editors:** John Wentworth and Phil Natividad; **Editorial Assistant:** Laura Seversen; **Copyeditor:** Cynthia Hastings; **Proofreader:** Jim Burns; **Indexer:** Prottsman Indexing; **Graphic Designer:** Nancy Rasmus; **Graphic Artist:** Tom Roberts; **Photo Editor:** Boyd LaFoon; **Cover Designer:** Jack Davis; **Photographer (cover):** © Claus Andersen; **Illustrator:** Tom Roberts; **Printer:** United Graphics

Printed in the United States of America                    10  9  8  7  6  5

**Human Kinetics**
Web site: www.humankinetics.com

*United States:* Human Kinetics
P.O. Box 5076
Champaign, IL 61825-5076
800-747-4457
e-mail: humank@hkusa.com

*Canada:* Human Kinetics
475 Devonshire Road, Unit 100
Windsor, ON N8Y 2L5
800-465-7301 (in Canada only)
e-mail: orders@hkcanada.com

*Europe:* Human Kinetics
Units C2/C3 Wira Business Park
West Park Ring Road
Leeds LS16 6EB, United Kingdom
+44 (0)113 278 1708
e-mail: hk@hkeurope.com

*Australia:* Human Kinetics
57A Price Avenue
Lower Mitcham, South Australia 5062
08 8277 1555
e-mail: liahka@senet.com.au

*New Zealand:* Human Kinetics
P.O. Box 105-231, Auckland Central
09-523-3462
e-mail: hkp@ihug.co.nz

# Contents

# Part III: Racing

# Foreword

Over the last thirty plus years, there has been a significant amount of research in exercise physiology and how it applies to running. This research was spurred on by two main influences:

1. the power of professional sports and the millions of dollars generated by them, and
2. the Cold War, during which the athletic field became another battlefield.

Consequently, there are numerous "experts" who have devoted their lives to exercise physiology as it pertains to runners. If I were to choose the most knowledgeable person in this area, I would have a hard time coming up with anyone more qualified than Jack Daniels.

Jack's background gives some hint of how he acquired his knowledge. He was first an elite athlete, competing in two Olympics and three World Championships in the modern pentathlon. He subsequently turned his attention to coaching and research and has written numerous articles and books on the physiological aspects of running. Jack became dedicated to testing champion runners such as Jim Ryun and Gerry Lindgren back in the 1960s. He continued testing most of the top American distance runners through the 1980s when he served as the full time exercise physiologist for the elite Nike track club, Athletics West, which included athletes such as Mary Slaney, Joan Benoit Samuelson, and myself.

I worked closely with Jack during this time and was amazed by his knowledge and how it directly applied to my training. When I first met him in 1981, he ran me through several tests to determine my potential times at different distances in order to help me to train appropriately. His predictions were unbelievably accurate! My only regret in working with Jack during this period was that I didn't follow his advice to cut back my workload when he thought I was overtraining. Unfortunately, he was right, as my running health deteriorated quickly by the mid-1980s.

Since that time, Jack has moved into full time coaching, continuing to apply his awesome store of knowledge about the human body. He has coached SUNY Cortland's women's cross country team to eight national titles—including 25 individual champions and 110 All-Americans—and has helped Jerry Lawson to become America's premier marathoner of the 1990s.

Whether you are a beginning runner or an aspiring Olympian, Jack Daniels' formulas can also help you achieve your full potential with the least risk of injury or illness along the way.

Yours in running,

Alberto Salazar

# Preface

There are many good personal reasons for taking up the sport of running: to improve health, to look better, to relieve stress, and to spend some time with friends and family. Some people also take up running to be part of a team, and look for satisfaction and accomplishment through competition. The great thing about distance running is that you don't need to be big or fast to achieve success—just determined. Some of the best runners in the world were cut from football, soccer, or other sports teams because the coaches thought they were too small or too slow. I was never a runner in my youth; I took up running in my early 20s to compete in modern pentathlon. I was pretty good at four of the five events but had to learn how to run if I was going to make it to the elite level of competition. This proved to be easier said than done.

When I was struggling to become a better runner, there was nowhere to turn for sound advice. I even searched the grocery checkout lines, but couldn't find anything that promised to improve my mile time by 20 seconds in 20 days. I attended coaching conventions to learn more about training, but most of the so-called experts were simply those coaches who happened to have a good runner at their school that year. Sadly, this was perceived to qualify them as instant authorities on training, and in later years their expertise suddenly extended to jumping events or whatever event their newly-recruited athlete excelled at.

Typically, these experts presented a standard week of training for their star athlete; unfortunately these programs weren't applicable or helpful to anyone else. Seldom did I hear about sound principles of training: how to set up a season program, how much or how fast to train, and how programs differ—why one method of training might suit some runners while a different approach might be better for others. Throughout my career as an Olympic athlete, exercise scientist, and running coach, I've been looking for answers to these questions, as are most coaches and runners today.

The results of my lifelong search are found in this book. I've put together training wisdom gleaned from years of coaching, advising, and studying people from all walks of life—including runners of all ages and abilities. I've been fortunate enough to work with some of the best runners in the world, including Jim Ryun, Tom Von Ruden, Tracy Smith, Lisa and Ken Martin, Gerry Lindgren, Jack Bacheler, Doug Padilla, Alberto Salazar, Joan Benoit Samuelson, Chris Fox, Penny Werthner, my wonderful wife, Nancy Jo, and many others. They provided me with invaluable training insights on which I still rely heavily. With this book I have an opportunity to pass these insights on to you.

I hope that the principles and programs in this book will answer all of your training questions, or at least will equip you with the tools to answer them yourself. My philosophy of training surfaces throughout the book: You should try to get the maximum benefit out of training with the least amount of discomfort possible. The chapters are written with this in mind.

Part I provides information on the principles of training, helps you set training and racing goals, and lets you determine your starting point for optimal training. The training tables found in these chapters are extremely valuable—they take all the guesswork out of pacing by providing exactly the right intensities for your current level of ability. Part II outlines my four phases of training, and shows you how to put the phases together in a program to meet your goals. I've also included a ranking system for the weeks within a training phase, so you can customize a program based on the number of weeks in your season or the amount of time left until your target race. Part III gives you everything you need to know to run your best race: tailored programs, intensity guidelines, peaking schedules, nutritional advice, and racing strategies.

Once you understand your abilities, the basic principles of training, and how to tailor your training to meet your goals, you can become the best runner possible for the time and effort you put into the sport. Running is a challenge. It should also be rewarding, and, believe it or not, it can be enjoyable—both for coaches and for every person who takes up the sport.

Finally, I want to offer my sincere gratitude to Graham Covington and Harry Turvey, who prodded me for over two years to compile my thoughts about training and helped me come up with a method of presenting the training schemes found in this book.

# The Ingredients of Success

*You will know when you are ready.*

There are four key ingredients for success in distance running, or any other pursuit in life, for that matter. In order, they are inherent ability, motivation, opportunity, and direction.

# Inherent Ability

It is easy to see the important role that genetics (inherent ability) plays in becoming successful in sports. Picture in your mind an Olympic female gymnast, a male shot-putter, an NBA center, and a jockey. You undoubtedly see a petite, trim girl; a large, powerful man; an extremely tall man; and a short, lightweight man or woman. These are simply the necessary body types for success in women's gymnastics, shot putting, rebounding basketballs, and riding a winner in the Kentucky Derby. Such athletes don't achieve their anatomical structure through training; they are born with bodies that adapted perfectly to their sport. The individuals have little control over their basic body designs. Their genetic makeup was inherited from their parents.

Now think about a successful distance runner. What do you see? Someone who is short, tall, muscular, or very lean? There have been, and still are, outstanding runners with a variety of body types, but physiologically they are as similar in their anatomic design as are female gymnasts or NBA centers. You can't see the physiologic characteristics that make some distance runners great and others not so great, but there are inherent qualities that separate one runner from another, just as surely as body size and composition are factors in shot putting or horse racing.

Genetic ability is the first ingredient of success. You have a certain amount given to you at birth on which you can, of course, improve, but the potential is set for you and it is up to you to do what you will with your particular gifts.

# Motivation

Motivation to use your God-given talent is the second ingredient of success, and must come from within. It is easy for a basketball coach to be motivated for a seven-foot-tall high school player, but if this seven-footer wants to be an artist rather than a basketball player, chances are that success will not be realized on the court.

© Ken Lee

Successful distance runners come in many shapes and sizes, but there are underlying physiological characteristics that they all share.

I believe that there are four kinds of distance runners:

1. Those who have inherent ability and the motivation to use that ability
2. Those who have the ability to do well, but are not motivated to use their ability
3. Those who are lacking in ability, but have great motivation to achieve success
4. Those who lack ability and are not motivated

The first group of people is made up of champions—they almost always perform well. The second group can be referred to as "coach frustrators." The coach sees the potential but little or no desire on the part of the athlete to use it. "If only you had some desire, you could be a champion," is often heard from the coach. The coach is motivated for the athlete, but intrinsic motivation is lacking and the coach becomes frustrated. The third type of people often can be categorized as "self-frustrators." This group has tremendous motivation to be great runners but doesn't have the necessary genetic makeup. These runners usually will do anything the coach says; they try every workout imaginable and run as much mileage as can be fit into a day. They are candidates for overtraining and for being beaten by the second category of runners. You probably have seen these two types in action—the "natural" athlete, who seldom trains, eats, or sleeps right but who still beats the highly motivated, nongifted, frustrated runner. It is sad but true.

I don't think coaches should remind Type 2 runners about their lack of motivation any more often than they castigate Type 3 runners for their lack of ability (which is almost never). It is very possible that the Type 2 runner is running only because of coach, family, or peer pressure. The coach should discuss options with the runner and the possibility that running may not be the right place to be spending time, even if there is obvious talent for such a pursuit. Having the coach on your side, in an understanding role, may go a long way in converting a Type 2 into a Type 1 individual, a transformation that is impossible for a Type 3 runner.

Finally, there are the no-ability, no-motivation individuals, who usually never even try running, nor would they be any good if they did give it a shot. Keep in mind, however, that Type 4 runners may be Type 1 people in some other, possibly more important, aspect of life.

# Opportunity

The third ingredient of success is opportunity. Opportunity includes a variety of factors, paramount among which may well be the environment in which you grow up or live. Someone born with outstanding ability for downhill skiing, but living in a warm, southern climate, may never have the opportunity to develop in the sport. Even if highly motivated (through movies and videos, for example), the person may fail due to inaccessible facilities.

Swimming pools are not available to much of our society. Horseback riding and jumping, yachting, and skating are unavailable sports for most individuals. A talented and motivated golfer or tennis player may see success become unattainable because a warm geographic location is not available during the important years of development.

Certainly, there are always individuals who, for one reason or another, break away from a prohibitive environment and unexpectedly achieve success in a particular sport. Still, the opportunity to participate in a sport is a very important ingredient of success.

In addition to having the climate, facilities, and equipment necessary for the pursuit of any given sport, an athlete also needs opportunity in terms of time and money. For example, merely living in a hotbed of golf doesn't guarantee all individuals access to the sport.

Finally, the opportunity to compete in a chosen sport is also important. A young fencer who truly loves the sport of fencing, has a good teacher, and possesses adequate time for training may still find the road to success a long one if there are few or no other fencers nearby with whom to compete.

Opportunity is an important ingredient of success, yet it is difficult for us to perceive it as a limiting factor in our affluent society. Nevertheless, it often is. In the United States, the business of providing opportunity in the sport of running is left primarily up to high schools and colleges. Schools with adequate finances have track facilities, good equipment, and travel expenses. Perhaps the greatest obstacle many aspiring runners face is the lack of opportunity outside the framework of the schools.

The lack of clubs for post-school competition also hurts American runners at the very time when they need the most support—in their early 20s. Another drawback of a school-based support system is the lack of continuity of coaching. A high school athlete may have more than one coach during early development, and may attend a community college before finishing at a four-year university; the athlete may run for three or four different coaches before reaching the best running years. American runners face a difficult task: consider the fact that learning a new training system often takes a full season to accomplish, and many athletes are not in a stable coaching environment for more than a couple of years at a time. Without steady, consistent guidance, many American runners falter and never have the opportunity to develop their full potential.

# Direction

Direction, the final ingredient of success, refers to a coach, a teacher, or a training plan that can be followed. Of the four ingredients of success, direction is probably the one of least significance, should one of the ingredients have to be eliminated. I say this because direction is the only ingredient that can have either positive or negative influence on the athlete.

© Ken Lee

The opportunity to participate in training runs and races is integral to long-term success in the sport. Look into joining a local running club and taking part in events and activities in your area if you have not already done so.

If you consider inherent ability, you'll realize that everyone has some degree of this basic ingredient. The same can be said for motivation and opportunity. However, it is possible for absence of direction to be better than bad direction. Examples of bad direction might be telling a beginning runner that anything less than 150 miles of running per week won't lead to success in distance running, or that one must do repetition work every day for the final two weeks leading up to an important marathon race.

When I think of all the great runners I have known who, at one time or another, had to suffer through a tough coach–athlete relationship, it is amazing to me that they reached the degree of success that they did. What we all tend to overlook more often than we should is the importance of positive individual attention given to each athlete on the team. Nothing can replace the encouraging comments or understanding words of support from a quality coach. To become an elite runner, an individual needs a support system, and this support system must have the best interests of each athlete in mind at all times.

## The Coach's Role in Providing Direction

It is easy to misinterpret the effectiveness of coaching when we reward or recognize major university coaches primarily for the level of performance of their athletes. A coach who uses all available scholarship aid on distance runners and wins a cross-country championship has a good chance of being voted coach of the year, even if the team is made up of newly recruited athletes who had no improvement in performance from the previous year when they each had a different coach.

If the term "coach" refers to the person who directs the improvement or refinement of running performance, then a good coach can answer the question, "Why are we doing this workout today?" A good coach produces beneficial reactions to training, creates positive race results, and transforms the athletes he or she brings into the program into better runners (and better human beings). In many large universities, however, the head coach is actually more of an administrator than someone who directs the training of the athletes. Even though the head coach reaps the glory when the team does well, and is probably deserving of some praise, it is often the assistants (or a written training system) who have guided the athletes throughout the season.

## Positive Direction Can Have Far-Reaching Effects

Talented athletes who have motivation and opportunity can usually perform well enough to mask the job being done by a poor coach.

Moreover, good coaches are not necessarily recognized for positive results when the available talent is not high caliber. Actually, a coach who provides good direction can do a lot to instill motivation and often has a good deal to do with providing opportunity as well, which in turn increases motivation.

# A Final Word

One could say that the four ingredients of success really boil down to two—ability and motivation, the latter being derived from one's intrinsic desire and drive plus the drive instilled by opportunities and direction provided by the coach. We can look at the four types of runners in this way:

Type 1: high ability and motivation—champions

Type 2: high ability, little motivation—"coach frustrators"

Type 3: little ability, high motivation—"self-frustrators" and potential overtrainers

Type 4: little ability, little motivation—in the wrong activity

Naturally, there are not clear-cut categories into which all athletes can be sorted. It is the varying amounts and combinations of ingredients that give runners their individuality. Be happy with what you have. Use your ability to its fullest. There are some basic principles of training that should be considered and applied on an individual basis, but don't be afraid to take some chances now and then. There are as many individual pathways to success as there are individual runners.

I am reminded of my fencing master, who, when I asked him, "When will I be ready for competition?" would reply, "You will know when you are ready."  Basically, if all went well, I was ready; if it didn't, I wasn't. You will know when you are satisfied with how well you run; you will know when you are a success.

# Part I

# Program Planning

# CHAPTER 1

# Focusing Your Training

*If winning is the only thing that rescues athletes from 'wasting their time training' then there are a lot of unhappy people wasting their time running.*

The transition from being a fitness runner, or just one of the members of a team in school, to approaching the sport more seriously as a competitive athlete is not always an easy one to negotiate. When someone decides to get more serious about training and competing, the person usually does several things:

1. Increases mileage (total distance run each week)
2. Tries to run on a more regular basis (by running six or seven days each week, if formerly spending less time at it, or by adding a second run to an already daily training routine)
3. Introduces some (or more) quality work into the current program of regular steady runs

Changing your training schedule in such a way increases considerably the likelihood of injury. Even if you are fortunate enough to realize the benefits (improved race times) without the negative effects (injuries), you are likely to suffer damage in the future if you continue a spontaneous approach to training. On the other hand, and just as often, a new dedication to running that is too enthusiastic leads to injury, and can cause you to turn away from the sport permanently. If not, it probably convinces you that competitive running is not for you and that you'll never be a serious runner, and therefore that you should return to your previous approach to running and hope you can avoid further setback.

What is really needed is some guidance; you need a plan to follow, a teacher, a coach. Probably what you least need is to read about the fantastic training program that some recent winner of the Boston Marathon followed, with the idea that if you follow that plan you will be a future winner at Boston.

The fact that distance running requires minimal technical skill yet high conditioning shouldn't prompt coaches and runners to escalate too rapidly the stress of training. Everyone has different physical and mental strengths and weaknesses, and must be treated accordingly. Take the time for a detailed evaluation of the factors, past and present, that contribute to a runner's training program.

In this chapter, I present some principles of training that will serve as the basis for any training system you develop. These principles are based on a combination of the physiology of the body's reactions to training and the environment, and on the many training responses

Jack Daniels has been providing sound coaching advice to his athletes for many years.

that I have seen in my 38 years of coaching, plus those passed on to me by other researchers and runners. It usually boils down to common sense being a very good teacher, along with a little willingness to experiment now and then.

# Getting to Know Yourself and Your Training Needs

The one question that needs to be answered on a regular basis regarding training is, "What is the purpose of this training session?" I wonder how many athletes can answer that question. I think I can answer just about any question that you may have regarding your training and racing (if racing is part of your plan). I am not, however, naive enough to believe that anyone has all the answers for every individual who takes up a running career. In fact, what works for one individual may not do so well for another. There are, however, some sound scientific principles that apply to everyone and some ways of doing things that certainly work better than others.

## TRAINING PRINCIPLE #1

# The Body Reacts to Stress

There are two types of reaction to the stress of exercise. The first is an acute reaction, such as you would experience if you got up from your seat, went outside, and ran to the corner. Heart rate speeds up, stroke volume (the amount of blood pumped with each beat of the heart) increases, ventilation rate and depth of breathing increase, blood pressure rises, and your muscles feel some fatigue. If you perform this ritual on a regular basis, then you will continue to get regular reactions to this activity. The second type of reaction to the stress of exercise is the training effect, which results from repeated, chronic exercise.

Training produces changes throughout your body that allow you to perform the daily run to the corner with less discomfort (and probably in less time, as well). The muscles that are stressed become stronger and blood flow to them becomes more generous. Changes inside the muscle cells provide more energy for the muscles, and less lactic acid accumulates during the bout of exercise. Your resting heart rate undoubtedly becomes slower (due to a stronger heart being able to pump more blood per beat and, therefore, needing fewer beats to deliver the needed blood). Also, you probably develop a lighter, springier step (due to fitter leg muscles), lower resting blood pressure, lower body weight, and less fat under the skin.

# What Works for Others May Not Be Right for You

Runners who train together often forget that they may not all be keying on the same event. Further, even if they are shooting for the same goal and same event, they may react differently to the same training. Tom Von Ruden, my friend and a great middle-distance runner, was in the final weeks of preparation for the 1968 Olympic Trials, to be held at altitude in South Lake Tahoe, California. He and the other finalists for the trials had been training together for several weeks in Tahoe and Tom was feeling a bit down about his chances, possibly as a result of watching the others seeming to float through various workouts. Tom asked me what I thought might be the best thing to do for his final preparation, and I suggested that he fly out to Leadville, Colorado, for a week or so and have some time to himself at an altitude that was a fair bit higher than what he would be facing at Tahoe in his Olympic Trials race. Out of trust in my scientific knowledge of the effects of altitude, or simply out of desperation for something different to do, Tom made the trip. Upon his return, he not only made the U.S. team, but also was a finalist in the 1500 meters at the Mexico City Olympics, where he finished ninth.

I believed in what I was advising, based on sound scientific knowledge about training. I also had spent time with Tom at altitude research camps and felt I understood his psyche to some degree. In any case, at that time, for that athlete, it was the right thing to do. Would it have been the right thing for all of the finalists training in Tahoe? Probably not. Certainly it would not have been right for the other finalists who made the U.S. team by staying in Tahoe.

## TRAINING PRINCIPLE #2

# Specificity of Training

The system that is stressed is the one that stands to benefit from the stress. Although training for one particular sport usually has little or no beneficial effect on your ability to perform a second sport, in some cases there may actually be a detrimental effect. An example of this is the negative effect that long-distance running has on explosive leg activities, such as sprinting and jumping. The same thing is true for bodybuilding and distance running: the extra muscle mass developed through bodybuilding can act as dead weight and interfere with distance-running capabilities.

To become accomplished at something, you must practice doing that thing, not some other activity. Another activity takes time away from your primary interest, and can also produce results that limit performance in the main sport. You must give considerable thought to every aspect of training, and you must know what everything you do is doing for you or to you.

© Richard C. Etchberger

Training in certain conditions may work well for others but not for you. You will want to be at your peak fitness for important races.

# What to Consider When Planning Your Program

The great miler Jim Ryun used to tell me about youngsters who wrote to him asking about his training program. They wanted to do what he was doing so they could run like he ran. They didn't want to wait until they were his age or until they had progressed to a particular performance level before launching into his program—they wanted to get the workouts and start doing them now. I receive similar letters and calls: "How should I adjust my (or my team's) training to have the success that you are having with your runners?"

While I appreciate these calls and letters and hope that I provide some help, it is difficult to work with only part of the picture. To give a workout without considering details such as the athlete's current status, goals, and available time makes it hard for the training advice to have a positive effect. I initially find myself asking more questions than I answer, in an attempt to figure out what type of individual or team of individuals I am dealing with. I go through a mental checklist before coming up with what I hope is a reasonable answer. Here are some of the questions that I consider to be important:

1. What is the runner's current level of fitness? What is his or her readiness for training and competing?
2. How much time (in weeks) is available for a season's best performance?
3. How much time (in hours per day) is available for training?
4. What are the runner's strengths and weaknesses, in terms of speed, endurance/lactate threshold, $\dot{V}O_2$max (aerobic capacity), economy, and reaction to different amounts (mileage) of running?
5. What type(s) of training does the runner like to do; to what type(s) of training does the runner respond well, psychologically?
6. For what specific event is the runner preparing?
7. How should periodic races fit into the training program (what are the race commitments)?
8. What are the environmental conditions, facilities, and opportunities that must be dealt with?

Usually, a coach or runner considers all of these questions at some level of conscious or subconscious thought, but it is not a bad idea to make a list that can be referred to when needed.

## TRAINING PRINCIPLE #3

# Specificity of Overtraining

Just as training benefits those body systems that are properly stressed by the exercise, overtraining has a negative impact on the systems that are overstressed.

It is possible for a single, overstressed system to affect a variety of activities other than the one that caused the damage. For example, a stress fracture in the leg, brought about by too much or improper running, can prevent a runner from performing other activities that stress the injured extremity. Too much running doesn't always mean you become overtrained in other types of physical activity, and it may be beneficial to limit running for periods of time in favor of other types of training. We quickly learn to appreciate the frailty of our bodies when we depend on everything to go right at all times in order to reach our goals.

## TRAINING PRINCIPLE #4

# Specific Stress Produces a Specific Result

This principle is common sense but is still important to bear in mind. The benefits that can be expected from doing three one-mile runs at eight minutes each three times a week, with five minutes recovery between runs, are specific to that frequency (three times each week), amount (three miles of running per session), intensity (8:00 pace), and recovery between runs (five minutes). Someone who carries out this training regimen regularly will reach a level of running proficiency that will remain stable (and that will be different from the proficiency level reached if the training program consisted of five-mile runs at a speed of seven minutes per mile). Figure 1.1 shows how a new level of fitness would be reached over time.

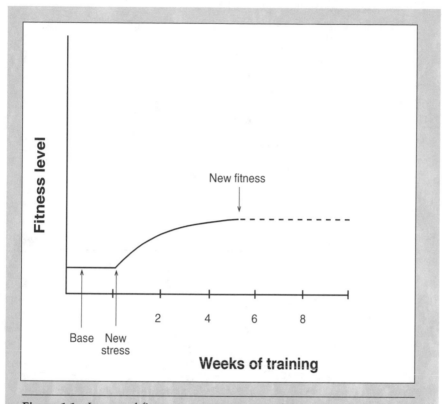

**Figure 1.1**   Increased fitness as a response to training.

Adding a new level of stress on top of your current training will further increase your fitness level. For a runner who has performed the training regimen regularly and reached a stable level of proficiency, there are many possibilities for training modifications. You could increase the training frequency from three to four or more days per week, the amount of training from three to four miles per session, or the distance of each interval from one mile to one and a half miles each. Another possibility is to increase the intensity (the speed of each mile) from 8:00 pace to 7:40 pace, for example. A final possibility is to change the recovery time allowed between the mile runs within a workout. Any one of these changes in training (frequency, duration, intensity, or recovery), or a combination of these changes, will affect the result of the program, leading to a new level of fitness (see figure 1.2).

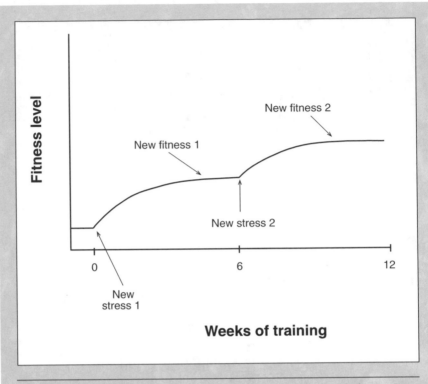

**Figure 1.2**    Increased fitness as a response to adding a new level of stress (new stress 2) onto prior training (new stress 1).

## TRAINING PRINCIPLE #5

# Rate of Achievement

You will notice in figures 1.1 and 1.2 that the rate of achieving the benefits of a training program is rapid at first and then tapers off over time. If you look at the time scale on these two figures, you will see that most of the benefits of a particular training regimen are adequately realized in about six weeks. Sticking with a training program for longer than six weeks, however, can produce more benefits. Without an increased stress of training, changes in body composition (loss of unnecessary fat, for example) can continue, leading to better performance.

Adequate benefits are realized in a matter of weeks, however, and if a runner wants to increase training, a good time is after six weeks. Changes imposed after fewer or more than six weeks of a specific program would follow curves depicted in figures 1.3 and 1.4, respectively. The primary danger of increasing training too often is escalated risk of injury and overstress caused by taking on too much too fast. It is difficult to get a feeling of what a particular training load is doing for you if you don't stay with it for awhile.

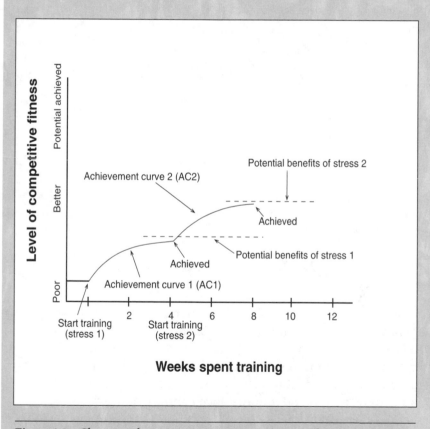

**Figure 1.3**   Changing the training stress you are doing within a specific phase of your program too soon will prevent you from achieving the maximum benefits from that phase of training.

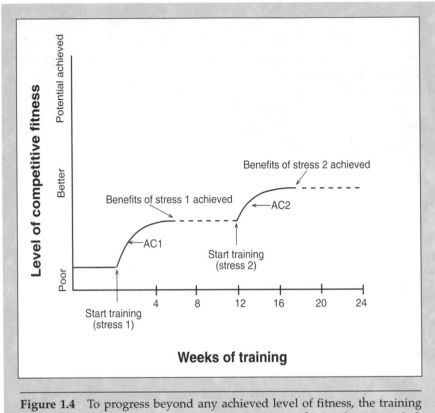

**Figure 1.4** To progress beyond any achieved level of fitness, the training stress must be increased or a fitness plateau will be reached and not exceeded.

# Set Your Own Pace

I would like to emphasize that each runner and coach should abandon the "copy the current champion" approach to training and challenge the runner's own body with training that is based on scientific principles. With your understanding of the runner's body, and with some common sense and a little creativity and boldness, set up a program that may well make you the next wonder of distance running or coaching.

On the other hand, don't ignore what the current champions are doing, because they may be supporting a training scheme that you also believe in but that you had been unable to prove would work. When you hear of a new approach to training, try to analyze it: evaluate what systems of the body are reaping the benefits, and why and how they are doing so.

It is important to keep in mind that what you read about a particular athlete's training may not be a regular or everyday training regimen. For instance, I'm sure every runner has been asked at one time or another how much running he or she does. The answer may be something like, "I do five miles a day," in hopes that the interrogator will interpret that to mean 35 miles a week, when in truth the individual runs three days a week and the longest run recently (or ever) was a five-miler. In other words, the runner may want to give the impression of a more demanding training schedule than is factual, either to gain some respect from others or to boost his or her own ego.

Sometimes the weekly training logs of champion runners are made public; what you usually see is a particularly great week of training, not a typical week. Or you may see a week in the strenuous phase of training, which is not at all the same as a week during a competitive phase of training. It's easy to talk about 150-mile weeks, even if only one was ever accomplished.

By the way, for those who think that high weekly mileage is a new approach to improved performance, let me relate the answers that one of my research subjects (an Olympian) gave me to the following questions in the late 1960s:

"What's the single longest training run you ever took?" Answer: 66 miles, on more than one occasion.
"What was your greatest week of running?" Answer: 360 miles.
"What was your greatest weekly mileage for a six-week period?" Answer: 300 miles per week.
"What was the greatest weekly mileage you averaged for an entire year?" Answer: 240 miles.

For all of you who like to copy what the great individuals do, try to resist replicating the accomplishments of this runner, because you may not have the same body type or the same ideal mechanics to deal with that much running, nor the same mental attitude toward the sport. We are all individuals and must be treated as such to achieve success in any pursuit.

The same principles apply to runners with little experience who are serious about reaching their potential and runners who have had some success but feel there is room for improvement: know your own body, identify your strengths and weaknesses, establish priorities, and try to learn more about why you do what you do and why you might consider something new in your approach to greater success.

# TRAINING PRINCIPLE #6

## Personal Limits

Another principle of training, which is related to the curves I have been presenting, is that each individual has unique limits. In fact, you could probably say that every system in a person's body has limits. For example, there is a limit as to how tall you will be, how

© Victah Sailer

Don't expect to be keeping up with elite runners if you are just beginning to train seriously. Let your body adjust to the increased stress of a well-structured training program. In the long run, being patient with yourself will pay off.

strong a particular muscle in your body can get (the heart being an important muscle for all of us), how much air you can breathe in and out of your lungs, how much blood can be transported to your running muscles, how much oxygen your running muscles can use in converting fuel to energy, and how fast you can run a mile, a 10K, or a marathon. Different people will reach different degrees of success, which are greatly dictated by what our limits are. The good news is that few people realize their limits, relative to running, and improvement is almost always possible.

Having limits puts us in the dilemma of testing the "no pain, no gain" theory. Let's say you've been gradually increasing your training every six weeks for the past six months, and your performances are steadily improving. After several weeks of even more difficult training, you feel tired and can't do the workouts very well. When a race comes along, performance is subpar. Your reaction is likely to be, "I need to train harder," but it should be, "Maybe I have reached some personal limit and need to reassess my training program." Something has to be done and the harder-training approach, although probably the most commonly used, is not the answer. Often the limit is seasonal and next year your performances will begin to improve again, to a new limit.

## TRAINING PRINCIPLE #7

# Diminishing Return

As training increases in duration and intensity, the benefit—or return—from the training decreases. This does not mean that increasing training decreases fitness; it means that the increases later in training are not as great or as beneficial as earlier in training. To clarify this principle, the benefits of increasing weekly mileage are shown in figure 1.5, with an all-inclusive term, competitive fitness, plotted against weekly mileage. Take the example of someone who starts training with 10 miles per week, doubles the weekly mileage to 20, doubles it again to 40, and finally reaches 80 miles per week, allowing a couple of months at each level. Regardless of how gradually the runner progresses from 20 to 40 to 80 weekly miles of training, the benefits reaped from 40 miles per week are not double those realized as a result of 20-mile weeks, nor are the results of 80 miles per week double the return of 40-mile weeks or four times the benefit of 20 miles per week. Adding more and more mileage to your weekly training does not produce equal percentages of improvement in competitive fitness. The same principle of diminishing return applies to increasing the amount of faster quality training.

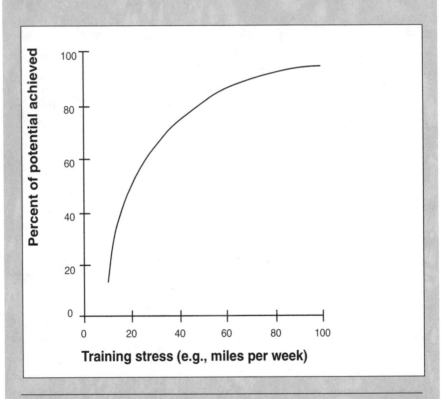

**Figure 1.5**  As specified by the principle of diminishing return, as you increase the amount of stress in your training, you get less benefit from that training. This is why beginning runners make vast improvements in their fitness as compared to elite runners.

# Be Flexible in Your Training

Education is a never-ending process, as is the search for improvement in any endeavor. I continue to learn about coaching and training by talking to other coaches and runners and by trying to answer their questions. Sometimes I don't have the answer, but the question prompts me to evaluate the situation and come up with what I consider a logical response—often a new approach to training.

Some local high school coaches asked me how their cross-country teams could get in some training when they were required to compete every Tuesday and Saturday. I don't like training (other than easy running) for two days before a competition, so that left only Wednesdays as the day for training. Further, because racing 5000 meters provides benefits similar to those of a good interval session, it was not necessary to add an interval session to the weekly schedule. Therefore, by treating Tuesdays (race days) as interval days, I opted for a threshold session (a few miles of comfortably hard running—see chapter 5 for details) on Wednesdays, creating back-to-back quality days each week. If a Tuesday race was not too demanding, the teams did some fartlek running (the mixing of fast and slow runs of various distances, as defined in chapter 7) over the race course following the race, making Tuesday a full-blown, quality interval day.

After a season or two, so many high school coaches reported success with this approach (back-to-back quality days on Tuesdays and Wednesdays) that I incorporated the same approach into my cross-country training system and have stayed with it ever since. Of course, we don't all have Tuesday races, so that becomes a good long-interval quality day, which I follow with another quality (threshold) day on Wednesday. I continue to follow this system to some extent during track season because the back-to-back training has several advantages. It allows my runners to adapt to having to race on consecutive days. Another advantage is that muscle soreness often is greater the second day after a stressful session than it is the very next day, so the follow-up quality day comes before the negative effects of the first day are realized. In addition, particularly for younger, overzealous runners, knowing that tomorrow will involve another quality day tends to calm their enthusiasm somewhat and they are less likely to overtrain.

# TRAINING PRINCIPLE #8

## Accelerating Setbacks

The setback principle states that low levels of training produce few setbacks (such as injury, illness, or lack of interest in training), and harder and harder training increases exponentially the potential for setbacks. The curve that depicts this principle is the mirror image of the diminishing returns curve. In figure 1.6, increases in training stress are plotted against the chance of encountering a setback. A setback is a setback and must be avoided at all costs.

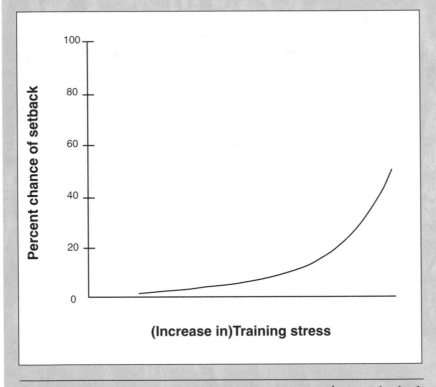

**Figure 1.6**   Increasing your training stress increases your chances of setback due to injury or illness.

## TRAINING PRINCIPLE #9

# Ease of Maintenance

This principle applies to maintenance of a level of competitive ability, which is, at least in part, a function of reaching a particular level of confidence. Although I am primarily referring to physiological fitness, it is no secret that psychological factors play an important part in how fast you can race. Once you break the barrier of the five-minute mile, or any other personal goal, the training effort required to repeat the task is usually well short of what was initially involved.

The maintenance principle is important when planning a long-term training program. It allows you to shift your training emphasis from one system (for instance, development of cellular adaptations that respond favorably to long, easy mileage) to another system (repetition work for the enhancement of economy, for example), and yet still maintain the cellular benefits through less frequent attention to the longer runs. Being able to improve a system and then maintain it while building up another system relies heavily on the maintenance principle.

## TRAINING PRINCIPLE #10

# Time Erodes Memory

Runners tend to forget how hard they trained earlier in their career, when they are disappointed by how difficult it is to make a comeback. This is the "time erodes memory" principle.

# A Final Word

As I have outlined in this chapter, I try to approach training runners by understanding the basic principles of training, the specific demands of the events being trained for, the types of training that confront these demands, and how to mix different types of training and racing into an overall training scheme. The chapters that follow are arranged to provide this information, and I hope that I present even the technical information in a practical and useful way.

# CHAPTER 2

# Training to Get Faster and Stronger

© Unicorn /Marie Mills

*We all get more practice losing than winning,
so it is as important to learn to be a good loser
as it is to be a graceful winner.*

The physiological components of greatest importance in distance running are the cardiovascular system, the muscular system, lactate threshold, aerobic capacity or maximum oxygen consumption, speed, and economy of running. I refer to these components as systems, but only the first two are body systems in the true sense of the word. Each of the six components involves the functioning of one or more of the traditional body systems (neuromuscular or metabolic, for example). Although it may be technically incorrect, the word "system" is useful when referring, for instance, to training the "lactate system" or lactate component of performance, rather than to break this difficult-to-define phenomenon into the multiple functions that lead to the production of lactic acid and its removal from the muscles. Therefore, I will sometimes refer to the six physiological components as systems in order to avoid long and tangential discussions of the body's complex functions.

After describing each component and the types of training that improve each component, I will explain how to create a personal profile in order to help you get the most out of each workout. I will then describe how to formulate your training goals and the types of training that will help you to attain those goals and to become a faster and stronger runner.

# Improving the Components of Running Performance

When a runner is at a low level of fitness, easy running will produce benefits to most of the components of running performance. To optimize the contribution of the components, however, it is necessary to understand how each component functions and to have a feeling for the factors that affect their role and capacity.

## Developing the Cardiovascular System

The cardiovascular system refers to the heart (cardiac) muscle and the network of vessels that carry blood to and from various parts of the body. For runners, the part of the body that needs a large blood supply is the part of the muscular system that does the running.

The function of the cardiovascular system is to provide an adequate supply of oxygen to the running muscles and to meet the increasing demands for oxygen as the runner becomes more fit. The delivery of oxygen depends on how powerful the pump (heart) is, how much oxygen a unit of blood can carry, how well the blood flows through the vessels, and how efficiently blood is diverted from less crucial areas of the body to the exercising muscles.

## The Heart as a Pump

Cardiac output (the amount of blood that the heart pumps in a given period of time, abbreviated "Q") is determined by heart rate (HR) and stroke volume (SV, the volume pumped by each beat):

$$SV \times HR / minute = \dot{Q}$$

At rest, the heart of a typical non-trained adult pumps 70 milliliters (ml) of blood at a rate of 70 beats per minute. Cardiac output is 70 × 70 or 4900 ml (4.9 liters) per minute. After training, the same heart's stroke volume might increase to over 80 ml, because training makes the heart muscle stronger and able to squeeze more blood with each beat. The same 4900 ml (4.9 liters) of blood needed to accommodate the resting metabolism of the body could then be met with a heart rate of 61 beats per minute: 61 × 80 = 4880 ml (4.9 liters). Further increases in stroke volume would result in an even slower resting heart rate.

Easy, steady running is the best type of training for desirable cardiovascular adaptations with the least discomfort. Think of time spent running as being more important than intensity of training. You will spend more time running if the intensity is not too great.

The maximum heart rate (HRmax) that a runner can reach doesn't necessarily change with training, but the stroke volume does. The intensity associated with easy runs best accomplishes the desired results. Consequently, the heart rate associated with any submaximal exercise task, such as an easy distance run, is slower following training just as heart rate at rest (a submaximal task in its own right) is decreased.

## Oxygen-Carrying Capacity of the Blood

The amount of oxygen that blood can carry is expressed in ml of oxygen carried per 100 ml of blood, and is a function of the hemoglobin concentration of the blood. Each gram of hemoglobin can transport 1.34 ml of oxygen; a person with a hemoglobin count of 15 (that is, 15 grams per 100 ml of blood) can carry 15 × 1.34 or about 20 ml of oxygen per 100 ml of blood, provided the blood is 100% saturated

Steady running allows your cardiovascular system to adapt to increased training stress with the least amount of strain on your body. Starting early in the year, long before you plan on running your first race of the season, will help to ensure that your cardiovascular system is ready when it's time to do harder types of training.

with oxygen. At sea level, blood is usually about 96% to 97% saturated, which, for the person mentioned above, would permit over 19 ml of oxygen to be carried by each 100 ml of blood. Therefore, for this person, the arterial blood (the blood that travels from the heart to the running muscles) has an oxygen content of 19 volumes percent (100 volumes of blood carry 19 volumes of oxygen).

If the hemoglobin concentration falls below normal for any individual, it is not difficult to calculate the difference in arterial oxygen content. Even small changes in the hemoglobin concentration can lead to significant performance discrepancies. In fact, the primary negative effect of running at altitude is that the lower atmospheric pressure results in a drop in the oxygen content of the arterial blood, which reduces its oxygen-carrying capacity. Both altitude and a reduced hemoglobin concentration have the same effect, but for different reasons (see chapter 10).

## Hemodynamics: The Characteristics of Blood Flow

Blood flow is determined by the diameter of the vessel through which the blood moves, the pressure difference between the heart and the destination of the blood, and the viscosity or thickness of the blood. The viscosity of the blood stays pretty constant, but vessel diameter can vary considerably depending on the tone of the muscular walls of the vessel, the nature of the tissue (particularly muscle tissue) surrounding the vessel, and the presence of deposits within the vessel that could inhibit flow. Basically, vessel diameter is the primary determinant of flow.

When exercise commences, the most desirable situation is for the vessels feeding the exercising muscles to relax and open up, which decreases the pressure in that area, increasing the pressure difference between the source of the blood and its destination. Blood flow to the needy muscles increases. Increased pressure of the blood leaving the heart as a result of faster and more powerful beating also increases the pressure difference, further enhancing flow. It is nice to be able to get large flow increases through drops in peripheral pressure (drops in resistance to blood flow) and moderate increases in central pressure (blood pressure as it leaves the heart), because this lowers the overall pressure in the system and reduces the energy expended by the heart to send blood, and therefore oxygen, to the muscles during exercise.

Also, blood flow to the exercising muscles increases as a result of a diversion of blood from areas of lesser need: the organs of digestion lose blood during exercise, as does the skin (unless weather conditions are so warm that large quantities of blood must be sent to the skin to help with body cooling).

As stated above, the viscosity of the blood doesn't change much under normal conditions. It does, however, change under conditions of dehydration, in which the blood thickens due to a partial loss of plasma (water) from the blood. Viscosity also changes when the red blood cell count changes; a lowered red cell count (usually associated with reduced hemoglobin concentration, as in the case of anemia) results in thinner blood, which to some degree allows for easier flow, but usually not enough to offset the loss of oxygen-carrying capacity caused by the lower hemoglobin concentration.

Maintaining optimal blood volume is very beneficial for races and daily training sessions. Doing so depends on maintaining good nutritional and hydration (fluid intake) habits. See chapters 10 and 11 for more details concerning hydration and nutrition.

## The Running Muscles

The cells (fibers) of the running muscles are the beneficiaries of the labors of the cardiovascular system. They make up the peripheral portion of the system, to which the heart is delivering fuel and oxygen, and from which carbon dioxide and lactic acid are removed.

Many adjustments take place in and around the muscle cells as a result of training, and relatively slow, easy running does an excellent job of promoting the desired results. Of particular importance is an increase in the number, size, and distribution of the mitochondria, the sites of aerobic metabolism. Another cellular adjustment is an increase in oxidative enzyme activity, which improves the rate at which the delivered oxygen can be processed. A third peripheral adjustment is greater perfusion of the exercising muscles with blood vessels: more capillaries become active and distribute blood to the muscle cells (an increased number of vessels distributing blood means a greater cross-sectional area of vessels, indicating enhanced flow; therefore, more oxygen can flow to more parts of the muscle). These adaptations to training improve the muscles' capacity for receiving and processing oxygen. The muscles also can become better at conserving stores of glycogen (their key stored carbohydrate fuel), metabolizing fat for energy, and dealing with lactic acid.

I have described quite a few central and peripheral benefits to comfortable training—speeds associated with 65% to 75% of an individual's aerobic capacity (70% to 75% of maximum heart rate). For most people this is a little slower than marathon race pace, or more than a minute per mile slower than 5K race pace. The benefits of slow, easy running are so important that I set aside an entire phase of training just for them (see chapter 4). I will now discuss components that benefit from more demanding (quality) types of training, which you will need to develop to improve your running performance.

# Improving Your Lactate Threshold

Runners must be able to work increasingly close to their maximum oxygen consumption without suffering from high accumulations of lactic acid in the blood. Blood-lactate accumulation is a function of how much lactic acid is being produced by the exercising muscles and the rate at which it is being cleared by the muscles, the heart, and the liver. Being able to hold down blood-lactate accumulation at faster and faster running speeds is a desirable attribute for a distance runner, and one acquired better by threshold (T) training (see chapter 5) than by other methods. Although the importance of threshold training increases with longer races, even middle-distance runners can use it with success because it provides quality training with limited stress. It also aids in recovery from the higher intensity training that often makes up much of a middle-distance runner's program.

The determination of blood-lactate accumulation became popular among athletes and coaches in the 1980s. The idea was to determine threshold training intensity by using a specific blood-lactate value (4.0 millimoles of lactic acid per liter of blood came to be commonly accepted as a desired threshold value). What is really being sought is an intensity of effort (which can be identified as a specific running pace known as threshold pace) that will be associated with a constant blood-lactate value. The constant blood-lactate value is produced during a steady training run of 20 to 30 minutes at a pace that most runners can maintain for about one hour in a race situation. For trained runners, this speed corresponds to about 88% of maximum oxygen consumption ($\dot{V}O_2max$) or 90% of maximum heart rate and 90% of $v\dot{V}O_2max$ (velocity at $\dot{V}O_2max$), as will be discussed later in this chapter.

For a large group of runners, the lactate value associated with this intensity might average about 4.0 millimoles per liter (blood-lactate accumulation or BLa), but individuals show vast variations from this 4.0 value. One runner might maintain a steady blood-lactate concentration of 2.8 and feel the same degree of stress as another runner who has a steady BLa of 7.2. They both may be at their lactate thresholds, even though the actual lactate values differ (and neither is at 4.0 millimoles). To ask these runners to train at a BLa of 4.0 would be overworking the former and underworking the latter, if the idea was to perform threshold training. It is much more valuable, in my experience, to use a given percentage of each runner's VDOT value

© Richard C. Etchberger

Steady running also promotes both the strengthening of the running muscles and the ability of your body to efficiently provide oxygen to the running muscles.

(an estimate of an individual's aerobic capacity based on actual race times; see chapter 3) to calculate threshold pace, rather than to try for a specific lactate value. Of course, if you have the equipment and time to do a thorough job of identifying the actual lactate threshold for each athlete, that's fine. Most coaches have neither the equipment nor the time. Improper use of equipment is another potential roadblock.

# Improving Aerobic Capacity ($\dot{V}O_2$ Max)

Improvements in the cardiovascular system and in the peripheral components referred to above enhance the body's capacity for consuming oxygen. Oxygen consumption can be specific to a muscle or group of muscles. The amount of oxygen an individual consumes when performing a particular activity (running, for example) depends directly on how much oxygen can be delivered to the muscles involved in the activity, how well the muscles process the delivered oxygen, and how easily the muscles can deal with the carbon dioxide and lactic acid produced during exercise. Exercising arm muscles trains the heart, but does little at the peripheral level to benefit the muscles needed for running. This is one of the main arguments in support of the principle of specificity of training (see principle #2, page 15).

To optimize $\dot{V}O_2$max, the runner must stress the oxygen delivery and processing system to its limit while performing the act of running. I assign a phase of interval (**I**) training (the most demanding phase of training for most people) to accomplish this goal. Interval training involves repeated runs of up to five minutes duration each, at about 3000-meter to 5000-meter race pace, with relatively brief recoveries between individual runs (see chapter 6).

# Developing Speed

I have heard coaches say, "Speed kills—all those who don't have any." It is true that many races are won during a final kick to the finish line. Those runners who win with a kick, however, were in a position to use it when the time came. In other words, having a great kick does you no good if you can't stay up with the pace during the bulk of a distance race. And staying up with the pace means having a high aerobic capacity ($\dot{V}O_2$max), a high lactate threshold, and good economy (discussed in the next section).

Still, I agree that speed wins many races. Bob Schul, the gold medal winner at 5000 meters in the 1964 Tokyo Olympics, had good speed. It paid off, particularly in the finals of the 5000 meters when the pace was slowed by the track conditions (this was during the days of natural track surfaces and rain could slow things down), which kept some runners from getting dropped earlier in the race. This was a race for kickers and Schul was the best of them. Others can only wonder what they may have done

## BOB SCHUL

**Bob Schul** was born in West Milton, Ohio, and remained in his home state throughout high school and college, where he attended Miami University. Bob took up running at the age of 12 because, as he puts it, "in games, I found I could outlast my peers." His initial goal as a runner was to be the best seventh grade 880-yard runner in his school. After college, Bob continued running during his tour of duty in the Air Force and later for the Los Angeles Track Club.

I became acquainted with Bob when he was training for the 1968 Olympic Trials and agreed to become a subject in my altitude research studies. I have never tested a runner with a lower maximum heart rate than Bob's, and during a 1993 follow-up test I discovered that it has not changed at all.

During his most successful years, Bob typically ran 80 to 90 miles per week and felt that "effort intervals" were the primary reason for his success. At various times in his career he held the world record for the 2-mile and American records for the 3-mile (both indoors and outdoors), 2-mile, and 5000. He was also national champion in the 5000 in 1964 and the 3-mile in 1965. Bob's greatest success was winning the Olympic 5000 in Tokyo in 1964, a feat that has received minimal recognition over the years but which certainly helped to fuel American interest in distance running.

Bob is probably the United States' greatest unsung hero of Olympic distance running. I have learned from Bob that there are a variety of approaches to success as a runner, but the one important ingredient is confidence in the plan you have chosen to follow.

**Bob's Bests**   Mile: 3:58.9   2-mile: 8:26.4   3-mile: 13:10   5000: 13:38

had conditions been different. I'm sure that Bob Schul would have had his kick under any conditions, but the slow track emphasized his advantage.

Many coaches feel that speed is inborn, but that endurance is earned through hard work. I believe that you are born with a certain gift for speed and a certain gift for endurance and that both can be improved with work. Sure, some people are physiologically more gifted than others in one area or the other, but a would-be 800-meter runner shouldn't give up on the 800 meters in favor of longer races just because the first attempt isn't particularly fast.

Everyone has fast-twitch muscle fibers that respond better to faster training than they do to endurance-type running; slow-twitch fibers are better suited for endurance running. Still, all muscle fibers respond to different types of training. Finding your particular strengths and weaknesses can be accomplished by letting your body experience various types of training.

Type of muscle fiber is only one factor in determining ability to perform well at a particular distance. Individuals with less desirable physiological makeups often keep up with runners with more desirable physiological makeups by having superior biomechanical characteristics or a tougher mental attitude. Many things determine success. Speed, however, is important for distance runners to train for. Fortunately, the type of training that best addresses speed also improves running economy; the intensity of the training may be the only variable from runner to runner (see the discussion of repetition (**R**) workouts in chapter 7).

## Improving Running Economy

Running economy refers to the amount of oxygen being consumed relative to the runner's body weight and the speed at which he or she is running. If one runner uses 50 ml of oxygen per kilogram (kg) body weight per minute (usually written $50 \ ml \cdot kg^{-1} \cdot min^{-1}$) to run at 6:00 pace and another runner uses 55 ml, the former is said to be more economical. If the first runner, as a result of training, can change oxygen consumption ($\dot{V}O_2$) at 6:00 pace from 50 ml to 48 ml, then the runner has improved his or her economy to an even better level. This is a highly desirable result of training, because the runner can now race at a faster speed than before without an increase in energy expenditure. Repetition (**R**) training (see chapter 7) improves economy by helping the runner to eliminate unnecessary arm and leg motion, to recruit the most desirable motor units while running at or near race pace, and to feel comfortable at faster speeds of running.

I have found that runners often have trouble linking to performance the concepts of $\dot{V}O_2$max, economy, and lactate threshold. The easiest way to bridge the gap between these physiological characteristics and running performance is to go through the steps taken when a runner evaluates his or her economy, aerobic capacity, and lactate response to different intensities of running.

# Creating Your Aerobic Profile

At any given time during your running career, whether in top shape or following a break in training when fitness is not so good, you will have a $\dot{V}O_2$max, economy curve, and lactate threshold curve. With the proper equipment, these variables can be measured and the resulting information used to describe your current capabilities and to identify all the training speeds that are necessary for optimizing $\dot{V}O_2$max, economy, and lactate threshold. The following discussion summarizes how $\dot{V}O_2$submax (running economy), $\dot{V}O_2$max (aerobic capacity), and lactate threshold (threshold) are determined and plotted for any distance runner. Should you have the opportunity to be tested, you would display a profile similar to those I have selected.

## $\dot{V}O_2$Submax

Let's say we have a runner who has reached a steady state by running for about six minutes at submaximal speed (marathon race pace, for example), and we collect a bag of expired air from this runner during the final minute or two of the six-minute run. Analyzing the expired air will tell us the aerobic (oxygen) demand of running at a certain pace for this particular runner. Heart rate (taken during the final minute or two of the run) and a small, finger-stick blood sample (drawn immediately on completion of the run) will provide information on the pulse rate and blood-lactate accumulation, respectively, that are associated with this velocity of running for this particular individual.

If the same procedure is repeated several times at increasingly faster (but still submaximal) running velocities, then the $\dot{V}O_2$, heart rate, and blood-lactate accumulation (BLa) responses can be plotted against running speed. Figure 2.1 on page 45 shows the data collected on one of the elite athletes whom I have tested. Notice that the $\dot{V}O_2$ response is relatively linear, as is heart rate. Blood-lactate accumulation, on the other hand, shows a different picture. Easy running speeds show little change in BLa, but as the speed of running becomes more intense, there is a dramatic increase in blood lactate. This lactate-response curve is typical for any runner. The better the runner, however, the faster would be the running pace at which the lactate-response curve would demonstrate the change from a gradual to a steep slope; a better runner's lactate curve is displaced farther to the right on the horizontal axis. The intensity at which the transition from a gradual to a steep lactate curve takes place is referred to as the individual's lactate threshold intensity.

If the runner being tested completes three or four submax tests (at increasingly faster speeds, up to about 10K race pace or a little faster), and then performs a "max" test, the response picture becomes adequate for determining current training, and even competitive intensities of running.

The body's ability to consume oxygen plays a very important role on running ability. Here, a runner has his $\dot{V}O_2$ measured on the track.

# $\dot{V}O_2Max$

In the max test, the runner starts running at the same pace as the final submax test (about current 10K race pace). This speed is held for two minutes on a treadmill (or for one lap on a 400-meter track). After the initial two minutes, a one-percent grade is added to the treadmill each minute (or the pace is increased to 5K race pace on a track). In a treadmill test, when the intensity of the ever-increasing treadmill grade becomes so great that the runner can't continue, then the test is over. In the case of a track test, after two or three laps at 5K race pace, the runner completes a final 400 meters at an all-out speed, after which the test is terminated.

In either case, expired air samples are continually collected, starting with about the third minute of the max test and ending when the runner stops. Heart rate is taken at the end of the test (or recorded during the final 30 seconds of the test if using a monitor). The final blood sample (used to detect maximum lactate accumulation) is drawn two minutes after completion of the max test (when blood lactate reaches its peak).

## Velocity at $\dot{V}O_2Max$

By adding the $\dot{V}O_2$max (the highest $\dot{V}O_2$ measured during the max test), the maximum heart rate (HRmax), and the maximum blood-lactate accumulation (BLamax) data points to the submax data shown in figure 2.1, we get what I refer to as a runner's aerobic profile (see figure 2.2 on page 46). $\dot{V}O_2$max is placed on an extension of the economy curve (the line drawn through the previously calculated $\dot{V}O_2$submax data points that show how much oxygen the runner consumed at diferent speeds), and this permits determination of the velocity at which $\dot{V}O_2$max would first be realized. This velocity is called $v\dot{V}O_2$max (velocity at $\dot{V}O_2$max) and is used to calculate a VDOT value, which, in turn, determines training paces and race potential (see chapter 3).

## The Importance of $\dot{V}O_2Max$

By now it should be apparent that the measurement of $\dot{V}O_2$max, by itself, provides limited information in terms of discriminating between groups of good runners. As a result, when I hear that some runner was found to have a$\dot{V}O_2$max of 90 ml·kg$^{-1}$·min$^{-1}$, I have two

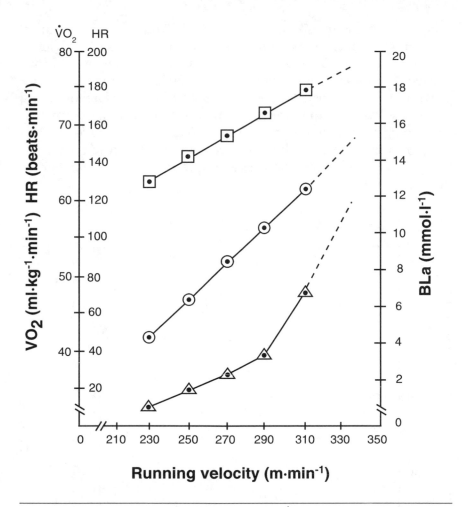

**Figure 2.1** Increases in oxygen consumption (V̇O—circles), heart rate (HR—squares), and blood-lactate level (BLa—triangles) in an elite runner as running speed is increased. The line marked with squares symbolizes HR, the line marked with circles symbolizes V̇O₂, and the line marked with triangles symbolizes BLa.

immediate reactions. First, the tests may have been poorly controlled (inaccurate reference gases used for the gas analyzers, or faulty equipment used in measuring ventilatory gas volumes, for example). Second, if the tests were well controlled, why doesn't this runner outperform everyone else?

Assuming that the runner with the high V̇O₂max does have an accurate assessment of his aerobic capacity, the most logical reason why he doesn't outperform everyone else is because his economy is poor.

When a runner with a 70 $\dot{V}O_2$max runs a 2:10 marathon and outperforms a 90-$\dot{V}O_2$max runner, imagine how poor the latter's efficiency must be. And who is to say that the 90-$\dot{V}O_2$max runner can improve efficiency (economy) any more than the 70-$\dot{V}O_2$max runner can improve his $\dot{V}O_2$max? Learning your $\dot{V}O_2$max can be useful for monitoring changes in response to training, but without supporting information concerning your economy, it can be misleading. Of course, there is another possible reason why a runner with high test results may not always beat "lesser" individuals: a simple lack of determination or motivation (guts).

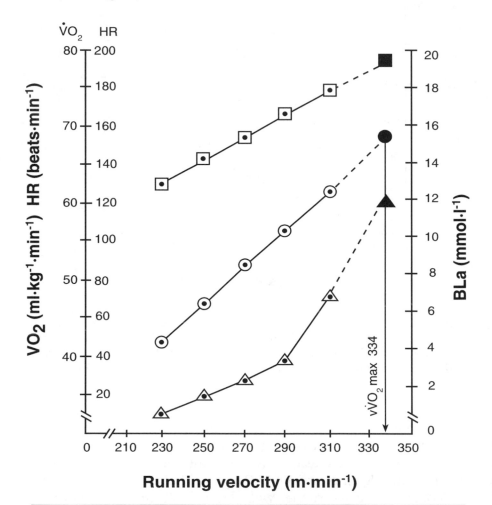

**Figure 2.2** An elite runner's aerobic profile, which includes submax (open symbols) and max values (solid symbols) for HR (squares), $\dot{V}O_2$ (circles), and BLa (triangles).

# Differences in Aerobic Profile

If the results of $\dot{V}O_2$ tests performed on different individuals or groups of runners are plotted, as is done in Figure 2.2, then some interesting information becomes apparent. Figure 2.3 on page 48 compares three female 3000-meter runners, all of whom I tested during the same week a few years ago. Notice that two of the runners have similar $\dot{V}O_2$max values (69.6 and 73.3); the third has a relatively low $\dot{V}O_2$max (60.4), but is much more economical than the other two runners (she has a lower economy curve, or a lower oxygen cost of running at submax test speeds). These facts suggest that if the three runners ran a 3K race at their $\dot{V}O_2$max, they would all finish in times of just about 9:00. In fact, their actual outdoor 3K times were in the predicted range, as shown in Figure 2.3.

# Male and Female Aerobic Profiles

Figure 2.4 on page 49 shows a comparison of many of the elite men and women distance runners whom I have tested. You can see that the typical elite male runner has a higher $\dot{V}O_2$max and is slightly more economical than the typical elite female runner (at comparable absolute running speeds). When running at the same absolute speeds, women are working at a higher intensity, relative to their $\dot{V}O_2$max, than are their male counterparts. When running at the same relative intensities (at the same percent of their $\dot{V}O_2$max), however, elite males and elite females do not differ significantly in economy. Still, the difference in aerobic profiles suggests that the men should outrace the women by about 14%, which is just a little greater than the typical percent difference turned in by these elite distance runners.

There is a great overlap in the $\dot{V}O_2$max and economy data for elite men and women, but the combination of the two ($v\dot{V}O_2$max) tends to favor the men. For example, two elite marathoners (one male and one female) whom I tested both had $\dot{V}O_2$max values of 78 ml·kg⁻¹·min⁻¹. However, the woman's best marathon was over ten minutes slower than the man's. The difference in performance was due to economy—the man was a fair bit more economical. On the other hand, I tested a woman whose economy was so good that her times were almost always better than the times of any man with a comparable $\dot{V}O_2$max. When I have compared elite male and female runners of equal aerobic profiles, performances are also equal.

## Changes in Aerobic Profile

Figure 2.5 on page 50 shows data collected on a runner at two different times of the year: early season, before the runner was fit, and midseason. Here you can see how the body responds to a season of training. Figure 2.5 shows that $\dot{V}O_2$max, economy, and lactate accumulation all responded well to training. Specific types of training should be used to optimize each of these components of performance.

## Using Race Performance to Determine Training Needs

There is an important relationship between $\dot{V}O_2$, HR, BLa, and $v\dot{V}O_2$max. The configuration of the economy curve (which plots $\dot{V}O_2$

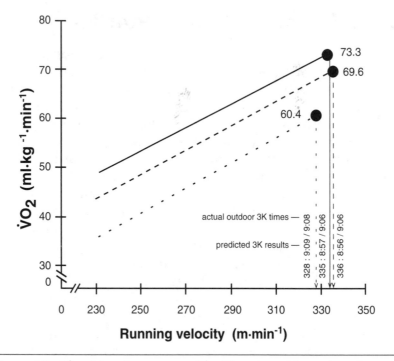

**Figure 2.3** Three female runners with diferent aerobic profiles that produce similiar predicted and actual 3000-meter times.

Adapted from Daniels, J. et al. 1986. "Elite and sub-elite female middle- and long-distance runners." In *Sport and Elite Performance—1984 Olympic Scientific Congress Proceedings, Vol. 3*, ed. D. Landers. Champaign, IL: Human Kinetics. First published in Daniels, J. 1985. "A case for running economy, an important determinant of distance running," *Track Technique*, Los Altosa, CA: Track & Field News.

against running velocity) is such that a 1% change in velocity is also nearly a 1% change in $\dot{V}O_2$. As a result, an intensity of 70% $\dot{V}O_2$max is equal to 75% of both $v\dot{V}O_2$max and HRmax, and an intensity of 88% $\dot{V}O_2$max is equal to 90% of $v\dot{V}O_2$max and HRmax. Both of these intensities are important and will be referred to in detail when I discuss training in Part II.

The relationship between velocities and intensities is extremely useful; it signifies that if $v\dot{V}O_2$max can be identified, there is no need for $\dot{V}O_2$max or economy testing for the purpose of setting training intensities. Fortunately, current $v\dot{V}O_2$max can be closely estimated from knowing the race performance capabilities of a runner.

What I am saying is that you can use current race information to determine how hard to train. Furthermore, I believe that this is better than relying on laboratory tests. There is a place for laboratory testing, but it is simply not necessary for the masses of runners and coaches who should be using more concrete

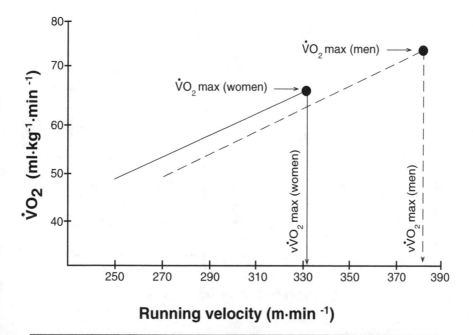

**Figure 2.4**   Comparison of aerobic profiles of elite male and elite female runners.

Adapted from Daniels, J. and N. Daniels. 1992. "Running economy of elite male and elite female runners." *Medicine and Science in Sports and Exercise* 24 (4): 483-489.

information to plan training intensities. After all, what is better than using how good you are as a measure of how fast you should train?

# The Goals of Training

What a runner is really trying to accomplish through training, based on the six components highlighted at the beginning of the chapter, are the following:

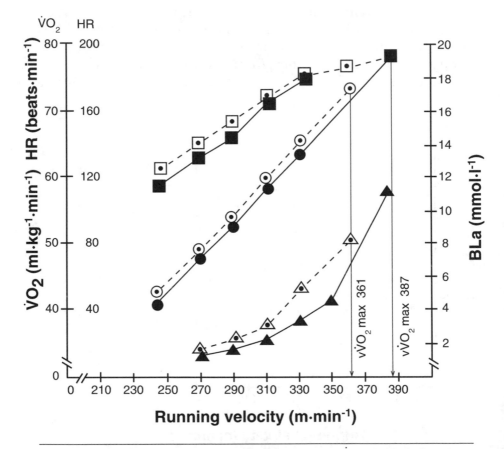

**Figure 2.5** The comparison of oxygen consumption ($\dot{V}O_2$—circles), heart rate (HR—squares), and blood-lactate level (BLa—triangles) of an elite runner during the early season and midseason. The open symbols delineate early-season measurements, and the solid symbols delineate mid-season measurements.

1. Improving the body's ability to transport blood and oxygen
2. Increasing the ability of the running muscles to effectively use their available oxygen (to convert carbohydrate and fat fuel into useful energy)
3. Shifting lactate threshold to correspond to a faster running speed
4. Increasing aerobic capacity ($\dot{V}O_2$max)
5. Improving speed
6. Lowering the energy demand of running (improving economy)

Naturally, there are other goals of training, such as improving race tactics, elevating self-confidence, changing body composition, and bettering self-image, but these less tangible factors will all result from improvement in one or more of the above-mentioned factors.

# Types of Training

Figure 2.6 on page 53 illustrates the various types of training and the associated intensities needed to stress the systems of importance to a distance runner. A brief description of these types of training follows (see figure 2.7 on page 54 for a comparative illustration of the types of training described below).

## Easy and Long Runs

When you do easy (E) runs to recover from strenuous periods of training or to carry out a second workout on a particular day, and when you do long (L) runs, you should run at a pace close to your E run velocity, which is about 70% of $\dot{V}O_2$max. Long runs improve cell adaptation, and lead to fluid loss, glycogen depletion, and the ability to spare glycogen and rely more on fat as fuel (all important considerations for distance runners), but should not be demanding in terms of the intensity (pace).

Be advised that the benefits of E-run pace are more a function of time spent exercising than intensity, and 70% $\dot{V}O_2$max, which corresponds to 75% v$\dot{V}O_2$max and 75% of maximum heart rate, is as hard as you need to go to get the benefits you want at the cellular level and in the heart muscle.

© Ken Lee

Using race performance to measure your fitness is a good way to judge what adjustments you need to make to your training intensities.

# Marathon-Pace Runs

The next faster intensity of training is marathon race pace (**MP**) and is pretty much limited to marathon training. Your **MP** is the pace at which you plan to race (or run, as the case may be) your next marathon, and is about 20 to 30 seconds per mile slower than threshold (**T**) pace.

# Threshold-Pace Runs

Threshold (**T**) pace is about 88% of $\dot{V}O_2max$ (90% of $v\dot{V}O_2max$ or of maximum heart rate). Subjectively, **T** pace is comfortably hard running—for most people, about 25 to 30 seconds per mile slower than current 5K race pace. When training at **T** pace, it is important to stay as close as possible to the prescribed speed; neither slower nor faster

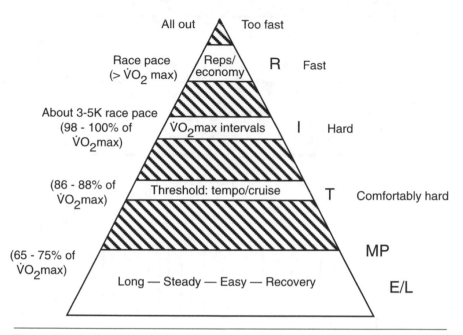

**Figure 2.6** Different types of training are associated with rather specific intensities of effort, and each has its place in a training program.

velocities work as well as the proper speed. In this case, going too fast—which many runners automatically try to do—is not as good as running at the right pace.

## Interval-Pace Runs

The training velocity that stresses $\dot{V}O_2$max is $\dot{V}O_2$max interval (**I**) velocity. The intensity should be equal to $v\dot{V}O_2$max. If using heart rate as a guide, I believe that most people should shoot for 98% to 100% of maximum heart rate, rather than demanding a 100% value. This is because if maximum heart rate coincides with 5:00 mile pace, for example, then a faster pace, such as 4:50 pace, will also elicit maximum heart rate, but is too fast for the purpose of the training session (which is to obtain the optimal result with the least possible stress). It becomes too easy to overtrain.

Interval (**I**) training is demanding (I refer to it as hard running), but is not all-out running. In the case of **I** pace, the harm of going too fast is that no better results are obtained and the excessive pace will probably leave you overstressed for the next quality training session.

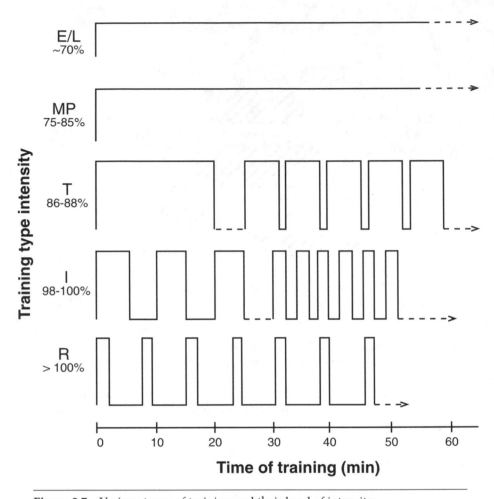

**Figure 2.7**    Various types of training and their level of intensity.

Adapted from Daniels, J. and N. Daniels. 1984. "Internal training and performance." *Sports Medicine* 1(4): 327-334.

## Repetition Pace

Repetition (**R**) velocity is faster than **I** pace, but unlike **I** and **T** running it is not based on $\dot{V}O_2$max. Rather, **R** pace is, to a great extent, based on the race for which you are training; it is designed for good mechanics at a fast pace.

A runner with a $v\dot{V}O_2$max of 300 meters per minute who is training for a 10K will have the same **T** velocity and $\dot{V}O_2$max **I** velocity as another runner whose $v\dot{V}O_2$max is 300 but who is training for a 1500-meter race. This is because **T** and **I** paces are related to the same v$\dot{V}O_2$max value, and runners with a 300 v$\dot{V}O_2$max would have identical training speeds for **I** and **T** training. On the other hand, **R** pace would differ for the two runners, because one is training for a faster race than the other, and needs good economy and speed for the faster pace. The purpose of **R**-pace training is to improve economy and speed; it is not to benefit $\dot{V}O_2$max or lactate threshold. It is important to keep in mind what every workout is designed to do for you, even if the benefit is pure relaxation.

## Avoiding "Quality-Junk" Training

In figure 2.6, there is a shaded area between **I** and **T**, and also between **T** and **E/L**. These areas are the "no man's land" of training. With the exception of **MP** runs and marathon races (which do fall in "no man's land" between **E/L** and **T**), if you select a training intensity that falls in "no man's land," your training is either too easy or too hard to reap the benefits you want. You are not achieving the purpose of training the two systems on either side of the chosen intensity. What you are doing might be termed "quality-junk" training. Also try to avoid the "no man's land" between **R** and **I**, which is faster than necessary for **I** benefits and questionable for **R** benefits. Training in these in-between zones is training with an unidentifiable purpose. Have a purpose for every training session. Ask yourself, "What system do I hope to improve by doing this workout?" and "What am I really trying to accomplish?"

# Support-System Training

Support-system training produces few direct benefits, but may mean the difference between success and failure. Support-system training includes flexibility, muscle strengthening, and mental and psychological approaches to performance enhancement. Runners benefit to varying degrees from the different types of support-system training. As with all types of training, be sure that what you are doing helps satisfy your needs and doesn't just add unproductive activity to your overall training program. Keep foremost in your mind what your goals are. For example, are stretching exercises used to improve your running, or just to become more flexible? Often, trial and error is the only way to see if something works for you. Remember to give a new approach to training a fair trial—more than just a few days.

The same thing can be said for the various types of training—are you doing a particular type of training because you like it and are good at it, or because it will produce the results you want in races? Be clear and realistic with your goals and expectations and you will almost always be happy with your performance.

# A Final Word

The information in this chapter may need some regular review so that you can keep in touch with what you are trying to accomplish and the types of training that work best in reaching your goals. Pay attention to the things that are often taken for granted, such as proper nutrition, rest, and total body conditioning. It is sometimes easy to get so involved in one aspect of your training that other important areas are overlooked.

# CHAPTER 3

# Measuring Your Starting Point

© Victah Sailer

*A great coach is the result of a coach and a great athlete getting along well.*

The physiological needs a distance runner should address are $\dot{V}O_2$max (through central and peripheral adaptations), lactate threshold, speed, and economy. In chapter 2, I discussed the types of training that best meet these needs (easy runs, intervals, threshold running, and repetitions). The next logical step in setting up a good training program is to determine your current level of fitness.

You could go to a lab somewhere and get a series of tests run on yourself to measure your $\dot{V}O_2$max, running economy, and lactate threshold, but that would probably cost a lot of money and may not be available. Or, you could use another measure of your current fitness—recent race performances—to establish how hard to train. As the result of many years of research involving runners of all ability levels, a former runner of mine, Jimmy Gilbert, and I came up with a comprehensive book of tables that associate race performances with a common measure of distance-running fitness. The book, *Oxygen Power*, allows runners of a wide range of abilities to identify where they are in their running ability by determining their aerobic profile (see chapter 2).

The purpose of this chapter is to expand on the idea of using race performances and their associated VDOT values to give you an idea of your current fitness, while avoiding laboratory testing. Further, I will provide some accurate and practical ways of determining how fast to perform the various types of training (intervals, reps, and threshold runs) that you will be doing in your quest for improved performances. Also, I will present a few useful "test session" workouts that you can use to compare your progress at various stages of a season.

# VDOT—The Key to Identifying Ability

An aerobic profile involves the identification of a $v\dot{V}O_2$max (velocity at $\dot{V}O_2$max) that represents the speed of running a race that lasts in the neighborhood of 10 to 15 minutes. This $v\dot{V}O_2$max reflects the runner's economy and $\dot{V}O_2$max, and will be the same for all individuals of equal race ability, although one runner may accomplish his or her $v\dot{V}O_2$max with great economy and a relatively meager $\dot{V}O_2$max and another runner with not-so-great economy and a high $\dot{V}O_2$max. It doesn't matter how the components vary if they combine

By determining your personal VDOT, you will always have a good sense of how hard you should be running for each type of training you are doing.

to provide the same end result. Basically, Gilbert and I forced every runner of equal performance ability onto a common economy curve, which meant that they would also have the same mathematically generated $\dot{V}O_2$max and a similar lactate-response curve. Equally performing runners are assigned equal aerobic profiles, which means that they would also have an identical pseudo$\dot{V}O_2$max, but not necessarily the $\dot{V}O_2$max they would come up with in a laboratory test.

Instead of referring to this pseudo$\dot{V}O_2$max (the one based strictly on performance) as $\dot{V}O_2$max, we use the term "VDOT." $\dot{V}O_2$max is properly stated "V-dot-$O_2$-max." By placing a dot over the V, the volume of oxygen is identified as a value measured over one minute. We shortened V-dot-$O_2$-max to VDOT. By doing this, each runner has a reference VDOT, a single number, that is easy to work with when comparing performances. It is also ideal for setting training intensities because intervals, threshold runs, and even easy long runs and marathon-pace runs are best performed at specific fractions (or percentages) of each runner's VDOT.

When you know your VDOT, you can eliminate a great deal of guesswork from training, and avoid overtraining. I'll go so far as to say that your VDOT takes into account your psychological input into racing, because we are using your race performances, which are affected by your motivation and willingness to deal with discomfort, to determine your ability level, rather than a lab test. VDOT reflects everything that an individual calls upon to perform in a race situation.

In addition to a generic economy curve, used to fit a variety of runners (see figure 3.1), Gilbert and I came up with another curve that represents the relative intensity at which a runner can race

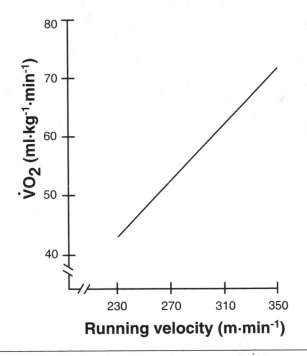

**Figure 3.1** Relationship between running velocity and $\dot{V}O_2$ demand.

Adapted from Daniels, J., R. Fitts, and G. Sheehan. 1978. *Conditioning for distance running: the scientific aspects.* New York: John Wiley and Sons, 31.

for various durations of time (see figure 3.2). Duration, not distance, is the key here, because the intensity (percent of current VDOT) at which any race can be run is a function of how much time it takes to complete the race. For example, one runner may complete a 10,000-meter race in 50 minutes; another runner may race 10 miles in 50 minutes. Both race at about the same intensity for 50 minutes. Intensity is of utmost importance, and the intensity that you can maintain reflects the various reactions that are going on inside your body, based on how long you are expected to be running in a race situation.

A runner learns to deal with a certain level of discomfort for a particular period of time, regardless of how many miles are covered in that time. For example, blood lactate accumulates at a certain rate, based on how fast you are running. At a fairly hard intensity (as in a five-mile or 10K race), lactate accumulation will be slow enough to allow you to go on for 30 minutes or so; at a higher intensity of effort (as when racing 3000 meters or two miles), lactate accumulation will be more rapid and you may be forced to stop after only 10 minutes of running. Each runner

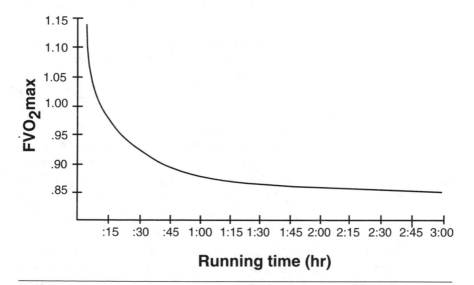

**Figure 3.2** Relationship between race duration and fraction of $\dot{V}O_2$max.

Adapted from Daniels, J., R. Fitts, and G. Sheehan. 1978. *Conditioning for distance running: the scientific aspects.* New York: John Wiley and Sons, 31.

learns to identify the intensity of effort that can be tolerated for different periods of time, with the better runners covering greater distances than would runners of lesser ability in the same time. By using the equations that generate the curves in figures 3.1 and 3.2, along with a few other calculations, Jimmy Gilbert and I developed the VDOT tables that have been used very successfully since the 1970s.

These tables can relate performances over an unlimited number of distances, and can be used to predict performances in races of any distance from a known performance in a race of any other distance. In addition, the formulas associated with the development of the VDOT tables allow a runner to identify the pace associated with a desired training intensity (such as $\dot{V}O_2$max intervals, threshold, or marathon pace; see chapter 2).

Table 3.1 presents a condensed version of the VDOT tables found in *Oxygen Power*. You can use the table whenever you want to find a VDOT value that is associated with either your race performances or examples that I will provide throughout the remainder of this book. A VDOT value can be generated for virtually any performance over any race distance, but is most desirable and accurate for races lasting from about three and one-half minutes to about three and one-half hours in duration.

To use the VDOT table, look up a recent time under any of the distances presented, and read across that row to find the corresponding VDOT. If you have more than one recent race distance to work with, the one that provides the highest VDOT is the one that describes your current state of fitness.

Make sure that the race from which you are predicting the VDOT was run on a flat course, with good footing, and under good weather conditions; when using a race run in difficult weather or terrain conditions, the time will be affected in a negative way and the VDOT will be lower than it should be. If, however, you are determining a VDOT on a cross-country course that will also be used for regular training sessions, then it is fair to use the VDOT value from that adverse course to set training intensities for the same type of adversity. You can use a time from a recent, moderate-distance road race to predict an upcoming marathon time, but the conditions of the two races must be similar for the prediction to be accurate; you can't expect to accurately predict a hot-day marathon time from a half-marathon time run under cool conditions. The "self-evaluation" form in figure 3.3 will be useful for establishing a personal VDOT.

## Table 3.1 VDOT Values Associated With Times Raced Over Some Popular Distances

| VDOT | 1500 | Mile | 3K | 2-Mile | 5K | 10K | 15K | Half-Marathon | Mara-thon | VDOT |
|---|---|---|---|---|---|---|---|---|---|---|
| 30 | 8:30 | 9:11 | 17:56 | 19:19 | 30:40 | 63:46 | 98:14 | 2:21:04 | 4:49:17 | 30 |
| 31 | 8:15 | 8:55 | 17:27 | 18:48 | 29:51 | 62:03 | 95:36 | 2:17:21 | 4:41:57 | 31 |
| 32 | 8:02 | 8:41 | 16:59 | 18:18 | 29:05 | 60:26 | 93:07 | 2:13:49 | 4:34:59 | 32 |
| 33 | 7:49 | 8:27 | 16:33 | 17:50 | 28:21 | 58:54 | 90:45 | 2:10:27 | 4:28:22 | 33 |
| 34 | 7:37 | 8:14 | 16:09 | 17:24 | 27:39 | 57:26 | 88:30 | 2:07:16 | 4:22:03 | 34 |
| 35 | 7:25 | 8:01 | 15:45 | 16:58 | 27:00 | 56:03 | 86:22 | 2:04:13 | 4:16:03 | 35 |
| 36 | 7:14 | 7:49 | 15:23 | 16:34 | 26:22 | 54:44 | 84:20 | 2:01:19 | 4:10:19 | 36 |
| 37 | 7:04 | 7:38 | 15:01 | 16:11 | 25:46 | 53:29 | 82:24 | 1:58:34 | 4:04:50 | 37 |
| 38 | 6:54 | 7:27 | 14:41 | 15:49 | 25:12 | 52:17 | 80:33 | 1:55:55 | 3:59:35 | 38 |
| 39 | 6:44 | 7:17 | 14:21 | 15:29 | 24:39 | 51:09 | 78:47 | 1:53:24 | 3:54:34 | 39 |
| 40 | 6:35 | 7:07 | 14:03 | 15:08 | 24:08 | 50:03 | 77:06 | 1:50:59 | 3:49:45 | 40 |
| 41 | 6:27 | 6:58 | 13:45 | 14:49 | 23:38 | 49:01 | 75:29 | 1:48:40 | 3:45:09 | 41 |
| 42 | 6:19 | 6:49 | 13:28 | 14:31 | 23:09 | 48:01 | 73:56 | 1:46:27 | 3:40:43 | 42 |
| 43 | 6:11 | 6:41 | 13:11 | 14:13 | 22:41 | 47:04 | 72:27 | 1:44:20 | 3:36:28 | 43 |
| 44 | 6:03 | 6:32 | 12:55 | 13:56 | 22:15 | 46:09 | 71:02 | 1:42:17 | 3:32:23 | 44 |
| 45 | 5:56 | 6:25 | 12:40 | 13:40 | 21:50 | 45:16 | 69:40 | 1:40:20 | 3:28:26 | 45 |
| 46 | 5:49 | 6:17 | 12:26 | 13:25 | 21:25 | 44:25 | 68:22 | 1:38:27 | 3:24:39 | 46 |
| 47 | 5:42 | 6:10 | 12:12 | 13:10 | 21:02 | 43:36 | 67:06 | 1:36:38 | 3:21:00 | 47 |
| 48 | 5:36 | 6:03 | 11:58 | 12:55 | 20:39 | 42:50 | 65:53 | 1:34:53 | 3:17:29 | 48 |
| 49 | 5:30 | 5:56 | 11:45 | 12:41 | 20:18 | 42:04 | 64:44 | 1:33:12 | 3:14:06 | 49 |
| 50 | 5:24 | 5:50 | 11:33 | 12:28 | 19:57 | 41:21 | 63:36 | 1:31:35 | 3:10:49 | 50 |
| 51 | 5:18 | 5:44 | 11:21 | 12:15 | 19:36 | 40:39 | 62:31 | 1:30:02 | 3:07:39 | 51 |
| 52 | 5:13 | 5:38 | 11:09 | 12:02 | 19:17 | 39:59 | 61:29 | 1:28:31 | 3:04:36 | 52 |
| 53 | 5:07 | 5:32 | 10:58 | 11:50 | 18:58 | 39:20 | 60:28 | 1:27:04 | 3:01:39 | 53 |
| 54 | 5:02 | 5:27 | 10:47 | 11:39 | 18:40 | 38:42 | 59:30 | 1:25:40 | 2:58:47 | 54 |
| 55 | 4:57 | 5:21 | 10:37 | 11:28 | 18:22 | 38:06 | 58:33 | 1:24:18 | 2:56:01 | 55 |
| 56 | 4:53 | 5:16 | 10:27 | 11:17 | 18:05 | 37:31 | 57:39 | 1:23:00 | 2:53:20 | 56 |
| 57 | 4:48 | 5:11 | 10:17 | 11:06 | 17:49 | 36:57 | 56:46 | 1:21:43 | 2:50:45 | 57 |
| 58 | 4:44 | 5:06 | 10:08 | 10:56 | 17:33 | 36:24 | 55:55 | 1:20:30 | 2:48:14 | 58 |

*(continued)*

## Table 3.1 (continued)  VDOT Values Associated With Times Raced Over Some Popular Distances

| VDOT | 1500 | Mile | 3K | 2-Mile | 5K | 10K | 15K | Half-Marathon | Mara-thon | VDOT |
|---|---|---|---|---|---|---|---|---|---|---|
| 59 | 4:39 | 5:02 | 9:58 | 10:46 | 17:17 | 35:52 | 55:06 | 1:19:18 | 2:45:47 | 59 |
| 60 | 4:35 | 4:57 | 9:50 | 10:37 | 17:03 | 35:22 | 54:18 | 1:18:09 | 2:43:25 | 60 |
| 61 | 4:31 | 4:53 | 9:41 | 10:27 | 16:48 | 34:52 | 53:32 | 1:17:02 | 2:41:08 | 61 |
| 62 | 4:27 | 4:49 | 9:33 | 10:18 | 16:34 | 34:23 | 52:47 | 1:15:57 | 2:38:54 | 62 |
| 63 | 4:24 | 4:45 | 9:25 | 10:10 | 16:20 | 33:55 | 52:03 | 1:14:54 | 2:36:44 | 63 |
| 64 | 4:20 | 4:41 | 9:17 | 10:01 | 16:07 | 33:28 | 51:21 | 1:13:53 | 2:34:38 | 64 |
| 65 | 4:16 | 4:37 | 9:09 | 9:53 | 15:54 | 33:01 | 50:40 | 1:12:53 | 2:32:35 | 65 |
| 66 | 4:13 | 4:33 | 9:02 | 9:45 | 15:42 | 32:35 | 50:00 | 1:11:56 | 2:30:36 | 66 |
| 67 | 4:10 | 4:30 | 8:55 | 9:37 | 15:29 | 32:11 | 49:22 | 1:11:00 | 2:28:40 | 67 |
| 68 | 4:06 | 4:26 | 8:48 | 9:30 | 15:18 | 31:46 | 38:44 | 1:10:05 | 2:26:47 | 68 |
| 69 | 4:03 | 4:23 | 8:41 | 9:23 | 15:06 | 31:23 | 48:08 | 1:09:12 | 2:24:57 | 69 |
| 70 | 4:00 | 4:19 | 8:34 | 9:16 | 14:55 | 31:00 | 47:32 | 1:08:21 | 2:23:10 | 70 |
| 71 | 3:57 | 4:16 | 8:28 | 9:09 | 14:44 | 30:38 | 46:58 | 1:07:31 | 2:21:26 | 71 |
| 72 | 3:54 | 4:13 | 8:22 | 9:02 | 14:33 | 30:16 | 46:24 | 1:06:42 | 2:19:44 | 72 |
| 73 | 3:52 | 4:10 | 8:16 | 8:55 | 14:23 | 29:55 | 45:51 | 1:05:54 | 2:18:05 | 73 |
| 74 | 3:49 | 4:07 | 8:10 | 8:49 | 14:13 | 29:34 | 45:19 | 1:05:08 | 2:16:29 | 74 |
| 75 | 3:46 | 4:04 | 8:04 | 8:43 | 14:03 | 29:14 | 44:48 | 1:04:23 | 2:14:55 | 75 |
| 76 | 3:44 | 4:02 | 7:58 | 8:37 | 13:54 | 28:55 | 44:18 | 1:03:39 | 2:13:23 | 76 |
| 77 | 3:41+ | 3:58+ | 7:53 | 8:31 | 13:44 | 28:36 | 43:49 | 1:02:56 | 2:11:54 | 77 |
| 78 | 3:38.8 | 3:56.2 | 7:48 | 8:25 | 13:35 | 28:17 | 43:20 | 1:02:15 | 2:10:27 | 78 |
| 79 | 3:36.5 | 3:53.7 | 7:43 | 8:20 | 13:26 | 27:59 | 42:52 | 1:01:34 | 2:09:02 | 79 |
| 80 | 3:34.2 | 3:51.2 | 7:37.5 | 8:14.2 | 13:17.8 | 27:41.2 | 42:25 | 1:00:54 | 2:07:38 | 80 |
| 81 | 3:31.9 | 3.48.7 | 7:32.5 | 8:08.9 | 13:09.3 | 27:24 | 41:58 | 1:00:15 | 2:06:17 | 81 |
| 82 | 3:29.7 | 3:46.4 | 7:27.8 | 8:03.7 | 13:01.1 | 27:07 | 41:32 | 59:38 | 2:04:57 | 82 |
| 83 | 3:27.6 | 3:44.1 | 7:23.1 | 7:58.7 | 12:53.0 | 26:51 | 41:06 | 59:01 | 2:03:40 | 83 |
| 84 | 3:25.5 | 3:41.8 | 7:18.5 | 7:53.7 | 12:45.2 | 26:34 | 40:42 | 58:25 | 2:02:24 | 84 |
| 85 | 3:23.5 | 3:39.6 | 7:14.1 | 7:48.9 | 12:37.4 | 26:19 | 40:17 | 57:50 | 2:01:10 | 85 |

# Establishing Training Intensities From a VDOT Value

Once you have established your VDOT, the next thing you need to do is to set training intensities, which can be done using the information in table 3.2. To use table 3.2, find the VDOT value from table 3.1 that best applies to you, and move across table 3.2 to see the various paces for the different kinds of training that you will be doing. For example, a runner with a best VDOT of 50 (based on a 5000-meter time of 19:57 in table 3.1) would shoot for the following paces:

Easy and long runs—5:07 per 1000 meters or 8:14 per mile

Marathon pace—7:17 per mile

Threshold (tempo or cruise-interval pace)—1:42 per 400 meters, 4:15 per 1000 meters, and 6:51 per mile

Interval pace—93 seconds per 400 meters, 3:55 per 1000 meters, and 4:41 per 1200 meters

Repetition pace—43 seconds per 200 meters and 87 seconds per 400 meters

In the 50-VDOT example cited above there is no mile pace noted for **I** training. A single bout of work in an interval session shouldn't last longer than about five minutes, and with a VDOT of 50, interval mile pace would be 6:12, which is too demanding. In this case, interval 1200s or 1000s would be the recommended distances for long intervals (4:41 per 1200 in the example above). For a list of over 40 race distances and their associated VDOT values, the book *Oxygen Power* can be a valuable guide.

## The Daniels "2.2 + Six-Seconds" Rule

As a result of constantly dealing with VDOT values and their associated training intensities (paces), it has become clear to me that a different rule can be applied to some race performances, and training intensities can be arrived at without referring to the VDOT tables.

Refer to table 3.3 on pages 70 and 71, one that I devised in the late 1960s to associate the times for 400-, 800-, 1500-meter, or mile race performances. If you put a mark by your recent race times for these

| Table 3.2 | Training Intensities Based on Current VDOT |

| VDOT | E/L Pace | | MP | T Pace | | | I Pace | | | | R Pace | | |
|:---:|:---:|:---:|:---:|:---:|:---:|:---:|:---:|:---:|:---:|:---:|:---:|:---:|:---:|
| | km | mile | mile | 400 | 1000 | mile | 400 | 1000 | 1200 | mile | 200 | 400 | 800 |
| 30 | 7:37 | 12:16 | 11:02 | 2:33 | 6:24 | 10:18 | 2:22 | — | — | — | 67 | 2:16 | — |
| 32 | 7:16 | 11:41 | 10:29 | 2:26 | 6:05 | 9:47 | 2:14 | — | — | — | 63 | 2:08 | — |
| 34 | 6:56 | 11:09 | 10:00 | 2:19 | 5:48 | 9:20 | 2:08 | — | — | — | 60 | 2:02 | — |
| 36 | 6:38 | 10:40 | 9:33 | 2:13 | 5:33 | 8:55 | 2:02 | 5:07 | — | — | 57 | 1:55 | — |
| 38 | 6:22 | 10:14 | 9:08 | 2:07 | 5:19 | 8:33 | 1:56 | 4:54 | — | — | 54 | 1:50 | — |
| 40 | 6:07 | 9:50 | 8:46 | 2:02 | 5:06 | 8:12 | 1:52 | 4:42 | — | — | 52 | 1:46 | — |
| 42 | 5:53 | 9:28 | 8:25 | 1:57 | 4:54 | 7:52 | 1:48 | 4:31 | — | — | 50 | 1:42 | — |
| 44 | 5:40 | 9:07 | 8:06 | 1:53 | 4:43 | 7:33 | 1:44 | 4:21 | — | — | 48 | 98 | — |
| 45 | 5:34 | 8:58 | 7:57 | 1:51 | 4:38 | 7:25 | 1:42 | 4:16 | — | — | 47 | 96 | — |
| 46 | 5:28 | 8:48 | 7:48 | 1:49 | 4:33 | 7:17 | 1:40 | 4:12 | 5:00 | — | 46 | 94 | — |
| 47 | 5:23 | 8:39 | 7:40 | 1:47 | 4:29 | 7:10 | 98 | 4:07 | 4:54 | — | 45 | 92 | — |
| 48 | 5:17 | 8:31 | 7:32 | 1:45 | 4:24 | 7:02 | 96 | 4:03 | 4:49 | — | 44 | 90 | — |
| 49 | 5:12 | 8:22 | 7:24 | 1:43 | 4:20 | 6:55 | 95 | 3:59 | 4:45 | — | 44 | 89 | — |
| 50 | 5:07 | 8:14 | 7:17 | 1:42 | 4:15 | 6:51 | 93 | 3:55 | 4:41 | — | 43 | 87 | — |
| 51 | 5:02 | 8:07 | 7:09 | 1:40 | 4:11 | 6:44 | 92 | 3:51 | 4:36 | — | 42 | 86 | — |
| 52 | 4:58 | 7:59 | 7:02 | 98 | 4:07 | 6:38 | 91 | 3:48 | 4:33 | — | 42 | 85 | — |
| 53 | 4:53 | 7:52 | 6:56 | 97 | 4:04 | 6:32 | 90 | 3:44 | 4:29 | — | 41 | 84 | — |
| 54 | 4:49 | 7:45 | 6:49 | 95 | 4:00 | 6:26 | 88 | 3:41 | 4:25 | — | 40 | 82 | — |
| 55 | 4:45 | 7:38 | 6:43 | 94 | 3:56 | 6:20 | 87 | 3:37 | 4:21 | — | 40 | 81 | — |
| 56 | 4:40 | 7:31 | 6:37 | 93 | 3:53 | 6:15 | 86 | 3:34 | 4:18 | — | 39 | 80 | — |
| 57 | 4:36 | 7:25 | 6:31 | 91 | 3:50 | 6:09 | 85 | 3:31 | 4:15 | — | 39 | 79 | — |
| 58 | 4:33 | 7:19 | 6:25 | 90 | 3:45 | 6:04 | 83 | 3:28 | 4:10 | — | 38 | 77 | — |
| 59 | 4:29 | 7:13 | 6:19 | 89 | 3:43 | 5:59 | 82 | 3:25 | 4:07 | — | 37 | 76 | — |
| 60 | 4:25 | 7:07 | 6:14 | 88 | 3:40 | 5:54 | 81 | 3:23 | 4:03 | — | 37 | 75 | 2:30 |
| 61 | 4:22 | 7:01 | 6:09 | 86 | 3:37 | 5:50 | 80 | 3:20 | 4:00 | — | 36 | 74 | 2:28 |
| 62 | 4:18 | 6:56 | 6:04 | 85 | 3:34 | 5:45 | 79 | 3:17 | 3:57 | — | 36 | 73 | 2:26 |
| 63 | 4:15 | 6:50 | 5:59 | 84 | 3:32 | 5:41 | 78 | 3:15 | 3:54 | — | 35 | 72 | 2:24 |

*(continued)*

## Table 3.2 (continued) Training Intensities Based on Current VDOT

| VDOT | E/L Pace km | E/L Pace mile | MP mile | T Pace 400 | T Pace 1000 | T Pace mile | I Pace 400 | I Pace 1000 | I Pace 1200 | I Pace mile | R Pace 200 | R Pace 400 | R Pace 800 |
|------|------|------|------|----|-----|-----|----|-----|-----|-----|-----|-----|-----|
| 64 | 4:12 | 6:45 | 5:54 | 83 | 3:29 | 5:36 | 77 | 3:12 | 3:51 | — | 35 | 71 | 2:22 |
| 65 | 4:09 | 6:40 | 5:49 | 82 | 3:26 | 5:32 | 76 | 3:10 | 3:48 | — | 34 | 70 | 2:20 |
| 66 | 4:05 | 6:53 | 5:45 | 81 | 3:24 | 5:28 | 75 | 3:08 | 3:45 | 5:00 | 34 | 69 | 2:18 |
| 67 | 4:02 | 6:30 | 5:40 | 80 | 3:21 | 5:24 | 74 | 3:05 | 3:42 | 4:57 | 33 | 68 | 2:16 |
| 68 | 4:00 | 6:26 | 5:36 | 79 | 3:19 | 5:20 | 73 | 3:03 | 3:39 | 4:53 | 33 | 67 | 2:14 |
| 69 | 3:57 | 6:21 | 5:32 | 78 | 3:16 | 5:16 | 72 | 3:01 | 3:36 | 4:50 | 32 | 66 | 2:12 |
| 70 | 3:54 | 6:17 | 5:28 | 77 | 3:14 | 5:13 | 71 | 2:59 | 3:34 | 4:46 | 32 | 65 | 2:10 |
| 71 | 3:51 | 6:12 | 5:24 | 76 | 3:12 | 5:09 | 70 | 2:57 | 3:31 | 4:43 | 31 | 64 | 2:08 |
| 72 | 3:49 | 6:08 | 5:20 | 76 | 3:10 | 5:05 | 69 | 2:55 | 3:29 | 4:40 | 31 | 63 | 2:06 |
| 73 | 3:46 | 6:04 | 5:16 | 75 | 3:08 | 5:02 | 69 | 2:53 | 3:27 | 4:37 | 31 | 62 | 2:05 |
| 74 | 3:44 | 6:00 | 5:12 | 74 | 3:06 | 4:59 | 68 | 2:51 | 3:25 | 4:34 | 30 | 62 | 2:04 |
| 75 | 3:41 | 5:56 | 5:09 | 74 | 3:04 | 4:56 | 67 | 2:49 | 3:22 | 4:31 | 30 | 61 | 2:03 |
| 76 | 3:39 | 5:52 | 5:05 | 73 | 3:02 | 4:52 | 66 | 2:48 | 3:20 | 4:28 | 29 | 60 | 2:02 |
| 77 | 3:36 | 5:48 | 5:01 | 72 | 3:00 | 4:49 | 65 | 2:46 | 3:18 | 4:25 | 29 | 59 | 2:00 |
| 78 | 3:34 | 5:45 | 4:58 | 71 | 2:58 | 4:46 | 65 | 2:44 | 3:16 | 4:23 | 29 | 59 | 1:59 |
| 79 | 3:32 | 5:41 | 4:55 | 70 | 2:56 | 4:43 | 64 | 2:42 | 3:14 | 4:20 | 28 | 58 | 1:58 |
| 80 | 3:30 | 5:38 | 4:52 | 70 | 2:54 | 4:41 | 64 | 2:41 | 3:12 | 4:17 | 28 | 58 | 1:56 |
| 81 | 3:28 | 5:34 | 4:49 | 69 | 2:53 | 4:38 | 63 | 2:39 | 3:10 | 4:15 | 28 | 57 | 1:55 |
| 82 | 3:26 | 5:31 | 4:46 | 68 | 2:51 | 4:35 | 62 | 2:38 | 3:08 | 4:12 | 27 | 56 | 1:54 |
| 83 | 3:24 | 5:28 | 4:43 | 68 | 2:49 | 4:32 | 62 | 2:36 | 3:07 | 4:10 | 27 | 56 | 1:53 |
| 84 | 3:22 | 5:25 | 4:40 | 67 | 2:48 | 4:30 | 61 | 2:35 | 3:05 | 4:08 | 27 | 55 | 1:52 |
| 85 | 3:20 | 5:21 | 4:37 | 66 | 2:46 | 4:27 | 61 | 2:33 | 3:03 | 4:05 | 27 | 55 | 1:51 |

distances, a straight line will probably connect the three performances. This line may slope down to the right, indicating better speed than endurance, or it may slope up to the right, which indicates better endurance than speed. A horizontal line suggests equal current ability in speed and endurance, which fits the profile of a surprising number of well-trained distance runners. Mathemati-

A. Enter best race times in past six weeks (or best guess) for events of 1500 meters or longer

| Distance | Time | Distance | Time |
|----------|------|----------|------|
| (1) _____ | _____ | (2) _____ | _____ |
| (3) _____ | _____ | (4) _____ | _____ |

Current (real or estimated) time for 800 meters, in total seconds (5) _____

Current (real or estimated) time for 400 meters, in total seconds (6) _____

Number in (5) $\times$ 2.20 = (7) _____ Number in (6) $\times$ 4.84 = (8) _____

Convert seconds in (7) to minutes:seconds (9) _____:_____

Convert seconds in (8) to minutes:seconds (10) _____:_____

B. Look up VDOT values for (1), (2), (3), and (4), and enter the highest number here (11) _____
If the 2nd highest of (1), (2), (3), and (4) is not within 2.0 of the value in (11), subtract 2.0 from the value in (11) and enter the difference in (12); if not, re-enter (11) in (12) _____

C. Look up the time in (9) under mile in the VDOT table and enter it here (13) _____
Look up the time in (10) under mile in VDOT table and enter it here (14) _____ Enter the lesser of VDOT's in (13) and (14) as (15) _____

D. If the VDOT in (15) is more than 2.0 greater than the VDOT in (12), then add 2.0 to the VDOT in (12) and enter that value in (16), below otherwise, use the average of VDOT's in (12) and (15) as (16) _____ current VDOT

E. Use table 3.2 and your current VDOT to set training paces for E/L, MP, T, I, and R

| | | | |
|---|---|---|---|
| E/L pace = | _____ per kilometer | _____ per mile | |
| MP = | _____ per kilometer | _____ per mile | |
| T = | _____ per kilometer | _____ per mile | |
| | _____ per 400 meters | | |
| I = | _____ per kilometer | _____ per mile | |
| | _____ per 1200 meters | _____ per 400 meters | |
| R = | _____ per 200 meters | _____ per 400 meters | |
| | _____ per 800 meters | | |

Complete this evaluation after any long layoff from running; otherwise use recent race performances to update the VDOT value used for determining training intensities.

**Figure 3.3** Self-evaluation form for establishment of a personal VDOT.

cally, times that fit a horizontal line are associated by a factor of 2.2 (multiplying a 400-meter time by 2.2 gives the corresponding 800-meter time, and multiplying an 800-meter time by 2.2 produces the corresponding 1600-meter time).

In addition, 1500-meter and mile race pace is essentially the proper speed for repetition (**R**) training, which is about six seconds faster per 400 meters than proper interval (**I**) pace. In fact, runners who can race a mile in 5:30 or faster can identify threshold (**T**) pace as being about six seconds slower per 400 meters than **I** pace, and marathon pace (**MP**) as six seconds slower per 400 meters than **T** pace. Using the six-seconds rule produces a **T** pace and an **MP** that are too aggressive for people whose best mile time is slower than 5:30; these people should stay with the VDOT tables all the way. On the other end of the scale, elite marathoners race at a pace closer to their **T** pace (about four seconds per 400 meters slower than **T** pace) and thus the six-second rule is not an accurate predictor of their **MP**.

# Adjusting Training Intensities

I suggest staying at a training intensity for at least three or four weeks, even if a race performance suggests that you have moved to a higher VDOT reference value. During a period of prolonged training, without races for evaluating improvement, it is safe to increase your VDOT value by a single unit after four to six weeks at the same value—if all is going well and workouts seem to be getting easier.

On a related note, a VDOT based on your best 1500-meter race, for example, doesn't necessarily mean that you can race a 10K at the equivalent VDOT value. It will tell you what an equivalent 10K time would be provided you adjust your training to prepare for a 10K race.

# Test Efforts

There are workouts that you can use as test efforts, with the idea of repeating the workouts later in the season to compare either performance times in the workout, or subjective feeling while repeating the same performance times. These test workouts are not set up to tell you how fast to train, but to give you a feeling of how your training is going.

## Table 3.3 Time Associations Between 400, 800, 1500, and Mile Runs

| 400m | 800m | 1500m | Mile | 400m | 800m | 1500m | Mile |
|------|------|-------|------|------|------|-------|------|
| 46.0 | 1:41.2 | 3:27.6 | 3:44.1 | 73.0 | 2:40.6 | 5:29.0 | 5:55.5 |
| 47.0 | 1:43.4 | 3:32.0 | 3:48.9 | 74.0 | 2:42.8 | 5:33.5 | 6:00.4 |
| 48.0 | 1:45.6 | 3:36.5 | 3:53.8 | 75.0 | 2:45.0 | 5:38.0 | 6:05.2 |
| 49.0 | 1:47.8 | 3:41.0 | 3:58.6 | 76.0 | 2:47.2 | 5:42.5 | 6:10.1 |
| 50.0 | 1:50.0 | 3:45.5 | 4:03.5 | 77.0 | 2:49.4 | 5:47.0 | 6:14.9 |
| 51.0 | 1:52.2 | 3:50.0 | 4:08.3 | 78.0 | 2:51.6 | 5:51.5 | 6:19.8 |
| 52.0 | 1:54.4 | 3:54.5 | 4:13.2 | 79.0 | 2:53.8 | 5:56.0 | 6:24.7 |
| 53.0 | 1:56.6 | 3:59.0 | 4:18.0 | 80.0 | 2:56.0 | 6:00.5 | 6:29.6 |
| 54.0 | 1:58.8 | 4:03.5 | 4:22.9 | 81.0 | 2:58.2 | 6:05.0 | 6:34.4 |
| 55.0 | 2:01.0 | 4:08.0 | 4:27.7 | 82.0 | 3:00.4 | 6:09.5 | 6:39.3 |
| 56.0 | 2:03.2 | 4:12.5 | 4:32.6 | 83.0 | 3:02.6 | 6:14.0 | 6:44.2 |
| 57.0 | 2:05.4 | 4:17.0 | 4:37.5 | 84.0 | 3:04.8 | 6:18.5 | 6:49.1 |
| 58.0 | 2:07.6 | 4:21.5 | 4:42.4 | 85.0 | 3:07.0 | 6:23.0 | 6:53.9 |
| 59.0 | 2:09.8 | 4:26.0 | 4:47.3 | 86.0 | 3:09.2 | 6:27.5 | 6:58.8 |
| 60.0 | 2:12.0 | 4:30.5 | 4:52.2 | 87.0 | 3:11.4 | 6:32.0 | 7:03.6 |
| 61.0 | 2:14.2 | 4:35.0 | 4:57.1 | 88.0 | 3:13.6 | 6:36.5 | 7:08.5 |
| 62.0 | 2:16.4 | 4:39.5 | 5:02.0 | 89.0 | 3:15.8 | 6:41.0 | 7:13.4 |
| 63.0 | 2:18.6 | 4:44.0 | 5:06.8 | 90.0 | 3:18.0 | 6:45.5 | 7:18.3 |
| 64.0 | 2:20.8 | 4:48.5 | 5:11.7 | 91.0 | 3:20.2 | 6:50.0 | 7:23.1 |
| 65.0 | 2:23.0 | 4:53.0 | 5:16.6 | 92.0 | 3:22.4 | 6:54.5 | 7:28.0 |
| 66.0 | 2:25.2 | 4:57.5 | 5:21.5 | 93.0 | 3:24.6 | 6:59.0 | 7:32.8 |
| 67.0 | 2:27.4 | 5:02.0 | 5:26.3 | 94.0 | 3:26.8 | 7:03.5 | 7:37.7 |
| 68.0 | 2:29.6 | 5:06.5 | 5:31.2 | 95.0 | 3:29.0 | 7:08.0 | 7:42.5 |
| 69.0 | 2:31.8 | 5:11.0 | 5:36.0 | 96.0 | 3:31.2 | 7:12.5 | 7:47.4 |
| 70.0 | 2:34.0 | 5:15.5 | 5:40.9 | 97.0 | 3:33.4 | 7:17.0 | 7:52.3 |
| 71.0 | 2:36.2 | 5:20.0 | 5:45.7 | 98.0 | 3:35.6 | 7:21.5 | 7:57.2 |
| 72.0 | 2:38.4 | 5:24.5 | 5:50.6 | 99.0 | 3:37.8 | 7:26.0 | 8:02.0 |

*(continued)*

## Table 3.3 (continued)  Time Associations Between 400, 800, 1500, and Mile Runs

| 400m | 800m | 1500m | Mile | 400m | 800m | 1500m | Mile |
|------|------|-------|------|------|------|-------|------|
| 1:40.0 | 3:40.0 | 7:30.5 | 8:06.9 | 1:45.0 | 3:51.0 | 7:53.0 | 8:31.3 |
| 1:41.0 | 3:42.2 | 7:35.0 | 8:11.8 | 1:46.0 | 3:53.2 | 7:57.5 | 8:36.1 |
| 1:42.0 | 3:44.4 | 7:39.5 | 8:16.6 | 1:47.0 | 3:55.4 | 8:02.0 | 8:41.0 |
| 1:43.0 | 3:46.6 | 7:44.0 | 8:21.5 | 1:48.0 | 3:57.6 | 8:06.5 | 8:45.9 |
| 1:44.0 | 3:48.8 | 7:48.5 | 8:26.4 | 1:49.0 | 3:59.8 | 8:11.0 | 8:50.8 |

# MONITORING HEART RATE TO GAUGE TRAINING INTENSITY

Can the knowledge of how fast your heart is beating be of use in reaching athletic excellence? As with any of our body's physiological functions, there are many interrelated factors in this regard. Heart rate is affected by blood flow, aerobic fitness, and the amount of oxygen being transported by the circulating blood. In addition, the temperature of the air around you, clothing being worn, the state of your health, and body-fluid status also affect heart rate.

Since cardiac output (amount of blood pumped per minute) is the product of heart rate and stroke volume (amount of blood pumped with each beat of the heart), it is useful to understand what affects the flow of blood around the body.

## Blood Flow

The body needs a particular amount of blood flowing to various parts at any given time. During exercise, blood flow increases dramatically to the exercising muscles and also possibly to the skin. Muscle demand is a function of how hard they are working, and skin demand depends on the body's need to hold down a rise in body temperature associated with exercise and climate.

Blood flow to any particular area is determined by cardiac output and resistance in the vessels which supply that area with its blood, and resistance is a function of where the body wants to divert blood by constricting some vessels and dilating others.

This in mind, the following are among the reasons that a change in heart rate may be noted:

1. a change in blood volume, often associated with degree of hydration or dehydration;
2. a change in blood available to be sent to the exercising muscles, which is dependent upon the amount routed to other areas, i.e., to the skin for cooling;
3. a change in overall fitness level; and
4. a change in the oxygen-carrying capacity of the blood, often dependent upon nutritional status.

## Measuring Heart Rate

Given the variety of conditions that affect HR, one must pay close attention to what exactly is being evaluated when monitoring it. Consider some of the times that athletes monitor their HR.

## Morning (Resting) Heart Rate

Some athletes use their "wake-up" HR to measure fitness, but keep in mind that resting heart rates can vary a great deal, even among highly-trained runners. A world-record holder I tested on numerous occasions never dropped below 60; others go well down into the 30s. Monitored on a regular basis, a slower morning HR can indicate improving fitness. Conversely, a consistent increase in wake-up HR often reflects overtraining, or possibly dehydration and/or poor nutritional status. In any case, measurements of resting HR can easily be performed with a finger on your pulse and a watch or clock with a second hand on it.

## Exercise Heart Rate

The idea in measuring heart rate during exercise is that by monitoring HR you know precisely how hard you are working. The problem with this assumption, as noted earlier, is that heart rate is influenced by many factors other than just how hard the body is exercising (working).

Therefore, if you adjust your work intensity to produce the same HR today that a previous workout suggests that it should, you actually could be working harder (or more easily) than you have set as a goal. Is your goal in training to produce a particular HR or is it to subject a specific system of the body to a certain amount of stress?

For example, if you have been performing particular workouts for a couple of months at sea level, will you try to reach the same HR in similar workouts at altitude? If so, you surely are understressing the exercising muscles, because at altitude less oxygen is being delivered with each beat of the heart, and to get the same oxygen delivery, HR must increase. Otherwise, you will be undertraining the muscles targeted by that particular workout.

## Recovery Heart Rate

Recovery HR is often monitored by athletes in both aerobic and anaerobic events. As with resting HR, recovery values are also subject to contamination by factors other than those directly associated with the workbout from which you are recovering. So given that under different conditions, the same HR may reflect different degrees of recovery, it may be better to subjectively measure when you have had enough recovery.

Further, using a particular HR as a guide for recovery must be geared to each individual. You need to know the individual's resting HR as well as maximum HR (HRmax). For example, a HR of 120 beats/min will reflect a different degree of recovery for a runner with a resting HR of 70 beats/min and an HRmax of 200 beats/min, than it will for a runner with a resting HR of 40 beats/min and an HRmax of 160 beats/min.

Another area in which using specific rule-of-thumb HR can get a runner into trouble is using a particular formula for determining max HR—220 minus age, for example. I once tested a 30-year-old elite athlete who had an HRmax of 148 beats/min; 220 minus age for this runner would suggest an HRmax of 190 beats/min. Certainly any training based on percentages of an estimated HRmax of 190 would greatly overstress this individual. In fact, telling him to shoot for an HR of 160 in a certain workout would be unreasonable. I have also seen several world-class 50-year-old runners with HRmax in excess of 190. In these cases, 220 minus age would suggest a max of 170, and targeting 153 beats/min as the appropriate HR to represent 90% of these runners' max would be impossible.

## Other Concerns

It is not uncommon for HR to be higher on stationary exercise equipment (particularly indoors where there is little air movement), than when exercising at the same stress outdoors, where movement of air can lead to better body cooling. The body's reaction to increased heat stress is to send blood to the skin, which usually leads to a higher HR. Setting up a fan that faces indoor exercise equipment can help in this regard.

Having to wear more clothes during winter running can also affect the HR associated with any particular speed of running. Of course, running against (or with) the wind, over hilly terrain, or on poor footing are all factors that can affect HR as it may relate to a desired running pace.

## Benefits of Heart Rate Monitoring

Heart rate monitoring can be of benefit if the user understands its limitations and trains accordingly. Some athletes do not have measured courses over which to monitor training pace, and HR can aid them in performing a series of repeated exercise bouts at similar intensities. Heart rate can help determine relative stress when running against the wind, up and down hills, or over difficult footing. Possibly the greatest use of HR monitoring is to help avoid overtraining. When standard workouts under ideal conditions produce HR values that are higher than typical, it is usually an indication that something is wrong and further evaluation should be made.

In general, when pace can be adequately monitored, then pace itself tells the best tale. But when pace is not easily monitored, then HR can be useful in controlling intensity. The best approach is to learn to read your own body based on your own perceived exertion scale, and to train within the constraints that you monitor by using a device you have with you at all times—the built-in computer in your head.

1. *Repeated 400s (8 to 10) with one-minute recoveries.* If the 400-meter times are slower than 70 seconds, use the one-minute recoveries; if faster than 70 seconds, start a 400 every two minutes, which permits the remainder of the time for recovery (for example, running 400s in 65 seconds would allow 55 seconds of rest).

After a good warm-up, run the 400s with the fastest possible average for the total number run. The best approach is to run the first few 400s at your current one-mile race pace. After the first three or four 400s, try to speed up the pace a little, and keep going as best you can until all are finished. Do not put on a kick for the final 400; keep the same solid effort. Complete 10 runs if your pace is 70 seconds or faster; do nine if running between 71-second and 80-second pace; and complete eight if slower.

When done properly, this is a demanding session, because it is faster than interval pace, but is performed with short, interval-type recoveries.

The average pace that you can run for this test set is probably the pace at which you can race one mile or 1500 meters. In fact, your race pace may be faster than your average pace for this set, so it is important not to start out too fast or the short recoveries will catch up with you and the overall average time will not be the best estimate of your mile fitness. I recommend that you try this workout only a couple of times in a season, when you need a test.

2. *Repeated 200s (16 to 20), with one-minute send-offs.* With this test session, a 200 is started every minute if the pace is 40 seconds or faster; if the pace is slower, take a 30-second break between 200s. This is similar to the repeated 400s test, but with shorter runs, less rest between runs, and same total distance run (16 repeats if going slower than 40 seconds, 18 repeats if running between 35 and 39 seconds each, and 20 repeats if running faster than 35-second.)

3. *Three-mile-plus tempo test.* After a good warm-up, run a steady three-mile tempo run at your proper threshold pace, followed immediately by a  test-effort 1000 meters or mile. If your typical

Whether a coach is assisting you or you are training on your own, retesting your VDOT throughout the season will ensure that your training intensity matches your current fitness.

tempo run is four miles, add one mile to the end of the three-mile tempo run; if three miles is your tempo distance, add 1000 meters.

This test is best run on a track, but could be done on a flat road, if you always use the same course. Run at threshold pace for the initial tempo effort and see how much better you can go for the final 1000 meters or mile. Hold a hard, solid pace throughout the final few minutes.

4. *Three- to four-mile tempo run.* Conduct your usual tempo run at your proper threshold pace and record your reactions to this run. Evaluate your fitness subjectively or objectively (by testing heart rate or blood-lactate values). If you use subjective measures, try to rate the effort at the end of each mile, starting with mile two.

5. *Cruise-interval test.* Run four to six miles of cruise intervals with one-minute recoveries. Record your subjective feelings or your heart rate and blood-lactate values after each mile, starting with mile two. Do as many miles of cruise intervals as you would normally run in a workout based on current training levels. Be honest with your evaluation of feelings. Use your prescribed threshold pace.

6. *Cruise-plus test.* This test is similar to the three-mile-plus tempo test; it lets you see what kind of mile you can add to the end of a cruise-interval workout. To perform this test, run one fewer than your normal number of cruise intervals, and, following the usual one-minute recovery, see what kind of mile you can add on. For example, if your usual cruise-interval session involves five miles at 6:00 pace, do four cruise intervals at 6:00 pace, take the one-minute rest, and then see what you can do on the fifth interval, which is the true test.

# A Final Word

In addition to knowing your starting point and keeping on top of your training intensities, it is important to evaluate other aspects of your overall training situation. Write down your long-term and immediate race goals. Determine how many days each week you can train, and how much time each day. Are you able and willing to train twice on some days? Include the conditions that you expect during various phases of your season, such as the weather and the availability of a track, grass, or trails to train on. Is a treadmill available for training sessions, and is there a pool that you can use for deep-water running? When setting up a season of training, you must address these concerns in addition to the paces that you will apply to your quality workouts and how much total mileage you expect to run.

# Part II

# Training

# CHAPTER 4

# Building Your Training Base

*Training itself must be rewarding.*

Regardless of the phase of training you are in, always know why you are doing what you are doing, and have some goals in mind. If you have not been running for a period of time, start out with only easy running. I call this initial period of E-pace training "foundation/injury-prevention training." This is a good time to develop a regular stretching and muscle-strengthening routine to supplement your more formal running regimen.

Participants in any sport need to spend some time subjecting the body to low-intensity stress, mainly to prepare the body for more quality training, but also to develop those components of fitness that respond well to low-stress training. In this chapter I will address the types of training that fall into the category of relatively low-intensity stress (this type of training could be called "conversational" because you can carry on a conversation with another runner while performing these intensities of running). I will also explain how to keep track of the amount of running you are doing, and how to increase mileage.

## STRIDE RATE: A STEP IN THE RIGHT DIRECTION

One of the first things I teach new runners is some basics about running cadence, or stride rate. Elite distance runners tend to stride at about the same rate, almost always 180 or more steps per minute. This means that they are taking 90 or more steps with each foot each minute, a rate that doesn't vary much even when not running fast. The main change that is made as a runner goes faster is in stride length; the faster they go the longer the stride becomes, with little change in rate of leg turnover.

Quite different from elite runners is the rate taken by many beginning runners. When I have my new running classes count their own stride rates, I find that very few (sometimes none out of a class of 25 or 30 runners) take as many as 180 steps per minute. In fact, some turn over as slowly as 160 times per minute. The main problem associated with a slower turnover is that the slower you take steps, the longer the time you spend in the air, and the more time you are in the air, the higher you displace your body mass and the harder you hit the ground on landing. When you consider that many running injuries are the result of landing shock, it is not surprising that experienced runners tend to turn over faster than do individuals who are new to the sport.

If a group of beginners were required to start running 100 miles a week, right at the start of their running careers, probably one of two things would happen: there would be a substantial number of injuries, and those who didn't get hurt would learn to take quicker, lighter steps. I figure I can save a lot of runners a considerable amount of grief by encouraging them to convert to a stride rate that is associated with less landing shock and more efficient use of energy.

Several studies have been conducted on the energy demands of different stride frequencies, and it turns out that experienced runners are most efficient at their chosen rate of turnover; longer or shorter strides (which mean slower or faster stride rates) result in greater energy demands. However, when not working with experienced runners, running economy can often be improved by converting slow-turnover runners into runners using a faster rate.

My wife and I spent most of our time at the 1984 Olympics counting and measuring stride rates and stride lengths of both male and female runners competing in all distance events from 800 meters up to the marathon. The results were convincing—the fastest turnover rates were among the 800-meter specialists, and next were the 1500-meter runners, but from the 3000-meter distance on up to the marathon, there was very little variation in turnover rate. In fact, the women took only a few steps more per minute than did the larger men, who often were running considerably faster (as a result of longer stride length).

Next time you watch a marathon race on television, count how many times the right arm of one of the runners swings forward in 20 or 30 seconds. Use the recorded number to calculate a one-minute rate (if, of course, you accept the fact that the runner is swinging his or her right arm as often as he or she is taking steps). Every time I suggest this to someone, I remember the marathon runner I once tested who told me that he always felt good up to about the 17-mile mark, at which time "one leg starts going faster than the other." I've tried my best to figure out how that can happen, but have yet to witness it. In general, counting arm swings is an acceptable way to count strides.

Also try counting steps of the same runner after various stages of the race. Chances are the good runners will not lose the cadence they began with. We often talk about getting into a good running rhythm, and the one you want to get into is one that involves 180 or more steps per minute.

If you count your own stride rate and it is considerably slower than what I am suggesting, try to work on a shorter, lighter stride. Imagine that you are running over a field of raw eggs and you don't want to break any of them—run over the ground, not into it. Try to get the feeling that your legs are part of a wheel that just rolls along, not two pogo sticks that bounce along.

If you feel that you need practice improving your stride rate, concentrate on it during easy runs. Rate usually goes up for slower-turnover people when they race shorter distances, so often you don't need to think about it during faster quality training. When practicing turning over faster on easy training runs, don't let the fact that you are taking quicker steps force you to run faster. Try to run at your normal training speed, but do it with a shorter, quicker stride rate. With some practice, you will soon find it becomes quite natural, and probably more comfortable.

# Determining Your Weekly Mileage

The best measure of how much work you are doing, as a runner, is how much distance you are covering. It costs just about the same amount of energy to run eight miles in 40 minutes as it does to run eight miles in 60 minutes—you are doing the same amount of work; only the rate at which you do it varies. Therefore, the amount of work (mileage) that you are performing is a useful way to keep track of the stress to which you are subjecting yourself. Over time, those runners who adapt to more work will be capable of more work. Therefore, the amount of mileage performed is a logical starting point for a discussion of training.

Mileage should not be the focal point of your training as a distance runner, but you should be aware of weekly mileage so that you can use it as a basis for how much of the various types of quality work you do and so that your training is consistent. Just as current VDOT or v$\dot{V}O_2$max (based on current racing ability) should guide training intensities, so should current weekly mileage be used to set limits on quality sessions.

In the case of weekly mileage, remember the principles of stress and reaction (principle #1, page 14) and diminishing return (principle #7, page 25) presented in chapter 1. Stay with a set amount of mileage for at least three weeks before increasing your mileage. This will give your body a chance to adjust to and benefit from a particular load before moving on to a more demanding one. When it is time to increase your mileage, add to your weekly total as many miles (or one and one-half times as many kilometers) as the number of training sessions you are doing each week, up to a maximum of a 10-mile (15-kilometer) total adjustment. For example, after at least three weeks of 20 miles per week spread over five training sessions, the maximum increase should be 5 miles or 7.5 kilometers—1 mile (or 1.5 kilometers) for each of the five sessions that you are doing each week. In this case, you would be moving from 20 to 25 miles per week.

Another person, doing 10 or more workout sessions per week, could increase the weekly total by 10 miles, after spending at least three weeks at the previous amount. Let a 10-mile (15-kilometer) weekly increase be the maximum mileage change, even if you are running two or more daily sessions, seven days a week.

## Account for Individual Limits

The principle of personal limits (principle #6, page 24) advises you not to increase mileage just because a three-week period at current mileage has elapsed. Everything you do must have a purpose and must be judged by how you feel and how you perform in training and in races. You might find that 45 miles a week is ideal for you, based on goals, available time, and injuries, for example. This means that mileage increases are not appropriate at this time. Also, you may not want to increase mileage as often as every third week, or by as many miles or kilometers as there are training sessions. That's fine; simply make smaller adjustments, but use the guidelines previously mentioned to prevent you from making too great a demand on yourself.

## How Much Is Enough?

When is it time to put a cap on the workload you are imposing on yourself? This is an individual matter and should be considered prudently while keeping your goals in mind. A mileage total that works for one person may be not enough, or too much, for another. Certainly, a new runner shouldn't copy a veteran runner's training program. In addition to daily and weekly considerations, training must be thought of in blocks of weeks, and even in yearly cycles. Weeks totaling 100 miles may be good for you, but only after a few years of lesser weekly mileage. Besides the daily stresses imposed by training, there are more gradual long-term stresses that take their toll (and can produce adaptations, as well). What you will be able to handle next year is a function of the stress you placed on yourself this year and the adaptations made by your body during the current season. The principle of personal limits (principle #6, page 24) applies in this case.

## Rest Periods

Longer-term adaptations depend partly on how you treat your body. You may need a full six-week rest period somewhere during the year. In fact, more than one "rest-from-running" period may be more appropriate for you than continuous training. Top-notch runners seem to take more breaks from running than do average or aspiring runners, but all runners can benefit from breaks in training. Unfortunately, most runners' breaks in training are of the unplanned variety. Many runners train too hard and find that an injury forces a furlough from running in order to recover. It is better to build lay offs into a yearly running schedule and enjoy them while injury free (see chapter 9).

## Event-Specific Training

Another factor that determines limits of weekly mileage is the event for which you are training. A marathoner needs more total mileage than a 1500-meter specialist. Some people overlook this obvious fact. It is true that the 1500-meter runner may reap considerable benefit by undergoing a period of high mileage training, and that the marathoner can benefit from periods of lesser mileage while working on a specific system, but basically, the marathoner should get in more distance than the shorter-distance specialist. The principle of specificity of training (principle #2, page 15) applies in this case.

Still, marathoners shouldn't necessarily run 120 miles per week, even if you polled the top 50 marathoner men and women and found they all ran between 100 and 150 miles per week. Consider how many years they have been running; it might have taken them eight years to build up to what they are currently doing. Maybe some of these top marathoners were once running higher mileage totals and have cut back to 120 miles per week. Also, remember that some of the top 50 marathoners

Training as hard as Lynn Jennings may not be very beneficial if you are not ready for that sort of load. Take into account your personal limits as you build your training base.

- may not be running as well as they could be on less (or more) mileage,
- have bodies that can handle more mileage stress than most people's bodies (the genetic factor), and
- have more time and financial backing to support the demands of the training program that they are following.

## CHRIS MCCUBBINS

**Chris McCubbins** took up running at age 15 because "it was the only sport I could do; as a teen I was very small and weak." His initial goal as a runner was to make his high school team. After graduating from high school, Chris attended Oklahoma State University where he ran track and cross-country.

During college Chris won the NCAA title in the 3000 steeplechase and continued his winning ways with a steeplechase victory at the 1967 Pan American Games. Chris also broke the NCAA steeplechase record and some years later the North American 15K record. The latter accomplishment came after Chris had taken up residency in Winnipeg and had become a Canadian citizen.

I became acquainted with Chris when he was in college and I was coaching at Oklahoma City University. He was recruited as one of my altitude research subjects and made one of the best adaptations to altitude of all the runners competing in the 1968 Olympic Games in Mexico City. In 1976, Chris made the Canadian Olympic Team in the 10,000. Chris's typical weekly mileage during his most successful years varied from 100 to 160 miles per week. He credits repeated runs of 800 to 2000 meters over undulating terrain as the key quality training he performed. He felt his major strength (and possibly also his major weakness because of injury potential) was his mental ability to relentlessly push himself.

Chris was a true free spirit who was extremely helpful to me during my days as an altitude researcher as both a research assistant and test subject. The most important thing I learned from Chris was that no matter how much better you are than the person you may be going on a run with, it is important to let the other person create a comfortable pace for himself or herself. You accomplish little by trying to run your workout partners into the ground.

**Chris's Bests**    5000: 13:44    10,000: 28:16

## Don't Do Too Much Too Fast

As with any type of training, monitor the results as you increase mileage and as you increase intensity. It is a long road to reaching your potential; rushing along that road too fast may send you on a detour and prevent you from taking the shortest path. Overtraining should not be your most common type of training. If you are doing well on a given amount of training and are eager to move up in mileage, it's okay to give it a try. If results are negative after several weeks, however, a mileage increase may not have been the right move for you at that particular time. Don't train harder for the sake of training harder; train harder to achieve better fitness and better performance. If you are not performing better, then realize that the harder work you are doing is not producing the desired results.

I wish I could say, "You must run x miles per week to be a good marathoner"; however, I just don't believe the picture is clear enough to make a statement like that. I feel comfortable saying that you must average somewhere between 70 and 120 miles (110 to 200 kilometers) per week to optimize your performance as a marathoner, but even 70 miles (110 kilometers) may be too much for some people, particularly during their first year or two of running. And some people may be able to go beyond what I have suggested as upper limits, like the elite runner I described in chapter 1 (not a marathoner, by the way) who ran an average of 240 miles per week one year and a 300-mile weekly average for one six-week stretch.

The inability to lay out specific training loads that can be applied to everyone is the very reason that we'll never be able to do away with coaches. Runners need someone to say, "You are starting to look real good running," or, "You are looking sort of dead-legged and I think you better cut back on the mileage for a while before an injury does it for you."

I am a strong believer in avoiding overtraining rather than spending lots of time and money to research at what point a runner is overtrained.

The more we try to identify overtraining, the more we will probably try to use the indices of overtraining as goals to shoot for. One of the best goals you can have is to race better, i.e., run faster times or race well and recover more easily. Trying to drive your body fat down to 4% and running on the brink of overtraining are not desirable goals.

Runners' and coaches' egos can get in the way of optimal training. It sometimes seems to mean more to talk about the great workouts you or your athletes have been doing than to watch the great race results come in. I am not impressed by the guy who brags about doing 150-mile weeks and can't hold a competitive marathon pace for 20 miles, nor by the guy with the lab-determined 90 ml·kg$^{-1}$·min$^{-1}$ $\dot{V}O_2$max who drops out at the 20-mile mark of a marathon because the pace was too fast. Both have been misled somewhere along the line.

Your training should bring you a certain degree of enjoyment (or satisfaction). Don't let training performance be your goal, but do enjoy the training and the satisfaction of being fit and healthy. It is disheartening to hear that "four years of training were wasted" because someone did not make the Olympic team. If you carry that reasoning to the extreme, you could say that four years were wasted because an Olympian did not win a gold medal; or three gold medals; or three gold medals, three world records, and a $1 million endorsement. If winning is the only thing that rescues athletes from "wasting their time training," then there are a lot of unhappy people wasting their time in sports. It is true that you train to improve performance, but there are lots of other benefits that come from training. Your training should be enjoyed, not just endured.

## Think Duration, Not Distance

I offer a final note about mileage: Although mileage is a convenient way to monitor work accomplished, it is often better to think in terms of total time spent training than in terms of distance covered. I think that two hours a day of running is quite a lot, and I can't imagine getting away with more than about three hours a day (about 30 miles a day for an elite distance runner). Remember, stress is a function of time spent doing something, so slower runners are often stressed more, even when completing lower mileage than their faster counterparts. That's why a 20-mile run is more stressful for a slow runner than for a faster individual.

A 20-mile run will take a slow runner three or more hours to complete; a fast runner will cover the same 20 miles in two hours. This means that

© Ken Lee

By measuring your training in duration instead of distance, you will help to prevent overtraining and injury. It's the number of steps you take that counts, not the number of miles.

the slower runner has taken 50% more steps than the faster person, even though they covered the same distance. It is the number of steps that can wear you down, and it is the extra hour in the heat or on slick roads that takes its toll. It's not just the 20 miles, it's the time spent completing those 20 miles. To avoid overtraining and injury, a slower runner may have to run less total mileage than a faster runner.

At the outset of this chapter, I referred to a few types of training sessions that fit into the category of running intensity. Following are some details regarding these types of sessions. Information about these training types was also provided in chapter 2.

# Easy Runs

Easy (**E**) runs are usually run in the morning, or are second runs in a two-a-day schedule. They also are used in the early phase of warm-up and cool-down sessions and during recovery between higher-intensity training bouts. An **E** run means running easily, and on many days that is all a runner needs to do. I suggest a minimum of 30 minutes for most **E** runs; the stress is not great and the benefits are substantial. With shorter **E** runs you are likely to spend more time changing clothes and showering than actually running. An **E** day of training could mean anything from no running (obviously easy) to two different runs lasting up to an hour or so each. The important point is that the intensity should be easy.

# Long Runs

The long (**L**) run is a steady run performed at **E** pace (based on your VDOT). (If you have no basis for determining a VDOT—if you have run no races recently or if you are unable to guess your current fitness—just make **E** pace a comfortable one, conversational in nature.) Set a long-run goal of 25% to 30% of your total weekly mileage, and place a two-and-a-half-hour limit on this run. An upper limit of 20 to 22 miles works well for many good runners. However, less talented or less fit runners who set 20 miles as their **L** run goal stand a greater chance of overstressing themselves (the run may take three hours or more to complete). Certainly, runs lasting three hours or more are not popular for elite runners, so why should they be useful for a less talented person? Ultramarathoners and some marathoners will benefit from runs in excess of 20 miles, but the improvement in performance for races like a marathon, half-marathon, 15K, and 10K is likely to be very slight (if it exists at all) in a physiological sense.

When I refer to setting the distance of the **L** run at 25% to 30% of weekly mileage, I am talking about the "long run" used by any runner, not just a marathoner. If you are doing 40 miles a week, your

L run would be about 10 miles (25% of 40 = 10). The 30% value is more likely to be used by people who train fewer than seven days per week at relatively low mileage. After all, someone who runs only four days a week is already averaging 25% of weekly mileage per training session.

# Marathon-Pace Runs

I got the idea of marathon-pace (**MP**) runs from one of my former subjects, Bob Williams, who is now a successful coach, and was a very successful runner. **MP** runs allow the athlete to spend time running at the pace at which he or she hopes to race an upcoming marathon. This type of training run is usually set aside for someone training for a marathon, but on occasion **MP** runs can be stimulating for just about any distance runner.

I like the duration of an **MP** run to be between one and one-half to two and one-half hours, but not to exceed 16 miles. To run fairly long at this pace can be demanding, so it is often best to perform this type of training session in a race situation. Find a half-marathon race you can run at **MP** pace, or a marathon race in which you can run part way. Being around other runners makes this type of training run much easier to handle. When you do an **MP** run as part of an official race, make sure you don't interfere with others and don't get caught up in the excitement and go too fast or too far. Doing an **MP** run is a great opportunity to practice drinking and otherwise preparing for an impending marathon race.

# A Final Word

Easy runs, long runs, and marathon-pace runs are all beneficial to the development of important physiological attributes that stay with you well and do not demand high-intensity stress to achieve. Not only do these types of training produce direct benefits, but they also contribute to the overall building of resistance to injury and to a solid foundation (base) from which to build faster training sessions in the weeks, months, and years ahead. Probably 80% to 85% of the running any runner does will be at an intensity associated with these types of runs. They are good opportunities to reap substantial benefits from relatively low-stress training. Also, these runs are almost always enjoyable to perform. Don't let total mileage dominate your training thoughts to the extent that other types of training are overlooked. The advantages of easy and long runs stay with you well; profit from them, then move on to other training as you carry the earlier benefits with you.

# CHAPTER 5

# Threshold Training

*Consistency is the key to productive training.*

The two types of threshold training that I will explain in this chapter are tempo runs and cruise intervals. Tempo runs, which are steady, moderately prolonged runs, have been around for some time, even though various runners and coaches define them differently. Cruise intervals are a series of repeated runs with a brief recovery between runs. I will address the differences and similarities between tempo and cruise-interval workouts and explain the danger of trying to perform at a faster pace than is adequate. It is very important to run threshold workouts at the proper intensity (speed). The correct pace for both tempo runs and cruise intervals is the same—a pace I refer to as threshold (T) pace.

The term "cruise interval" is one that I introduced to the running community in the 1980s. I heard the term used by swimmers when I was involved in testing many of our national and Olympic team members. About the same time, Bertil Sjödin, a Swedish researcher and running coach, told me about the benefits of threshold training, both in the form of steady tempo runs and when performed as an interval session. So, the term that I borrowed from swimming was attached to the type of training that Sjödin told me about, and cruise intervals became a common type of training for runners.

Whether you are doing a tempo run or a set of cruise intervals, the proper pace is about 86%-88% of $\dot{V}O_2max$, or 90% of $v\dot{V}O_2max$ or maximum heart rate. One of the most productive types of training that distance runners can do is T-pace running. It does a great job of helping runners to avoid overtraining, and thus leads to more satisfying training and better consistency. You can find your T pace in table 3.2.

# Tempo Runs

A tempo run is nothing more than a steady 20-minute run at T pace. Subjectively, the intensity of effort associated with T-pace running is comfortably hard. The effort should be one that you could maintain for about one hour in a race.

It is important to perform tempo runs under desirable weather conditions and on relatively flat terrain with good footing, because the goal of this workout is to maintain a steady intensity of effort for a prolonged period of time. Hills, rough footing, and wind all play havoc with the ability to maintain a steady pace, and interfere with achieving the purpose of the workout. You could monitor your heart rate, but a steady rhythm under constant conditions is the desired approach to a tempo run.

Possibly the biggest challenge in doing tempo runs is to hold the proper pace and to resist making the tempo run into a time trial. Remember, the proper pace is more beneficial than a faster (or slower) one. This is a good type of workout for practicing your ability to concentrate on a running task and to keep in touch with how your body feels while running comfortably hard.

Begin a tempo workout with a good warm-up. Follow the tempo run itself by a cool-down, which should include some strides—four or five 20- to 40-second runs at about mile race pace. You'll be surprised how good you feel about 10 minutes after a tempo run.

## Variations on Tempo Running

The ideal duration of a tempo run is 20 minutes, but this can vary somewhat to accommodate a particular course. For example, if your T pace is 6:00-mile pace, and you choose a three-mile course, this will give you an 18-minute tempo effort; or you may go four miles for a 24-minute tempo run. Naturally, you could go exactly 20 minutes, using the mile markers to set proper pace, and stop between three and one-quarter and three and one-half miles. It is not a bad idea to do tempo runs on the track (or even a treadmill, now and then) so that pace can be closely controlled.

## Don't Push Yourself Past the Proper Intensity

I offer some words of caution regarding how often to repeat identical workouts and monitor progress in a particular type of workout: With human nature being what it is, runners often want to see progress in their workouts and often try to perform a particular workout at faster and faster speeds over the course of a fairly short period of time. Trying to compete against yourself in this way is inadvisable. It does not conform to the principle of letting your body react and adjust to a particular type of stress before increasing the amount of stress (principle #5, page 20). So, perform the same workout quite a few times at the same speed, or until a race performance indicates that you have achieved a higher fitness level.

Richard C. Etchberger

Maintain proper pacing during your tempo runs. Running faster than your current VDOT stipulates will do more harm than good.

One of the best ways to monitor how your training is progressing is to see how much more easily you can perform a particular workout as time goes by. If what used to be a tough workout becomes not so tough after several weeks of training, then that is a great sign that your training is paying off in a positive way. At this point, you are usually ready for an increase in intensity or amount of training. In contrast, always trying to see if you can go faster in a workout that you have done before (the "always hurt as much as possible" technique) can be very misleading in trying to determine how much progress you are making. With this approach, you always hurt the same (or more), and you never get to experience doing a standard workout with diminishing discomfort. Doubts begin to set in as you ask yourself, "Am I really getting better or just learning to tolerate more pain?" If you often hurt badly in practice, a race won't be anything special; you should be able to take on more discomfort in a race than you do in daily training.

A more sophisticated way to monitor the degree of stress of a workout is to check heart rates or blood-lactate values at various points during the effort or during recovery. Relying on these more scientific means of keeping track of your progress, however, can prevent you from learning how to do a good job of it on your own. Whether or not you use mechanical or electronic devices to monitor body responses, you should still learn to read your body's feelings and reactions to the various types of workouts that you do.

# Cruise Intervals

Cruise intervals are repeated runs of anywhere from about 3 to 10 or even 15 minutes each, broken up by short recovery periods (usually one minute each, or less). The great advantage of the brief recoveries is that blood-lactate levels remain fairly constant and the runner experiences threshold effort throughout the entire training session, which can last a fair bit longer than could be accomplished with a steady tempo run. Even though it involves more T-pace running per workout than does a tempo run, a cruise-interval session is usually easier to do because the runner looks forward to the little breaks that come periodically throughout the workout.

A typical cruise-interval workout might consist of 5 repeated miles at T pace, with one-minute recoveries. Another possibility is 8 or 10 repeated 1000-meter runs at T pace with 30-second to one-minute recoveries. Miles, and 1000-meter, 1200-meter, 2000-meter, and even 2-mile runs are pretty common distances to repeat in a cruise-interval workout. Slower runners would usually select shorter distances, and, in fact, may find repeated 800s to be a good cruise-interval workout.

The total amount of quality running for a cruise-interval workout is up to 10% of your current weekly mileage, with a maximum of 8 miles or 13,000 meters, and a minimum of 4 miles or 6000 meters. A runner averaging 40 miles per week would do the 4-mile minimum; a 120-mile-per-week runner would do up to 8 miles or 13K of T-pace running in a session. I think that elite marathon runners are best suited for the upper mileage extremes, as opposed to the average runner, who may be well advised not to exceed 6 miles or 10,000 meters in a single cruise-interval session. I have found, with several of the marathoners I have coached, that mixing 8 miles of T-pace running with an hour (or up to 10 miles) of easy running in the same workout satisfies the needs of a long run and a threshold session. The idea behind this demanding workout is that the T-pace running forces the running muscles to use up glycogen stores

Cruise intervals are an excellent way to prepare for the rigors of upcoming races.

## BREATHING RHYTHMS

Most elite distance runners breathe with what is referred to as a 2-2 rhythm—taking 2 steps (1 with the right foot, 1 with the left foot) while breathing in, and 2 steps while breathing out. This gives the runner about 45 breaths per minute (remember that most good runners take about 180 steps per minute, 90 with each foot), because with 4 steps for each respiratory cycle (2 steps breathing in, 2 breathing out), 180 divided by 4 equals 45.

This is an ideal rate because it gives the runner adequate time for a substantial amount of air to be moved in and out of the lungs with each breath.

In the latter stages of an intense middle-distance race, 45 breaths per minute may not be enough. In this case, due to the desire to maintain some regular rhythm of breathing, the tendency is to shift to about 60 breaths per minute, which means either taking 1 step while breathing in and 2 while breathing out, or 2 in and 1 out. These would be referred to as 1-2 or 2-1 rhythms. The latter seems to be preferred by most good runners.

When not breathing particularly hard, slower breathing rhythms are sometimes used. An example is a 3-3 rhythm (3 steps breathing in, 3 steps breathing out), which is often used during easy runs, but becomes stressful at **T** pace or faster. A 4-4 rhythm can be used, but is not recommended, since the depth of breathing is energy-consuming, and ventilation is not as relaxed. A 1-1 rhythm is often used by runners who try to increase rate rather than depth of breathing, in an attempt to get more air into their lungs. However, 1-1 breathing leads to very shallow breathing (more like panting) and is not an efficient way to ventilate the lungs. This is not a recommended pattern of breathing.

Actually, a runner can use different breathing rates in various ways, an important one being during a warm-up. Start your warm-up with a 4-4 rhythm, switch to 3-3 after a few minutes, and then to 2-2 for the remainder of the warm-up. This often gives you something to concentrate on when going through an otherwise boring warm-up period.

Breathing rate can also be used to monitor intensity of effort while running. You should be comfortable with a 3-3 pattern on an easy run, and maybe even a 4-4 pattern, if so desired. However, if 3-3 does not provide you with enough air on an easy run, then it's not an easy run. Slow down to where 3-3 is comfortable. You may prefer 2-2 on an easy run, but be able to go 3-3 if necessary, if for no other reason than to prove it is an easy run. On the other hand, 3-3 is not fast enough to meet the demands of a distance race; the recommended rhythm is 2-2.

Knowledge of breathing rhythms can assist you in races, by helping you determine how fast to run up hills, for example. If you are trying to maintain a constant intensity while going up and down hills, focus on adjusting speed so that the 2-2 rhythm feels equally demanding (or comfortable) during all terrain changes. Naturally, this means slowing down on the rough terrain (or up hills) and being able to speed up going down hills.

Another situation when knowledge of breathing rhythm can be useful is when you get a side stitch. Usually stitches are aggravated by a fast, shallow breathing rate; a slower, deeper pattern can aid or eliminate a side stitch. Next time you get one of these sharp pains in the side or gut, try going to a 3-3 breathing rhythm and see if that helps.

About the only time a 1-1 rhythm may not be detrimental is during the final minute or so of a race. Keeping a 1-1 pattern for longer than a couple of minutes is usually counterproductive. In general, you will use a 2-2 rhythm in most races, possibly switching to 2-1 the last third of the race. In a marathon, 2-2 should be possible throughout the race (and 3-3, if need be).

Another situation in which knowledge of breathing patterns is of considerable aid is when you first are exposed to running at altitude. Let your typical rhythms guide you on easy runs and T runs in particular. If you usually use a 3-3 or 2-2 on these intensities, respectively, then adjust your speed of running at altitude to allow the same degree of discomfort as is normal at sea level. This is better than trying to reproduce the same speed of running you are used to at sea level.

During all types of training, the same principles apply. A 2-2 breathing rhythm is preferred for most quality training. Even though 3-3 can be used on easy runs, I suggest using 2-2, just to be consistent. Further, 2-1 may be called upon during the latter stages of an interval session in which workbouts (the repeated runs that make up a session of intervals) last several minutes each. It should not be necessary to rely on a 2-1 rhythm during T-pace or R-pace work; in fact the ability to avoid this faster pattern can be used to keep you from going too fast at times, particularly on a tempo run.

more rapidly than would be the case in a steady, easy, long run. By the latter stages of the workout the feeling you get mimics the feeling during the final stages of a marathon race—but you haven't had to run so far. This is a pretty rugged workout, and I don't recommend that it be done weekly.

# Using Both Tempo Runs and Cruise Intervals

Although tempo runs and cruise intervals are designed for the same purpose (raising the lactate threshold), I recommend using both in a training regimen. The steady tempo runs are probably a better value for the time spent training, because of the concentration factor—you must keep up a quality pace for a prolonged time. On the other hand, cruise intervals provide a break from the mental rigors of the tempo run and offer an opportunity to get more physical work done in a session.

# A Final Word

Please remember not to run faster than the prescribed **T** pace when doing tempo and cruise-interval workouts. When you are having a good training day, it is not that tough to beat a previous time over a 4-mile tempo course, and it is tempting to want to make each mile in a cruise-interval workout just a little faster than the previous one. It is very important, however, to let your ability, based on competitive efforts, determine training intensities. When a particular workout begins to feel easier, use that feeling to support the idea that you are getting fitter. Then, prove that you are getting better in a race, not in a workout.

If you are in a prolonged phase of training, with no races scheduled or desired, it is reasonable to increase training intensity without the supportive evidence of better competitive performances. In this case, a good rule of thumb is to increase VDOT 1% every four to six weeks. This would be the same as improving your 5000-meter race time by about 10 to 15 seconds, a substantial improvement in my opinion. If you are in a maintenance program, which is designed to require the least possible training stress that will allow you to stay at a particular level of fitness, there is no need to increase training intensity (VDOT) or distances. In this case, the best goal is to see how easy standard workouts can feel over time.

When setting up the phases of training, the placement of threshold training may vary in the overall order of the program, based on the individual involved and the specific event being trained for. Unlike **E** and **L** runs, which almost always fall in the earliest phase of a program, threshold training may be emphasized early, at the mid-point, or late in a runner's training schedule (see chapters 12-14).

# CHAPTER 6

# Interval Training

© Victah Sailer

*Remember, the finish line is at the end of a race.*
*Don't use up all your energy before reaching it.*

Of all the types of training, interval training takes on the greatest number of meanings, and it would be inappropriate for me to try to cater to them all. In fact, because of its many meanings I have chosen to carefully define what I mean by interval (**I**) training, or "$\dot{V}O_2$max interval (**I**) training," as I often refer to it. I will use this definition because optimizing $\dot{V}O_2$max is, in my opinion, the greatest benefit of **I** training, especially when performed according to my description in this chapter. In this chapter I identify, and explain my reasoning behind, the ideal intensity for **I** training, the duration of individual workbouts, the optimal amount of recovery between workbouts, and some guidelines as to how much total quality running is desirable for a session of intervals.

I define $\dot{V}O_2$max **I** intensity as a speed of running that could be kept up for about 10 to 15 minutes in a race situation. For an elite athlete this is about 5000-meter race pace, but for most people it is closer to 3000-meter to 4000-meter race pace. Using the pace of a current 5K race to approximate **I** pace is acceptable for less gifted or unfit runners, even though they take more than 15 minutes to race a 5K, because the pace factors in a more conservative intensity, which may not be a bad idea for this population of runners.

# Determining the Duration of Your Intervals

Interval intensity is demanding for anyone, 50 individual workbouts in an interval workout should not be over five minutes each. Going for longer than five minutes at a time leads to too great an accumulation of blood lactate, which usually ends up causing the runner to cut the workout short or to run the last few intervals too slowly (and not accomplish the purpose of the workout). At the other extreme, 30 seconds is a good, practical lower boundary for the duration of work intervals during a $\dot{V}O_2$max **I** workout.

The fact that five minutes is the longest recommended duration for individual workbouts in an interval session means that if your VDOT is less than 66, you should not repeat miles or 1600-meter runs in an interval workout. Proper **I** pace would require you to take longer than five minutes to complete a mile. For people who fall into this category (VDOT under 66), 1200-meter or 1000-meter runs are the longest distances that should be used for work intervals. Stay under the five-minute limit whenever possible.

Actually, five-minute runs are excellent for an interval session, regardless of how far you get. I call this type of interval training "non-structured" because even though you are timing the duration of each quality run, you are relying on feeling the degree of stress rather than going a set distance in a predetermined time. The same type of thing can be done with one-, two-, three-, or four-minute runs. Concerning interval miles, it is possible to do mile repeats even if the time is a few seconds over five minutes, but try to be reasonable about the duration of repeated workbouts.

## TOM VON RUDEN

**Tom Von Ruden** was born in Coeur d'Alene, Idaho. He took up running "to stay in shape for basketball and other sports," and a keen interest in general fitness certainly paid big dividends during his competitive running years. Following success as an all-around track and field athlete, Tom attended Oklahoma State University where he enjoyed considerable success as a middle-distance runner and member of numerous record-setting relay teams. It was during this time that I became acquainted with him, recruiting him as a subject in several altitude research projects.

Following college, Tom continued competing in the Army and then as a member of the Pacific Coast Club. He was 1967 Pan American Games champion in the 1500, and in 1968 he made the Olympic Team and placed ninth in the same event. In fact, Tom individually and as a relay member broke nine world and American records in indoor 880- and 1000- yard races, indoor and outdoor 1000-meter and 2-mile relay, and distance-medley relay events. He was twice Amateur Athletic Union (AAU) indoor national champion at 1000 yards and won the

the Indoor National AAU and NCAA 880-yard titles. He also managed good finishes at the Outdoor Nationals in the mile and 880-yard races. During the U.S. Track and Field Federation Championships, Tom once ran both the leadoff and anchor legs of the mile relay. Typical training during his best competitive years included 70 to 80 miles per week, with quality interval and repetition workouts. Tom was also a successful cross-country runner.

In my opinion, Tom is one of the greatest all-around athletes ever involved in middle-distance running. But Tom's ability was not limited to the middle distances. The two of us also competed in our first marathon together (I thought I had him when he stopped for a pit stop, but his good speed finished me off in the final miles). The main thing I have learned from Tom is that you never lose interest in an activity you enjoy.

**Tom's Bests**    800: 1:46.8    Mile: 3:56.9    1500: 3:38.5

# Recovery Time

The amount of recovery you should take between repeated runs in an interval session should be equal to, or a little less than, the time spent performing the preceding workbout. For example, if you are doing 1200-meter intervals in four minutes each, you should take up to four minutes of recovery time prior to the next 1200 meters; 40-second intervals would allow recoveries of no more than 40 seconds each. Generally, the longer the workbouts, the less you need to concern yourself with the brevity of the recovery time.

Because the purpose of interval training is to stress your $\dot{V}O_2max$, it is important to spend time running at $\dot{V}O_2max$. A five-minute run does this well (see figure 6.1). When running at proper **I** pace, it takes your body about two minutes to reach the point where it is operating at maximum oxygen consumption (the purpose of the workout). Therefore, when you run five minutes at **I** pace, the last three minutes will be at $\dot{V}O_2max$. A relatively short recovery before the next run will speed up the process of reaching $\dot{V}O_2max$ somewhat, but three high-quality minutes (out of a total of five) is a good return on your investment. That's why it doesn't

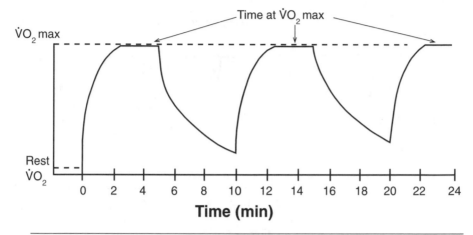

**Figure 6.1** Interval running allows you to train at maximum aerobic capacity ($\dot{V}O_2$max) for a good portion of the workout while still getting necessary rest periods.

Adapted from Karlssen, J. et al. 1970. *Energikraven vid Löpning*. Stockholm: Trygg, 39.

matter much if recoveries after five-minute runs are a little longer, relative to the recoveries following shorter intervals.

# Shorter Intervals Demand Shorter Recovery Periods

Figure 6.2 shows what happens when 400-meter workbouts at 80 seconds each are used during an interval workout. Because a single run doesn't last long enough to allow your body to reach $\dot{V}O_2$max, the short recovery helps you to achieve $\dot{V}O_2$max more quickly in subsequent workbouts. The short rest doesn't permit full recovery back to resting $\dot{V}O_2$, so with each new workbout $\dot{V}O_2$max is reached more quickly than in earlier bouts or if longer recoveries were used. By repeating the short intervals and short recoveries over and over, you can accumulate a fair amount of time running at $\dot{V}O_2$max.

A good way to handle interval 400s is to start one every two minutes, which means that 80-second 400s would allow for 40-second recoveries. This doesn't work so well for people who do interval 400s in 90 seconds or longer, because they get so little recovery time that they have trouble running the 400s at the proper speed. Interval 200s on a one-minute send-off (starting a 200 every minute) are also good for variety.

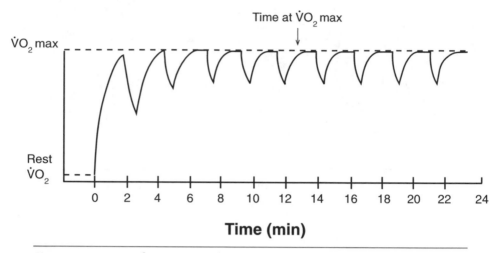

**Figure 6.2**    To reap the benefits of short interval training, the recovery periods must be kept even shorter.

Adapted from Karlssen, J. et al. 1970. *Energikraven vid Löpning*. Stockholm: Trygg, 41.

## Active Recovery

Runners often ask, "What should I do during the recovery?" When performing I-pace training, it is best to use active recovery (easy running) because low-intensity activity helps to clear blood lactate, and also brings you to the next workbout at a slightly elevated $\dot{V}O_2$, making the attainment of $\dot{V}O_2$max a little quicker. Jogging during recoveries also helps keep muscles loose and flexible for the demanding runs yet to come.

# Maintaining Proper Pacing

It is very important to maintain the proper pace during each quality run that makes up the I session, regardless of the duration of these individual workbouts. It surprises a lot of runners to learn that you should not run interval 400s any faster than interval miles. Remember, the basic purpose of the workout is to boost your $\dot{V}O_2$max, not to convert you into a workout fanatic. Many runners tend to try for a faster pace when doing shorter intervals, but you should save your speed for repetition workouts (see chapter 7).

Running faster than $v\dot{V}O_2$max cannot produce a greater aerobic involvement than does running at $v\dot{V}O_2$max. The stress of shorter intervals comes from shortening the recoveries, not from running at faster speeds. If you feel that interval 400s at **I** pace are too easy, shorten the recoveries, or use 1000-meter instead of 400-meter workbouts, but don't play with intensity. Please remember, you can introduce variety into your interval training by adjusting distances and recoveries. Don't introduce higher intensities into your workouts unless you are certain you have moved up in fitness. If you want to train faster, prove you are fit enough by racing faster.

# Setting Your Weekly Amount of Interval-Pace Training

The amount of quality running in an interval session should be up to 8% of weekly mileage, with a 6-mile or 10K maximum. Even if you are logging 120-mile (200-kilometer) weeks, you shouldn't exceed the 10K cap, because $\dot{V}O_2$max intervals are without doubt the most demanding training you can do. This is another reason why you shouldn't go faster than prescribed during a workout—the excess speed may prevent you from accomplishing another quality workout on the day that you had planned.

The idea of holding interval mileage to no more than 8% of current weekly mileage is to prevent individuals with low training loads from performing interval sessions with others who are doing a lot more training. You should never ask a 20-mile-per-week runner to go through a 6-mile interval session with a 75-mile-per-week person, even if they have the same **I** pace. They can run their workout together up to the point that the lower-mileage person must drop out due to quality-training limits imposed by the lower total training stress. Six miles of running at **I** pace, plus warm-up, recovery, and cool-down running could easily add up to half of the lower-mileage runner's weekly total. That is just too much.

One of the nice things about interval training (and it is good to find something nice about intervals) is the variety of training sessions that can be done, all of which accomplish the purpose of stressing

© Beth Schneider

Being totally spent at the end of a race shows that you are able to push your body to the limit. Intervals help you to learn how to give your all.

$\dot{V}O_2$max. Keep in mind that the one thing that shouldn't vary is the intensity, or speed, of the quality portion of an interval session, regardless of the length or duration of the various workbouts. Speed of intervals should only be changed when race performances so dictate, or, if there is no race by which to judge improvement, after four to six weeks of consistent training. If you do increase the stress of training, don't go over a 1% VDOT increase, unless your races indicate that a larger increase is acceptable. If you are in a nonracing mode, use the same rule of thumb used with threshold training—increase VDOT by 1% not more often than every third or fourth week of consistent training.

# Varying Workbouts Within a Single Training Session

Not only can you change the makeup of an interval workout between one session and another, you can also vary the workbouts within a single interval training session. For example, if your **I** pace is 268 meters per minute (6-minute mile pace or 90-second

400-meter pace) and you want to total 24 minutes (four miles) of quality running in an interval session, you could run six 2-minute runs with 1-minute recoveries, followed by eight 1-minute runs with 30-second recoveries, followed by eight 30-second runs with 15-second recoveries. All of the runs should be at 90-second 400-meter pace, so that $\dot{V}O_2$max is stressed properly, and the recovery times should be equal to or less than the times of the related workbouts. The total session would last 36 minutes, with 24 minutes of I-pace running and 12 minutes of easy recovery running. In this particular workout, the feeling of stress should remain pretty constant as the workout progresses, because the individual workbouts get shorter as the total amount of quality running accumulates.

Actually, you can make up almost any type of interval workout as long as you stick to the rules of interval training that I have mentioned, and that are summarized here.

1. Run between 30 seconds and 5 minutes per workbout.
2. Stick to **I** pace for all aspects of quality running.
3. Run easily during recoveries.
4. Keep recovery periods equal to or shorter than the workbouts they follow.
5. Let the quality portion of an interval session total up to 8% of your current weekly mileage with a nonnegotiable upper limit of 10,000 meters.

## Optimal Interval Duration

Experience tells me, and researchers agree, that the optimal duration of individual workbouts in an interval session is between three and five minutes each. As a result, I most often use mile and 1200-meter intervals for men and 1000-meter and 1200-meter intervals for women to get the best results. Still, varying the durations of the workbouts adds interest and helps to minimize the mental stress of interval training. As in all types of training, there must be a balance between accomplishing the physiological and biomechanical goals of a training session and optimizing the psychological factors.

# A Final Word

Perform an interval session with some thought as to what the workout is going to accomplish for you in the long run. Intervals are challenging, but do not look at I pace as something you have to surpass. Consistent training is the key to success, and trying to set a record in an interval workout is not the best way to achieve consistency. Use the interval workout to meet your long-term goals with as little effort as possible; don't overtrain.

A phase of training set aside for emphasis on intervals will vary depending on the event being trained for and the individuals involved. I typically position interval training as the next to last phase in a season's program. This allows for a solid period of buildup in preparation for the rather demanding interval phase, and it also lets the runner leave the interval phase behind as the more important racing part of the season arrives. It is logical to drop most interval training when serious race time arrives, because many middle-distance races (particularly those that last 10 to 30 minutes) provide the same benefits as a good interval session.

# CHAPTER 7

# Repetition Training

*Sometimes picking up the pace feels better than staying
with the same pace; always try speeding up before you drop
back from a tough pace.*

All of the types of training that I have detailed so far can be nicely identified by an intensity associated with the individual's VDOT. Other types of training, however, are aimed at anaerobic factors. Repetition (**R**, or rep) training is the major type of training whose purpose is not aerobic. The benefits of **R** training are associated more with mechanics and anaerobic metabolism than with aerobic factors.

The intensity of running reps usually puts considerable stress on the body to provide energy anaerobically, which in turn produces beneficial changes in anaerobic pathways, where fuel is converted to energy in the absence of adequate oxygen. Also, by practicing at **R** pace you learn to run relaxedly and fast, and race pace becomes more familiar and comfortable. In **R** training, you recruit the exact muscle fibers that you need for economical running. These are the muscle cells that allow you to run fast, with the least effort, wasted movement, and energy. Repetition workouts involve practicing running at race pace or faster, while making sure that each workbout is done with proper technique and adequate recovery.

In describing **R** training, one of my objectives is to improve the understanding of the various types of training that runners use. The training terms "interval" and "repetition" carry with them a multitude of definitions, and, in fact, are sometimes used synonymously. I like to separate **I** and **R** training based on the benefit a runner is trying to achieve. I have clear definitions for these two types of training. In this chapter I present the importance of recovery between **R** workbouts. I address the intensity and duration of the workbouts and the amount of quality running to do in an **R** session. I also introduce hill training and fartlek training.

# Determining Recovery Time

Let me approach **R** training in a somewhat unusual manner—by considering the recovery periods first. This is a key difference between reps, intervals, and cruise intervals—the recovery activity and time for reps are not so structured. The type and amount of recovery following each individual workbout is determined subjectively. You simply recover until you feel you can perform the next run as well as you did the previous one. If you need five minutes to recover from a one-and-a-half-minute run, then take five minutes. Don't rush into the next rep feeling tired. Some people use heart rates to determine how long recoveries should be, but I prefer to leave it up to the individual. The purpose of reps is to improve speed and economy, and the best way (almost the only way) to run fast and with good technique for repeated workbouts is to be fully recovered from the previous run before starting the next. There are only two negative aspects of recovering too long between runs in an **R** session: you might become stiff, cold, and tense before embarking on your next fast rep, and the workout might take too long on a day when you are pressed for time.

A guideline for planning **R** recoveries is to rest four times as long as you work; for example, a one-minute run followed by a four-minute recovery period. At least part of the recovery period should consist of easy running. Whatever brings you to the start of the next rep feeling ready to run at **R** pace is what is best for the recovery period. If that involves running, walking, or even some stretching, that's fine. In reps you should always feel you are ready to perform the next run as the best one of the series.

## JACK BACHELER

**Jack Bacheler**, a lanky 6-foot 6-inch 160-pounder when I first tested him, was born in Washington, D.C., and first ran during his senior year of high school. Bacheler's initial goal was to beat the first and third best runners on his high school cross country team. "They were a couple of jerks," he recalls. Jack quickly found that not only could he beat his teammates, he could also beat his competition. This success led to his continued participation in running at Miami University in Ohio. Bacheler continued to run in graduate school for the Florida Track Club (for which he designed the orange logo). He is currently a professor at North Carolina State University and a coach. He has produced numerous national champions and All-Americans.

As a collegiate runner, Jack was a three-time NCAA finalist in the steeplechase, with a second place finish during his senior year. After college, Jack concentrated on flat distance events and racked up wins in the 10,000 at the 1969 Nationals; the 6-mile on the track in 1970 (in which he tied with Frank Shorter); and also placed first, second (twice), third, and sixth at various national Amateur Athletic Union (AAU) cross-country championships. He also had the distinction of beating the American record in the 10,000 but was not credited with the record because he was beaten by three other Americans in the race. Jack typically ran 140-mile weeks during his most productive years. He lists consistency, volume, quality, and lack of injuries as factors in his success as a runner.

Jack was one of my subjects in sea-level and altitude studies in the months leading up to the 1968 Mexico City Olympics. He not only qualified for the 5000 final in Mexico City, he also ran a great marathon (finishing ninth) at the 1972 Olympics in Munich. Jack has always struck me as a great example of a person committed to excellence in every endeavor. The main thing I learned from him is that great runners' bodies can come in a variety of sizes.

**Jack's Bests**   Mile: 4:01.3   2-mile: 8:31.8   5K: 13:37.4
10K: 28:12   10-mile: 47:10   Marathon: 2:17:36

# Determining Your Repetition Pace

Another important difference between reps and intervals is that each **R** workbout usually takes less than two minutes and is 600 meters or less in length (800-meter reps are acceptable for faster competitors). Shorter run times and longer recoveries are used for reps than for intervals because **R** pace is faster than **I** and **T** paces. Repetition pace is partly a function of the event you are training for. If your event of primary interest is 1500 meters, then your reps will be faster than if you were training for a marathon.

# Race Pace

I identify at least two **R** paces. The first is equal to current race pace if your primary event of interest is shorter than 5000 meters. For example, a 1500-meter runner who currently races the 1500 at 75 seconds per 400 meters would do reps at 75 seconds per 400 meters (37.5 seconds per 200 meters). Repetitions at race pace are clearly faster than **I** pace for this particular runner.

The second **R** pace is for people whose primary event is 5000 meters or longer, in which case **R** pace is set at 6 seconds per 400 meters faster than current **I** pace. A 10K runner who races at 85-second pace per 400 meters (about 35:25 for the 10K) would have an **I** pace of 81 seconds per 400 meters. Because **I** pace is faster than race pace for this 10K runner, **R** pace would be about six seconds per 400 faster than the 81-second **I** pace—75 seconds per 400 meters. Table 3.2 provides you with a basic **R** pace, based on a standard relationship with **I**-pace training.

Another **R** pace that works well for runners who want to key on a good mile or 1500-meter race is to pick a pace that is 3 seconds per 400 meters slower than the goal pace that they hope to achieve by the end of the current season. It is certainly possible to experiment some with **R** intensities, but keep in mind the need for adequate recoveries and good mechanics.

# Cruise Repetitions

"Cruise repetition" is my term for a modification of usual **R** running. A cruise-rep workout involves a series of runs performed at **T** pace for anyone preparing for races 10K or longer, or at **I** pace for runners preparing for races shorter than 10K. As opposed to the very brief recoveries used in cruise-interval workouts, use full recoveries between runs in a cruise-rep workout. Cruise reps are usually longer in duration than the two-minute limit for reps. It is typical to run 800s, 1000s, or 1200s in a cruise-rep workbout (usually a total of 2 or 3 miles), allowing complete recovery between runs. Cruise reps are not true reps by definition but are a relatively low-key set of reps at a comfortably hard pace. They are best used in the final days leading up to an important race, because they provide some quality with minimal stress.

# Setting Your Weekly Amount of Repetition-Pace Training

The amount of quality running in a true **R** session should be up to 5% of current weekly mileage, with an upper limit of 3 miles or 5000 meters. For example, a 5K runner who is running 60 miles per week and whose **R** pace is 70 seconds per 400 meters might run 12 × 400 meters at 70 seconds each, or 24 × 200 meters at 35 seconds each, or some combination of 200s and 400s that would total 3 miles (5% of 60). On the other hand, 5% of 100 weekly miles would be 5 miles of reps, which is a bit demanding and, since recovery time is about four times as long as quality time, very time consuming. Thus my recommendation for an upper limit of 3 miles or 5000 meters. Please keep in mind that the 5%–3-mile figure represents an upper limit for reps and need not be the required amount.

Repetitions are pretty intense for many people, and often leave runners dead-legged and without much of a kick for races. This is true particularly during a phase of training when reps are being emphasized. When going into a period of important competitions, you can drop true **R**-pace running in favor of cruise reps, or cut back considerably the total amount of quality running at **R** pace. Surprisingly, cruise-reps seem to aid the development of a kick and for some runners produce greater speed than do the faster reps. Before trying the more demanding reps, I recommend using cruise reps for a season, especially if you are a young runner or a beginner.

## POINTERS ON TREADMILL TRAINING

I have personally been using treadmill (TM) workouts since 1960, when I first worked in a lab where a TM was available; it was also the year that I first started coaching runners at the collegiate level. I used to make up workouts that would just about stress me to the limit in hopes of making a regular outdoor session seem easy in comparison. I also used to set up standard workouts on the TM that

I could repeat during different times of the season to check my progress or digression.

All these years of measuring $\dot{V}O_2$, HR, and blood-lactate levels, at different TM speeds and grades, led to an interest in how different combinations of speeds and grades can be used to produce the demands of a variety of running paces on flat ground. The importance of having this information is that some well-controlled workouts can be carried out on a TM that won't go very fast, but whose grade can be adjusted to impose the desired degree of stress.

A big advantage of TM running is that pace can be accurately monitored. Being able to set the desired pace on a TM allows the runner to concentrate on other things like good technique, breathing patterns, and leg cadence. One of the disadvantages of TM running is not being able to share a run with a partner. However, this can be overcome if you pick the right kind of workout. One of my favorites is to run a series of repeated 30-second or 1-minute runs at a pretty steep grade and slow speed with equal amounts of recovery time between runs. This accomodates two people very nicely—while one is resting the other is running.

I have realized over the years that some injuries are not aggravated on a TM when running slowly up a steep grade. A workout of the same intensity (stress) on the flat could exacerbate the injury. In a sense, graded TM running can be a specific type of cross-training (for those who cross-train in an attempt to avoid too much running while still stressing physiological systems of importance).

## Types of Treadmill Training

There are really only two general types of training a person can do— steady running and intermittent running. Within these two general categories, intensity can be varied to stress different systems in need of development.

Another big advantage that TM running has over over-ground running is in the area of hill training. In overground training, hill work involves both going up and coming down. On the TM, it involves going up or resting to go up again. There's none of the potentially damaging downhill stuff. This is of particular importance to a runner who is nursing a landing-shock injury.

Even downhill training (to prepare for the downhills of the Boston Marathon, for example) can be accomplished on a TM. Just jack up

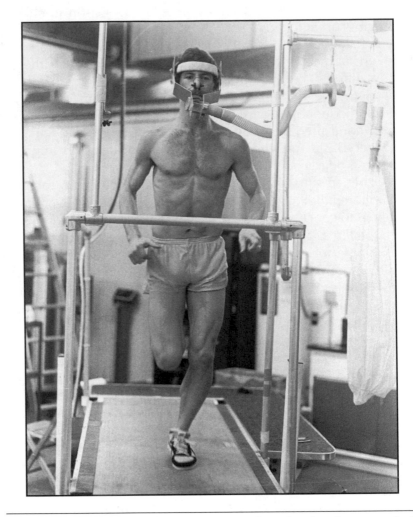

My many years of studying the varying effects of speed and grade on a treadmill has allowed me to create some very effective treadmill workouts.

the rear support of the TM and lower it onto a solid block of wood. Then you will have to elevate the grade just to reach level running. I wouldn't try more than a 6% or 8% downhill grade for any training sessions because it is easy to run very fast and the quads can take a beating, and recovery is slow from this training. Also, set up a fan so that the layer of hot air that inevitably builds up around your body when on a TM can be moved away and replaced with cooler, less humid air.

## Equating Workout Intensities

Table 7.1 allows for the use of a wide variety of speeds and grades to accomplish desired training stresses. Be aware that any speed of running on a TM is slightly less demanding than it would be on a track or level road, yet because of the greater chance for heat buildup you may get an equal or even higher heart rate. To adjust for the lack of work that you would experience by running against a headwind, it is advisable to add a 1% to 2% grade to the TM; this also reduces landing shock slightly, and is better than adjusting the workload by running faster than you would during overground running. Table 7.1 takes into account the need for a slight grade to equate TM to overground running.

Table 7.1 shows the grade that, if applied to the miles per hour (mph) speed (shown at the top), will produce an effort equal to running at the mile pace shown in the left column. For example, a 6:11 mile effort could be accomplished by running at 6 mph on a 10.2% grade, 7 mph at a 7% grade, or 9.5 mph at 2.3% grade. A 4:13 mile effort (63 seconds per 400 meters) could be done at 6 mph on a 21.2% grade, or any combination of values in that row, ending with 12 mph at a 4.3% grade.

## Calibrating Your Treadmill

If you train on the same TM regularly, you might want to determine the accuracy of the speedometer by measuring the running belt length to the nearest centimeter, and then timing 10 revolutions (while running on the TM) to determine how fast you are actually running in meters per minute. Then you can use table 7.2 on page 123 to identify mph and pace per mile.

# Hill Running

Hill running is a type of R training. It involves intense, short workbouts separated by relatively long recovery periods. Hill work produces some of the same benefits as reps—better economy and the strength that aids speed.

My preferred method of incorporating hill training into a program is to use a treadmill, so that you can eliminate the downhill running generally associated with a hill session (the downhill running between harder uphill runs can lead to landing-shock injuries, if you are not careful).

# Fartlek

Another type of training that can involve **R** running is fartlek (pronounced "fart-lake"), a Swedish term translated as "speed-play." Fartlek workouts mix several types of running—easy running, hills, reps, and even **T**-pace bouts—into one session.

There can be long fartlek sessions or short ones, hard ones or easy ones, depending on what you want to accomplish. It is important to remember the purpose of the session. If a fartlek workout is planned as an easy day, don't let it become a hard day just because various aspects of the session lend themselves to getting into a race with

## Table 7.1 Determining Desired Mile Pace Using Treadmill Grades and Miles per Hour

| Pace | Treadmill grade | | | | | | | | | | | | |
|------|------|------|------|------|------|------|------|------|------|------|------|------|------|
|      | 6.0  | 6.5  | 7.0  | 7.5  | 8.0  | 8.5  | 9.0  | 9.5  | 10.0 | 10.5 | 11.0 | 11.5 | 12.0 |
| 9:19 | 2.9  | 1.9  | —    | —    | —    | —    | —    | —    | —    | —    | —    | —    | —    |
| 8:15 | 4.8  | 3.5  | 2.5  | —    | —    | —    | —    | —    | —    | —    | —    | —    | —    |
| 7:24 | 6.6  | 5.2  | 4.0  | 3.0  | 2.2  | —    | —    | —    | —    | —    | —    | —    | —    |
| 6:44 | 8.4  | 6.8  | 5.5  | 4.4  | 3.5  | 2.6  | —    | —    | —    | —    | —    | —    | —    |
| 6:11 | 10.2 | 8.5  | 7.0  | 5.8  | 4.7  | 3.8  | 3.0  | 2.3  | —    | —    | —    | —    | —    |
| 5:43 | 12.1 | 10.1 | 8.5  | 7.2  | 6.0  | 5.0  | 4.1  | 3.3  | 2.6  | 2.0  | —    | —    | —    |
| 5:19 | 13.9 | 11.8 | 10.0 | 8.5  | 7.3  | 6.2  | 5.2  | 4.3  | 3.6  | 2.9  | 2.3  | —    | —    |
| 4:59 | 15.7 | 13.4 | 11.5 | 9.9  | 8.5  | 7.3  | 6.3  | 5.4  | 4.6  | 3.8  | 3.2  | 2.6  | 2.0  |
| 4:42 | 17.5 | 15.1 | 13.0 | 11.3 | 9.8  | 8.5  | 7.4  | 6.4  | 5.5  | 4.7  | 4.0  | 3.4  | 2.8  |
| 4:27 | 19.4 | 16.8 | 14.5 | 12.7 | 11.1 | 9.7  | 8.5  | 7.4  | 6.5  | 5.6  | 4.9  | 4.2  | 3.6  |
| 4:13 | 21.2 | 18.4 | 16.0 | 14.1 | 12.4 | 10.9 | 9.6  | 8.5  | 7.5  | 6.6  | 5.7  | 5.0  | 4.3  |
| 4:01 | 23.0 | 20.0 | 17.5 | 15.4 | 13.6 | 12.1 | 10.7 | 9.5  | 8.5  | 7.5  | 6.6  | 5.8  | 5.1  |
| 3:51 | 24.8 | 21.7 | 19.0 | 16.8 | 14.9 | 13.2 | 11.8 | 10.5 | 9.4  | 8.4  | 7.5  | 6.6  | 5.9  |

someone else or yourself.

A type of fartlek session that works well, especially if you don't have known distances to cover or a watch to keep time, is counting steps as you run. Run 10 steps (counting one foot, not both) then jog 10, run 20 and jog 20, run 30 and jog 30, and so on up to running 100 and jogging 100 (or more if you wish). Then descend the "ladder" by tens until you run and jog 10 steps again. This is a good workout

## Table 7.2   Conversions for Miles per Hour (mph) to Mile Pace and Meters per Minute (m/min)

| mph | Mile | m/min | mph | Mile | m/min | mph | Mile | m/min |
|-----|------|-------|-----|------|-------|-----|------|-------|
| 6.0 | 10:00 | 161 | 8.1 | 7:24 | 217 | 10.1 | 5:56 | 271 |
| 6.1 | 9:50 | 164 | 8.2 | 7:19 | 220 | 10.2 | 5:53 | 274 |
| 6.2 | 9:41 | 166 | 8.3 | 7:14 | 223 | 10.3 | 5:49 | 276 |
| 6.3 | 9:31 | 169 | 8.4 | 7:09 | 225 | 10.4 | 5:46 | 279 |
| 6.4 | 9:22 | 172 | 8.5 | 7:04 | 228 | 10.5 | 5:43 | 282 |
| 6.5 | 9:14 | 174 | 8.6 | 6:59 | 231 | 10.6 | 5:40 | 284 |
| 6.6 | 9:05 | 177 | 8.7 | 6:54 | 233 | 10.7 | 5:36 | 287 |
| 6.7 | 8:57 | 180 | 8.8 | 6:49 | 236 | 10.8 | 5:33 | 290 |
| 6.8 | 8:49 | 182 | 8.9 | 6:44 | 239 | 10.9 | 5:30 | 292 |
| 6.9 | 8:42 | 185 | 9.0 | 6:40 | 241 | 11.0 | 5:27 | 295 |
| 7.0 | 8:34 | 188 | 9.1 | 6:36 | 244 | 11.1 | 5:24 | 298 |
| 7.1 | 8:27 | 190 | 9.2 | 6:31 | 247 | 11.2 | 5:21 | 300 |
| 7.2 | 8:20 | 193 | 9.3 | 6:27 | 249 | 11.3 | 5:19 | 303 |
| 7.3 | 8:13 | 196 | 9.4 | 6:23 | 252 | 11.4 | 5:16 | 306 |
| 7.4 | 8:06 | 198 | 9.5 | 6:19 | 255 | 11.5 | 5:13 | 308 |
| 7.5 | 8:00 | 201 | 9.6 | 6:15 | 257 | 11.6 | 5:10 | 311 |
| 7.6 | 7:54 | 204 | 9.7 | 6:11 | 260 | 11.7 | 5:08 | 314 |
| 7.7 | 7:48 | 207 | 9.8 | 6:07 | 263 | 11.8 | 5:05 | 317 |
| 7.8 | 7:42 | 209 | 9.9 | 6:04 | 266 | 11.9 | 5:02 | 319 |
| 7.9 | 7:36 | 212 | 10.0 | 6:00 | 268 | 12.0 | 5:00 | 322 |
| 8.0 | 7:30 | 215 | | | | | | |

© Richard C. Etchberger

Hill running improves running economy and strength, and can also stress aerobic capacity if the hills are long enough.

when you feel lethargic but want to get in some decent running. In this workout, there is no pressure to achieve certain splits, and the very nature of the workout gets you going at a pretty good pace.

# A Final Word

I often introduce what I call "mix" sessions into the phases of training, especially toward the latter part of a season (see the training tables in chapters 12 and 13). A typical mix workout might include a few cruise intervals, followed by a few 200-meter or 400-meter reps and a couple more cruise intervals. It is like a fartlek session, but it is not as long and certainly not as varied.

A good measure of a successful workout that involves **R** running is that you end the workout feeling that you have accomplished some relatively fast, quality running and that you could have continued a little longer without struggling with the pace. Being in control of the pace you are setting is the key to successful **R** training.

# CHAPTER 8

# Designing Your Performance Program

*No one has all the answers to running success.*

No one has all the answers to what works best for any individual runner. Further, everyone reacts differently to a particular type of training. The amount of coach feedback that each runner needs also varies tremendously. The approach presented here is as simple and effective as possible, and lends itself to runners who want to coach themselves as well as to athletes under the firm control of a coach.

In this chapter I present the concept of breaking a season down into phases of training, with four phases being the ideal model, but with consideration given to shorter or longer seasons. In the case of inadequate time for four full phases of training, I provide a way to decide how much of each phase to keep, or what you might eliminate altogether. After considering the season's training scheme, I discuss the ways of arranging quality days of training within each week of the season, taking into account weeks with no competition as well as weeks with races.

# Setting Up a Training Program

Any time that you set up a running training program—be it for yourself, an individual whom you are coaching, or a team—there are several questions that must be answered relative to each runner in the program. I presented a list of these questions in chapter 1 (page 17), including such considerations as available time, strengths and weaknesses, likes and dislikes, and current fitness.

Next, draw up a block of time on a sheet of paper (see figure 8.1). Start at the far right of the time block and mark this as your goal or peak-performance date. This is the period of time when you want season-best performances, such as in a single championship meet, or at the beginning of a series of competitions lasting several weeks. The training that you will perform during this final quality (FQ) phase is geared to prepare you for your best performances of the season.

This time plan is influenced by many factors. For example, many high school runners participate in different sports during different seasons. The amount of time available for running training varies greatly from person to person, from school to school, and from one region of the country to another. For all runners, weather and

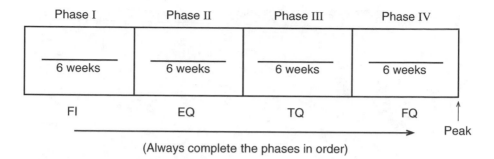

**Figure 8.1** Sample plan for setting up a 24-week training program. Insert the dates (into the four boxes) that you want to train in each phase starting with your peak-performance date and working backwards.

facilities are two big factors that dictate, at least to some degree, how the various training blocks can be set up.

## Marathon Training

Runners training for a marathon are usually in a simpler situation than runners training for a series of middle-distance races. Marathoners know the exact date of competition, and can focus all their training on the race; they do not need to worry much about races prior to or following the marathon. Still, there are various schemes of training that can be used successfully in preparing for a marathon; an approach that is useful this year may not be chosen next time around. The blocks of training depicted in figure 8.1 can be set up for any particular marathon and adhered to quite nicely.

## Peaking for More Than One Race

Unlike the marathoner, the typical high school and college runner has many important races to contend with on the way to the peak period. If the races along the way can be worked into the training program, the general plan can still be followed with success.

In figure 8.1, I show four 6-week blocks of training (24 weeks) leading up to the peak period. This is a desirable amount of time to set aside for preparation, but is not necessarily workable within the framework of a school program. School seasons often are more likely

Working races into your training schedule will help satisfy overall fitness needs.

to cater to a 12-week program (some may be shorter and some slightly longer).

# Creating Your Training Program

My preferred approach to a 24-week season of training, which I believe is the ideal length, would be four 6-week phases. The first phase would be a foundation / injury prevention (FI) phase. For most runners the second phase, which I call early quality (EQ), would be for working on mechanics, economy, and some speed—a rep phase. Phase three, transition quality (TQ), would be the toughest and would concentrate primarily on long intervals. The final phase, final quality (FQ), would involve a fair amount of threshold running, along with lesser amounts of reps or intervals, and, of course, races.

In other words, my generic approach to a 24-week program is easy running, followed by reps, then intervals, and finally threshold running and racing. Obviously, this would not be the same for every type of runner but would suit most middle- and long-distance runners. But the ideal is not usually how things work out, and adjustments must be made. I have prepared a way of fitting the best possible training scheme into the time available for any particular individual.

Figure 8.2 shows four blocks (phases) of training, progressing from Phase I at the left to Phase IV at the right. Within each block I have listed 6 numbers, 24 in all. Consider these numbers "priority" weeks of training. I arrived at this prioritization by asking myself, "If an individual, who has logged no training whatsoever up to this point, has only one week available to prepare for the final race of the season, what should that individual do for training?" My answer is that only FI running should be performed during that week; therefore, place this one-week priority number (#1) in the Phase I column. I feel the same about anyone with only two or three weeks available prior to racing in the last race of the season—only Phase I training should be performed—so #2 and #3 are also placed in the far left column.

| Phase I | | | Phase II | | | Phase III | | | Phase IV | | |
|---|---|---|---|---|---|---|---|---|---|---|---|
| 1 | 2 | 3 | 10 | 11 | 12 | 7 | 8 | 9 | 4 | 5 | 6 |
| 13 | | | 18 | | | 14 | | | 17 | | |
| | 21 | | | 19 | | | 15 | | | 22 | |
| | | 23 | | | 20 | | | 16 | | | 24 |

| FI | EQ | TQ | FQ |
|---|---|---|---|

(Always complete the phases in order)

Figure 8.2 Priority weekly numbering system to determine the number of weeks of training per phase according to how many weeks you have available.

Adapted from Daniels, J. June 1993. "World's best peaking program." *Runner's World* 28 (6):43.

If a runner has six weeks available, allocate three weeks of Phase I training (priority weeks #1, #2, #3) and thr ee weeks of Phase IV training (priority weeks #4, #5, #6). The practical way to identify the weeks of training for each phase would be to circle the numbers 1 through 6. In the event of 10 weeks of training being available, then you would circle numbers 1 through 10, which would give you three weeks of Phase I, one week of Phase II, three weeks of Phase III, and three weeks of Phase IV. If you feel that only one week of Phase II is not worth the change of training, you can push the week into Phase III and not have a Phase II. Whatever the number of weeks assigned to each phase, and regardless of the priority numbers, the number of weeks set aside for Phase I must be performed before going to Phase II, which must be done before Phase III, and so on. If the one week of Phase II was moved to Phase III, then the runner would have three weeks of Phase I, followed by four weeks of Phase III and a final three weeks of Phase IV. Once you identify how many weeks you have available for training, simply circle the numbers in the blocks that correspond to the number of available weeks and then progress through the phases in order, spending the specified amount of time on each.

If you have a season or period of time longer than 24 weeks, then decide which phases should receive the extra time and go from there. If you are coming into a season with a background of running or some other sport that is adequate to minimize Phase I, you may circle as many numbers in Phase I as you feel are legitimate and start the priority circling beyond the Phase I level.

When determining where a runner's training priorities should be, I feel the FI phase must be first and Phase IV (FQ), which is associated with final race preparation training, should be second. If either Phase II or Phase III must be sacrificed, get rid of Phase II. Phase III is more likely to prepare you for FQ than will Phase II.

Naturally, some people (coaches and runners alike) may feel that the ideal season is not 24 weeks, and I agree in certain cases. Whether a longer or shorter season is preferred, it still fits this type of approach. You need to ask yourself: "If I have only x weeks available, how will I prepare?" "X" can be any number of weeks. Once you have decided the ideal amount of time to prepare, map out your program; then go through each phase of training completely before going to the next phase (all of the weeks circled for a particular phase must be completed before you move to the next phase).

Up to now, I have presented two concepts:

1. A way to look at a season in terms of phases of training: Phase I (FI), easy, steady running for cell adaptation and injury prevention training; Phase II, early quality (EQ) training; Phase III, transition quality (TQ) training (the most demanding phase); and Phase IV, final quality (FQ) training (during and following which best performances should be attained)

2. A way of determining how many weeks of attention each of the four phases of training should receive, taking into account the total number of weeks available for the season

Some of what I have discussed stems from my personal coaching philosophy. Obviously, there is more than one approach to the number of phases of training that should make up a season, the length of each phase, the type of training that should be emphasized in each phase, and the order in which the various types of training should be performed. In fact, I will present different approaches to a season for runners preparing for different events when I discuss how to structure full training seasons in Part III.

This said, I will now analyze further my four phases of training, with some suggestions regarding what you might accomplish with each. Overall, the season should be set up with various phases of training that will

1.  build resistance to injury,
2.  prepare you for different types of training yet to come,
3.  develop the systems that are beneficial to the races of primary importance, and
4.  bring you into races with confidence and a feeling of freshness, not fatigue.

Each phase of training should include primary (P) training, which develops the component of fitness that you want to focus on at the time. There is usually enough time available each week for a secondary (S) emphasis, and occasionally, some maintenance (M) work can also be performed. However, I don't believe in trying to include every type of training (**MP, T, I,** and **R**) into each week of training, a method I refer to as a "shotgun" approach.

When setting up the various phases of training, arrange them so that they build on each other. Some coaches may require (and some events dictate) that reps precede intervals (I usually do); others demand the opposite, always going from slower to faster training. It is important to have a plan in which you have confidence, and to follow that plan. My suggestion is that you focus first on the workouts that will go into the final phase of training (FQ), because this is the period of time during or immediately following which you plan to perform at your best.

## GERRY LINDGREN

**Gerry Lindgren** was born in Spokane, Washington where he started running at age 15. His initial goal as a runner was to run fast enough to make other members of his team better runners, maintaining a "go-out-hard" approach throughout his entire career (I remember asking Gerry in 1993 what his best time for a 440 was. "52 seconds...on the last lap of a 5K"). At one point in his career, Gerry ran over 30 consecutive races faster than world-record pace for the first half of the race. I guess you could say he was the ultimate rabbit, but he frequently didn't relinquish the lead.

During college at Washington State University, Gerry won 11 NCAA Championships and placed ninth in the 10K in the Olympics. During his peak running years he logged between 200 and 350 miles per week. He presently runs for "Gerry's Joggers" and still puts in some pretty long runs when motivated. He has no plans to stop running. Gerry is one of a kind, the most determined runner I may have ever met. I learned from Gerry that serious world-class athletes are just as interested in having fun as are the rest of us.

**Gerry's Best**     3-mile: 12.53     6-mile: 26:11.6

# Phase IV: Final Quality Training

The final phase of training should be geared toward preparing each runner for actual race conditions. There are several items to consider for this phase.

## Account for the Elements

Make your Phase IV preparations as specific as possible to the conditions of the coming races. If the peak race will be in warm weather, then heat acclimatization should be part of this phase. If the all-important race will be at altitude, spend time at altitude during this phase (see chapter 10 for more on altitude). Participation in a race in a faraway time zone must be considered and plans made accordingly. If important races are to be in the morning hours, then quality workouts (if not all workouts) should be performed during similar times of the day.

## Focus on Your Strengths

The next thing to consider relative to the FQ block of training (and possibly the first thing for those who will not have to travel far from their training site) is the type of training performed. To do this, you must consider your individual strengths and weaknesses. In general, strengths should be taken advantage of during the final weeks of training, with weaknesses attended to earlier in the season. For example, a distance runner who is weak in the area of speed would be better served by approaching that weakness early in the season. If the same individual is well known for endurance and tenacity in a race, then this should be the type of training to emphasize during FQ training. In other words, concentrate on what you do best when the chips are down; don't spend a lot of time on aspects of your personal arsenal that don't serve you well at this critical time of the season.

## Don't Forget About Your Races

In addition to concentrating on what works best for you, some thought must be given to the events of importance during this racing phase. For example, FQ training usually will differ between runners

© Victah Sailer

By concentrating on the specific needs of your chosen event, you have a much better chance of being in peak shape for important races.

preparing for a marathon and those concentrating on racing a fast 1500 meters. The marathoner most likely will have left faster, rep-type training behind in favor of more threshold and long runs, whereas the 1500-meter specialist may be doing just the opposite during his or her final preparations.

# Pay Attention to Your Likes and Dislikes

Take into account each individual's likes and dislikes during FQ training. Some marathoners may like to continue doing some reps or intervals this late in the season because it builds their confidence or because a particular fast workout can be used as a reference point to help evaluate fitness. Muscle makeup may partly determine how some runners treat their final weeks of preparation. Some find that faster training leaves them with little spring in their stride; others like what fast strides do for their psyche.

# Phase III: Transition Quality Training

Because Phase III (TQ) training involves the most stressful, event-specific training, and because it also sets you up for the less stressful FQ phase, I like to focus on it next. Emphasis during the TQ phase is on workouts that build on what has already been accomplished in

## LET EACH STAR SHINE ITS BRIGHTEST

When dealing with a group of athletes who train together and are treated alike during the final weeks of training, it shouldn't be a surprise that their race performances may vary considerably. Some runners race best off of one type of training, while others perform optimally with another type. The results of this lack of individualized training can be seen every year when some distance runners do very well during cross-country season but perform in a mediocre manner during track season. Often, this is the result of different types of training imposed on the runners during the different seasons, more than it is the result of differences in how some individuals run cross-country as opposed to how they run track.

Almost every year I get new runners on my roster who say they like cross-country better than track (and who also perform better in the former), but by the end of their first track season, they are doing a much better job than ever before in track (and enjoying it more, as well). The opposite also holds true, of course, and some runners learn to improve their cross-country performances more than their track races. I attribute most of these differences in cross-country and track performances, and preferences, to the differences in training (or coaches) that the runners were exposed to during their early years of competing.

> Tradition has played a major role in how distance runners are treated throughout the school year. Typically, the early part of the cross-country season (if not the entire season) is devoted to mileage, and late cross-country and nearly all of track season is set aside for speedwork. (I would like to point out that I reserve the term "speedwork" for reps, but many runners and coaches consider all types of structured workouts as speedwork, even if the bouts are run at threshold or interval pace.) When following the traditional approach, cited above, it is assumed that every runner has the same strengths and weaknesses, that all have the same responses to training, that all have the same personal goals, and that all are best suited for the same event. Individual desires, strengths, and weaknesses must be taken into consideration, and the overall development of each runner must be of primary concern if optimal progress is to be made.

earlier weeks of training and that provide a good transition into the final phase of training.

## Stress the Proper Systems

During Phase III training your goal is to optimize the components of training (that is, stress the proper systems) that apply to your event of primary interest. For example, $\dot{V}O_2$max training (intervals) usually demands your primary attention when training for a 5K, 10K, or similar distances. On the other hand, 800-meter and 1500-meter runners may be better off with more anaerobic training, accomplished via primary emphasis on repetition training. The type of training to which each individual responds best (some 1500-meter runners respond better to intervals than to reps, for example) is of primary importance during Phase III.

## Don't Overdo It

By the time they reach Phase III, many runners have enough FI and EQ training under their belts that they feel very fit and sometimes invincible. This is not a good time to show how tough you are by training faster or more than the program has scheduled you to do. It is a good time to pay particular attention to hitting the proper training paces and taking good care of yourself. It is late enough in the season that injury and illness must be avoided at all cost. Good nutrition and adequate rest are of utmost importance now. Also, since Phase III is usually the most stressful in terms of quality training sessions, it is not a good idea to further stress yourself by increasing mileage at this time. Presumably, you have had adequate time to have reached your mileage goal by the time you move into the TQ phase of training.

## Accept the Challenge

Phase III challenges a runner's mental and physical toughness. It is tempting to slack off on some of the tough workouts that you will be facing in this phase. I believe in being flexible, even to the extent of rearranging the days on which your various quality sessions are performed. For example, Tuesday's session may be moved to Monday or Wednesday to avoid nasty weather. Make every effort, however, to get in all scheduled training sometime during each week.

## Use Races to Your Advantage

Races can produce breakthroughs in performance and boosts in confidence during this phase of training, often because a serious race can replace a dreaded training session, and may produce a surprisingly good result at a time when you are not peaking for a top performance. This is a good time to race distances that are either shorter or longer than your primary event of interest. Off-distance races can stress you in a way that makes a normally difficult workout seem much more tolerable. For example, racing 1500 meters or a mile, when your primary event is 3000 or 5000 meters, will often make subsequent interval and repetition sessions seem easier than before.

# Phase II: Early Quality Training

I prefer to approach early quality (EQ) training by thinking of two things: what type of training can be handled with what has been done so far, and what will best prepare the runner for the next phase. This means that the type of running that you feel is most important in the TQ and FQ phases of training must be prepared for in this EQ phase.

In a rather short season, some coaches may find that there is not enough time to include an EQ phase in the overall scheme of the season. A formal Phase II, however, can go a long way in making your season's goals more attainable.

# Time to Start Running Faster

Early quality training is designed to introduce faster workouts into a season's program. During this phase, I like to include strides and reps in the weekly schedule. Reps (primarily 200s and 400s at current mile race pace, with plenty of recovery time between runs) and strides (20- to 40-second runs at about mile race pace, using a light, quick leg cadence) go a long way in building good mechanics early in the season. Improving mechanics (which improves running economy) and strength, which are associated with faster running, can also minimize the chance of injury related to improper technique. I usually recommend five or six strides as part of at least two or three workouts each week (during warm-ups and cool-downs and in the middle of or at the end of long runs).

# Use Phase II to Minimize the Stress of Phase III

The faster, usually **R**-pace, running used for most Phase II programs prepares the muscles mechanically for the more stressful **I** training that is typical of Phase III quality workouts. Phase II reps are not very taxing on the cardiovascular and aerobic systems, so the overall stress imposed on the body is not great. During Phase III, when more demanding intervals are involved, the new stress will be primarily limited to the aerobic systems of performance. On the other hand, if intervals are performed in Phase II, then mechanical and aerobic stresses will be introduced at the same time, with a high chance of overload. In this type of situation, coaching philosophy, tempered by the needs of each runner, will ultimately determine the type of training that goes into a particular phase of the season's overall plan.

# Phase I: Foundation/Injury Prevention Training

Knowing that steady, easy running produces many desirable cellular benefits, while minimizing the chance of injury (as long as the amount of running is not increased too rapidly), makes the FI phase the ideal type of training for early in the season. As the season progresses, the benefits of steady, longer running are maintained physiologically, even with reduced emphasis on this type of training.

## Listen to Your Body

During Phase I training it is important not to increase stress too rapidly, a real temptation because there has yet to be any really stressful training, in terms of intensity, and it is easy to want to increase mileage too rapidly. Stick with my recommendation that weekly mileage not be increased more often than every third week and you'll seldom run into trouble in this regard. Learn to recognize signs of fatigue or too much running too soon and don't be afraid to take a day off now and then to keep yourself feeling in control of your running.

## Establish a Good Routine

Phase I is the time to get yourself into a good daily schedule of running, eating well, and sleeping regularly. If morning runs are to be a part of your overall program, schedule some, even if they are very short, just to get in the habit of it.

## Avoid the Mileage Syndrome

It's a mistake to get caught up in letting mileage become so important that it dominates your training, especially if you maintain this attitude when moving into subsequent phases of training when various types of quality running are of primary emphasis. Of course, marathoners and ultramarathoners often view long runs as being of primary importance during most of their season, and, keeping with the priorities I set for determining types of training, I would say many of them are right. As mentioned, the benefits of high mileage are well preserved once attained, so don't fear dropping some mileage later to allow other types of training to receive more emphasis.

# How Much Quality Training Is Necessary?

The next step in introducing details into a season of training is to determine how much of each type of training to include in each of the chosen phases. I try to include two or three types of quality training in each week of each different phase of the overall program. This usually means I give primary emphasis to one system, secondary emphasis to another system and, occasionally, maintenance emphasis to a third system. In many school situations, one of these emphases (and sometimes more than one) is, by necessity, a race, which still should be worked into the overall scheme of training.

## Plotting a Weekly Schedule

When plotting out each week's schedule, the workout of primary emphasis should be considered first. If, for example, you are in a Phase III, where interval training is of primary concern and midseason races limit you to just one quality session for the week, then that workout should be at **I** pace (unless, of course, the races you are performing replace or offer the same benefits as does interval training). When possible, the primary-emphasis workout should be done under desirable conditions, so that you have a good chance of completing a positive primary workout. It is also usually best to schedule the primary workout for earlier in the week, so that you are more likely to get it done and thus relieving the worry that poor weather later in the week may interrupt your plans.

When your competitive schedule permits, each week will usually include another session on the system of secondary emphasis. For example, when **I** running is of primary emphasis, a secondary emphasis might be on **T** runs, which are lower stress

© Victah Sailer

Working some races into your schedule will not only supplement your quality training, it will also give you a good indication of your current form. This, in turn, will allow you to keep good tabs on how well your training program is working for you.

but still of good quality and of importance to another component of fitness. In addition, a long run or some reps added to the end of a **T** session would help maintain the benefits of an earlier emphasis on easy running or an **R** phase of training.

# Alternating Hard and Easy Weeks of Training

If you follow the idea that there will be one primary and one secondary workout each week and a maintenance workout every other week, this means that in a six-week block of training, you will have six primary, six secondary, and three maintenance sessions—15 quality workouts over a six-week phase of training. This can also be viewed as having three quality sessions one week, followed by two quality sessions the next week, and so on. In effect you are alternating harder and easier weeks of training. When there is a weekly competition during this type of training scheme, then the (usually Saturday) competition would replace the scheduled Saturday training session.

## Mixing In Competitions With Quality Training Sessions

Another approach would be to schedule three quality sessions each week, with the primary (P) emphasis being the first quality day, the secondary (S) emphasis being the second quality day, and the maintenance (M) day scheduled for Saturday of each week. The advantage of this scheme is that each week has a primary and a secondary session and some weeks will also have the maintenance emphasis,

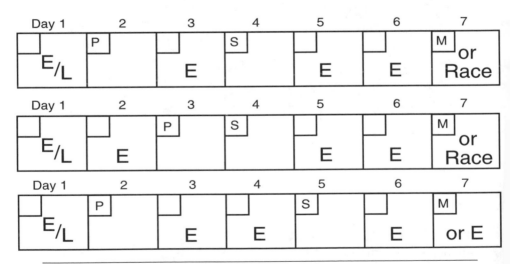

**Figure 8.3**  Three possible weekly schemes for primary (P), secondary (S), and maintenance (M) workouts.

Adapted from Daniels, J. March 1987. "Gimme five." *Runner's World* 30.

again depending on whether or not a competition is scheduled for that week. In fact, to assure both a primary and a secondary session each week, in the event of a midweek competition, the secondary session could replace the Saturday maintenance session to free up the midweek date for competition.

The key factor is to always give top priority to a primary workout and then to secondary and maintenance workouts in that order, with competitions first replacing the maintenance then secondary sessions, in that order. However, keep in mind that the events being performed in a competition may better replace one type of training than another, which can also dictate the type of training session that can best afford to be dropped for that particular week. Figure 8.3 presents a variety of possibilities regarding the placement of easy primary, secondary, and maintenance sessions in weeks with and without a Saturday competition.

# The Benefits of Back-To-Back Quality Days

In looking over figure 8.3 you will notice that one of the examples I have provided involves back-to-back quality days on Tuesday and Wednesday each week. I have found this to be a particularly good way of arranging a schedule when you want two quality sessions in the same week and you also have a Saturday competition to end the week. The advantages include the following:

1. You get two easy days of training after a Saturday race and before another quality session.

2. You get two easy days before a Saturday race.

3. Knowing you have to come back with a good session on Wednesday keeps you from getting carried away with Tuesday's workout and trying to set a workout record of some kind.

4. Having finished a solid day of training on Tuesday also tends to keep you from falling into the same overtraining trap mentioned above, on Wednesday.

# Keeping Long Runs In Perspective

Throughout these weeks of training, it is assumed that Sunday will probably be a long run, but unless you are getting in very long runs (one and one-half hours and longer), this run is still considered an easy day

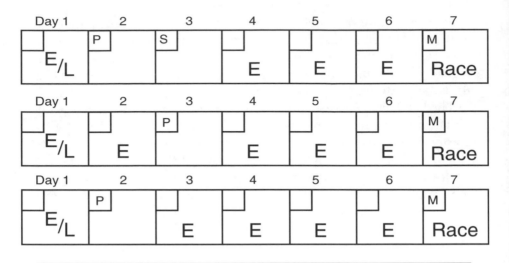

**Figure 8.4**   Three sample weekly training schemes when preparing for an important competition.

Adapted from Daniels, J. March 1987. "Gimme five." *Runner's World* 30.

and not particularly a quality day. On the other hand, there are times when performing long runs is a primary or at least a secondary or maintenance emphasis and they would be counted as a quality day.

# Training During the Peak Competitive Season

What I have described refers mainly to weeks of training when competitions are not high priority (qualifying and championship meets). Figure 8.4 shows a few examples of a weekly training scheme when the weekend competition is particularly important. Remember, even though you may continue with a good quality session in the week leading up to an important competition, the usual tactic will be to lower the weekly mileage and amount of quality training, but not necessarily the intensity.

Sometimes it is best to make the one quality day of the week leading up to an important competition four days before the race; other times it may be even better to go with the final quality session five days before the race day. In either case, you can still include a few quality strides or 200s up to three days before the important race, but be especially careful not to run anything faster than is usual for you, regardless of how little of that type of running you do. Keeping some light, quick strides as part of the final days can be particularly useful if the coming important competition is a meet lasting several days. On the other hand, a single day effort (such as a cross country national or state championship) can very nicely be approached with more days of just easy running.

# Setting Up Your Weekly Training

Once you have written down which days of each week will receive primary, secondary, and maintenance emphasis as is shown in figures 8.3 and 8.4, the next step is to indicate what type of workout goes with which day. For example, if you are in Phase II of training, with primary emphasis on **R** running, place an **"R"** on the calendar where there is a "P" in the schedule. If your current secondary emphasis is at threshold pace, then you simply place a **"T"** in each day marked with an "S". Do the same thing for maintenance days (possibly a long run, or a race).

When your program switches to a new phase of training, you merely change what primary, secondary, and maintenance stand for and go on to the new schedule. I have provided sample training programs for different events of interest in chapters 12 through 14.

## Training Variations From Different Coaches

Keep in mind that this is where coaching philosophy plays a major role in setting up a program. Different coaches like different system emphases during various phases of a season's program. Following the plan outlined here helps keep the coach (and runner) focused on the idea that particular systems are receiving primary, secondary, and maintenance emphasis for predetermined periods of time throughout the season.

Part of my coaching philosophy is based on the premise that it takes a long time to attain greatness and that skill should come before conditioning. By this I mean that it is better to develop speed (skill) before endurance (aerobic conditioning). I should clarify, though, that I believe in this approach over a number of seasons of training, not necessarily within every season. So, what I really believe in is helping runners to

1. learn good technique as youngsters,
2. work toward speed development without high mileage during the developmental years of high school and college, and
3. progressively carry out more endurance work later in their careers.

I would consider this to be an ideal approach. Unfortunately, in our scholastic-based athletic system such an approach can rob young runners of athletic scholarships because the endurance needed to demonstrate good distance times may not be adequately developed by the time the runner reaches college age. But there can still be some compromises made in today's society with high school coaches working more for speed in early years and adding some endurance as the runners move into their final year or two of high school competition.

This ideal approach, of moving from faster to endurance training can also be envisioned and used as a model for seasonal programs, which for some runners and coaches may appear to throw the various training components out of order (or out of order according to traditional training ideas). For example, faster training is often

# PARTICIPATING IN OTHER SPORTS

Sometimes, alternative sports are better in the long-term development of future distance runners than is more and more running. This is true since muscle weakness often leads to injuries, and performing only easy, long-distance training does little for muscle strength. Without good strengthening programs (which often come with participation in other sports, and should always accompany a physical education program), aspiring distance runners are set up perfectly for injuries. Add to this the desire of young runners (and often their coaches and parents) to reach outstanding performances as soon as possible, and it is no wonder that young distance runners (females in particular) have a high incidence of injury, which leads to a high dropout rate. Individuals who take up running after they have reached physical maturity usually avoid injuries that plague young beginners, because the mature runners are physically stronger and often not so driven (by themselves or by a coach).

A beginning runner probably will fall into one of three categories:

1. Runners who start before reaching physical maturity
2. Runners who begin in their early years of physical maturity
3. Runners who take up running well after reaching physical maturity and after they have completed their years of formal education

Very young beginners would do best to follow the 1500-meter–3K program (see table 8.1 and chapter 12), possibly downgrading interval training to nothing more than maintenance emphasis during any phase of training.These youngsters need reps and threshold training to learn good mechanics and to get in good quality with limited stress. More mature youngsters can handle a slightly tougher approach, but are still better off in a 1500-meter–3000-meter program. On the other hand, older beginners may find the marathon approach—but with limited mileage—to be a good start to formal training. This latter group may also want to extend Phase I training (see table 8.1 and chapter 14).

For runners who do another sport during the winter, consider the demands of the other sport and figure a way to work it into your overall running plan. Many runners who do another sport in the winter are involved in basketball, which demands some fast running and jumping. From a physiological point of view, these activities accomplish some of the same things as rep training. A runner involved in basketball can spend less time on reps and more time on other systems once formal running training commences.

Some runners are involved in cross-country skiing or ice hockey in the winter. The explosive, speed training of hockey, and the endurance factor of cross-country skiing are useful in determining what to include in, or possibly leave out of, an upcoming outdoor track season.

seen as needing increased emphasis later in the season. However, it usually takes several weeks to rebound from a phase of fast workouts, and better races often come after the bulk of fast training has been discarded for the season. One of the real keys to taking advantage of repetition work is to lessen total weekly mileage as well as the amount of quality work being done. A program of some fast running (but not faster than usual), coupled with threshold training, works well at the end of a season for distance runners who like to maintain some quality running with minimal stress and good day-to-day recovery.

Again, I want to remind you that for athletes who have only a few weeks of training available to them because of participation in other sports, the final phase of training must get close scrutiny, because that may be the only chance to get in some event-specific training. Under such circumstances, other desirable aspects of an ideal season may have to be scrapped for lack of time. Often, multisport athletes miss out on a good muscle endurance base. But if running is an important long-term goal for this athlete, then it is better to ignore endurance at an early age than it is to neglect speed.

# Working Races Into Training

A note about replacing workouts with races. In general, you can consider a race of about 3000 meters to 10,000 meters to stress aerobic capacity greatly enough that races within this range of distances would normally replace a good interval workout for the week in question. For races shorter than 3000 meters, and particularly when an athlete competes in several races in the same meet (say the mile, 800 meters, and a leg on a 4 × 400 relay), then this type of session would replace a rep workout. Sometimes, when using a meet to replace a particular workout you can add some to the races, making the day a full-blown workout. For example, you might race a mile and run a leg on a relay. After that formal racing, it may be desirable to get in a set of six or so repeat 200s at **R** pace. This makes a full **R** session out of the day. For an interval day, you may follow a 3000-meter race or maybe a shorter cross country race (5000 meters or less) with a trip around the course doing one-minute or two-minute **I**-pace runs.

Too often the tendency is to say, "We didn't do much at that meet today, so we better try to get in some quality training tomorrow and avoid missing out on our scheduled training this week." I prefer to extend a race day's demands a little to fill out a full session, thereby eliminating the need to add another quality day to the week. However, I always say that when you are in doubt as to whether or not to add something (to a workout or to a week's schedule), don't. Take the conservative approach and prolong your interest in the sport.

# Programs for Less Experienced Older Runners

A word to those of you who take up running later in life. I have been gearing most of this chapter's discussion toward younger runners, particularly in regard to spending the early years focusing on developing technique and speed. This particular approach may not be best for those who take up the sport as adults. In this case, starting with easy, aerobic running often works best, primarily because racing is usually not the first thing on the minds of older people who take up running; good healthy aerobic exercise is more likely the motivation.

Once they have reached a reasonable level of fitness, however, many older runners want to test themselves in a race of some kind. This often leads to wanting to run faster, and it is at this time that the idea of quality workouts starts to become a reality. I still think some repetition training can be beneficial, but I have found that there is

| Table 8.1 Identification of Training Emphasis for the Four Phases | | | |
|---|---|---|---|
| Training Phase | 1500m-3000m | 5K-15K | Marathon |
| I | Easy runs/strides | Easy runs/strides | Easy runs/strides |
| II | P - Reps<br>S - Threshold<br>M - Interval | P - Reps<br>S - Threshold<br>M - Interval | P - Reps or Interval<br>S - Threshold<br>M - Long or T/L |
| III | P - Interval<br>S - Reps<br>M - Threshold | P - Interval<br>S - Reps<br>M - Long | P - Interval or T/L<br>S - Threshold<br>M - MP |
| IV | P - Reps<br>S - Threshold<br>M - Interval | P - Threshold<br>S - Interval/Reps<br>M - Reps/Interval | P - Threshold<br>S - T/L<br>M - MP |

*Note:* **T/L** is a combination of threshold and long running in one session. **MP** denotes running a steady distance at projected marathon race pace.

more enjoyment (and still desirable results) from a program that minimizes intervals and repetitions and focuses more on threshold training as the main quality emphasis.

Table 8.1 gives examples of how training might be broken down for runners interested in different events. Always keep in mind that individual differences must be catered to, which may alter the way different phases of training are arranged. I encourage coaches and potential runners to work on general body conditioning, basic leg speed, and good running mechanics, particularly during early phases of each season.

# A Final Word

Whatever type of training program you decide on, follow one that is enjoyable enough (or at least rewarding enough) that you will stay with it long enough to find out how good you are capable of becoming. Be able to look back and say you enjoyed the training as much as you enjoyed the outcome of a well-run race. That is the real sign of a good training program.

# CHAPTER 9

# Taking Time Off

© Richard C. Etchberger

*Don't let the indices of overtraining
become the goal of your training.*

At some point or another, most runners experience a setback in training that requires them to take time off from training. Most runners should also take an occasional scheduled break. While a break and a setback both involve a reduction in training, a break is usually planned while a setback occurs unexpectedly, often as the result of an injury or illness.

This chapter addresses the issue of time off from running, whether planned or as the result of too much training, injury, or illness. I will give you some ideas about coping with time off from running, including advantages and potential disadvantages of cross-training. In addition, I'll offer some advice about avoiding future unwanted setbacks, how to plot out a return to normal training, and how to rearrange an interrupted season's schedule.

# Maintain a Positive Attitude Toward Breaks

While runners fear setbacks and are often reluctant to take breaks, I like to look at the bright side of time off. All breaks and almost all setbacks are actually beneficial to a runner in terms of overall development. A break gives both the body and the mind some time to regroup from what may have been a pretty strenuous period of training and competition. Good health, both mental and physical, is more likely to occur when a runner is training moderately and leading an unstressful (or low-stress) lifestyle. Continuous exhaustive training can place too much wear and tear on runners' bodies and can also have an adverse psychological effect.

It is true that runners sometimes pick up bad habits—such as overeating—during a break from training. However, sometimes these bad habits can be productive. Overeating, for example, can actually enable some runners to build up depleted iron stores that will serve them well when strenuous training is resumed. Breaks in training also allow little injuries to heal, injuries that may not have been serious enough to stop a runner's training but that could have become much worse if hard workouts had continued.

## The Benefits of Taking Time Off

Most individuals approach their running programs with great eagerness following a break in training. After a break, runners are fresh physically and mentally and usually feel enthusiastic about new goals they have set for themselves. While fitness has been reduced during the break, big improvements can occur once training resumes. Remember the principle of training that says maintaining fitness is easier than achieving it in the first place (principle #9, page 29)? The same truth applies to regaining a previous level of fitness; it's easier to regain fitness than it is to attain that fitness in the first place. You have been there before and experience is on your side.

Another reason why runners benefit from training breaks, involves the "determination factor." Setbacks can make runners determined to prove that great things were just about to happen had training not been unexpectedly interrupted. What serious runner hasn't been "on a roll," only to have training suddenly curtailed by a setback? Injuries are an inevitable part of distance runners' careers. But , they are not always as bad as they are made out to be.

In fact, it's best to look at these setbacks positively, as "career prolongers." As a setback-induced break ends, a runner's enthusiasm for running is renewed and the runner is more knowledgeable about what type of training is and is not stressful to his or her body. Wiser, better rested, and more determined, a runner is actually in a position to have a longer career because of the imposed break.

## The Hunger Factor

To better understand this point, consider for a moment the situation faced by many swimmers. Injuries occur much less frequently during swimming than in running, primarily due to the lesser physical trauma associated with gliding through the water compared to pounding the pavement. In swimming, there is no landing shock, no struggle against gravity, and not as much heat stress due to the cooling water environment. All this means that swimmers can train for long periods of time without injury-induced setbacks.

Think about it for a moment. If you were a swimmer and you could train continuously, free from injury for 8 or 10 years, wouldn't you feel that you had given yourself a good chance to see if swimming were really your sport? Let's say that you started as a 10-year-old, trained and competed without setbacks until you were 18, and all of a sudden kids younger than you, with fewer years of training and less experience, started beating you. What would your reaction be?

How about runners? If you start at age 12, by the time you are age 20 you probably have enjoyed only a couple of years of uninterrupted training. You are still hungry and still thinking that you have not come anywhere near your potential. Not many younger kids are beating your times, and when an injury occurs, you simply say, "As soon as I get over this problem, I'll show everyone what kind of a runner I really am."

In a sense, runners stay more like young swimmers, because of the setbacks they sometimes experience during their careers. Setbacks can be terribly disappointing, but they also have a way of keeping us hungry. Temporary training stalemates can actually rekindle competitive fires, revitalize worn and tired body parts, and minimize the chance of burnout that seems to occur more often in some other sports.

# Unplanned Setbacks

Unlike contact sports, in which it is normal to know just how and when an injury occurred, runners are quite often unable to relate an injury to a specific incident. An injury is often the result of overstressing an imperfect body part, such as a leg length discrepancy or a tendency toward overpronation. Many running injuries just seem to progress slowly over time.

## Logging the Specifics

My first recommendation is to record every setback in a special diary or log book that you can refer to easily when needed. Particularly when injuries have occurred, enter all the details leading up to the problem.

Categorize the injuries according to the parts of the body in which they occur—knee, ankle, foot, hip, hamstring. Enter the date that you first noticed the injury and the date that you think the injury actually occurred (probably the same day, but not necessarily). Also write down what you think caused the injury, or at least the training, competition, accident, or incident that was associated with the malady. Finally, keep track of what you do to remedy the problem, both at the onset of the injury, and in later days and weeks until you feel that the traumatized body part is healed.

The logged information can help you handle future injuries; you'll have a permanent record of what helped you to alleviate knee pain or Achilles tendon soreness, for example. Some injuries seem to go away after a couple weeks of no training; others disappear even though training continues. The log book will help you remember how your own body responded to different types of injuries and will help you save a lot of worry, time, and maybe even some money (on various treatments) in the future when similar injuries crop up again.

Of the 26 elite distance runners whom I tested in the late 1960s and again 25 years later, the individual who had the best results in his $\dot{V}O_2$max test as a 47-year-old (76 ml·kg$^{-1}$·min$^{-1}$) had recorded the nearly 100 setbacks that had plagued him over the years, along with the time he had taken off to care for each problem. He had done a magnificent job of learning to rest when needed and was a highly successful masters competitor. Therefore, setbacks can even lengthen your running career.

## Let Your Experience Guide You

When an injury occurs for the first time it is always a little scary, but most running injuries do respond to treatment and many can be prevented. A trip or two to a doctor may be necessary for a first-time injury, but the treatment (unless it is a prescription) may be something you can do yourself in the future, especially if you have written down the treatment or rehabilitation in your log book.

Frequently, a few strengthening and stretching exercises can do wonders in clearing up injuries and in preventing recurrences of the injuries. If a particular injury in one leg is cleared up and prevented with a few exercises, it is wise to use the same exercises on the other leg. Many runners I have coached who were prone to knee pain had their knee problem corrected by faithfully doing some final 10- to 15-degree knee extensions with moderate resistance. Other runners have been able to clear up hamstring problems by doing knee curls regularly.

In my early pentathlon days, I suffered from terrible shins-plints, but I kept pounding away in training until both legs throbbed in pain. I quickly learned that my left leg would always show symptoms sooner than the right leg, and I found that if I backed off certain types of running (especially speed running on my toes) and stretched the appropriate muscles whenever the

Documenting what has caused an injury can help you to avoid a reoccurrence of the injury and can also give you insight into how to handle recovery if and when another injury occurs.

pain began in the left shin, the right shin never flared up and the left shin pain would go away. I learned to use my left shin as a warning signal that I was doing too much of the wrong kind of training and wasn't stretching properly. It's not that I cured myself from ever getting shinsplints; I'm sure I could still bring them on with some "shinsplint-specificity" training. I simply learned about the body signals that warned me of approaching injury and took appropriate steps to stay well.

It is not my purpose to present cures for various types of injuries— that is a task for trained specialists in the field of sports medicine. Nevertheless, I think that all runners can do themselves a favor by learning to keep in touch with their bodies and by not always relying on someone else to do it for them. I can say the same thing about nutrition and training. A competent sport nutritionist can be a great asset, as can a qualified coach, but you must learn to use their teachings in order to become the healthiest, happiest, most successful runner you can possibly be.

# Prevention Is the Best Plan

My approach regarding injury and illness is rather cautious. I strongly believe in the "ounce-of-prevention" philosophy. I think that more time and effort should be spent on identifying optimal (injury preventing) training instead of identifying overtraining, which usually receives a great deal of attention. It sometimes seems that the goal of many training programs is to strive for a state of excess training. With some coaches the attitude seems to be, "May the strongest survive and let the others find another sport." The sad part of this attitude is that it discourages many potentially outstanding runners at a time when they are not physically ready for the stress being imposed. Instead of shooting for signs of fatigue and physical stress, I strongly believe that runners should strive for improved performance. If improved performances result from easier training and a healthier, stronger body, then I'm not disappointed that my training program did not produce the magical signs of overtraining.

Injuries can't be taken lightly; even the slightest injury can become a major problem. It is not at all unusual for a little ankle pain in one leg to cause a slight limp during running. Continued favoring of one leg can easily put enough extra stress on the other leg that a new, more serious injury occurs in the "good" side of the body—in the hip or knee, for example. It is never a good idea to try to hobble through an injury, even if that injury seems to be one that will clear up soon. The danger of a second injury being caused by a limp is just too great.

# When Those Inevitable Injuries Do Occur

When overuse injuries occur, a runner can't just return to training as usual. Something has to be changed. It may be a matter of reducing mileage or intensity of training; it may involve adding some stretching and strengthening exercises to the overall program; or it may mean having some corrective devices put in one or both of your running shoes. Again, become familiar with your own body (or the bodies of the runners you coach), and try to avoid situations that have caused injuries in the past.

No matter how careful and thoughtful you are about your training, occasionally injuries will occur and must be dealt with. One of the key aspects of dealing successfully with an injury is making sure you don't return to your normal amount and intensity of training or competition too quickly. My first rule in this regard is not to run a race after an injury until you have done at least one good-quality workout to prove that you are capable of handling the physical demands of race-intensity stress. In other words, don't use a race to test your recovery.

Of course, in the case of a season-ending championship, you may be able to afford taking a chance if you know that following the race there will be plenty of rehabilitation time, in the event of recurring injury. However, it is better to bypass most competitions in favor of full recovery from an injury or illness, especially if this means giving someone else an opportunity to participate. I'll be forever grateful to a teammate who was our national champion, but who suffered an injury just before the Olympics. Although not entirely by choice, his not competing afforded me (as the team's alternate) the opportunity to be in my first international competition, the Olympic Games, and I performed well enough to win a silver medal. That success led to my staying with the sport and most certainly was the main reason I was able to compete in another Olympics (where I won a bronze medal) and three World Championships (another bronze medal), and to twice win the United States National Championship.

## Setbacks Only in Quality of Training

Sometimes an injury produces a setback only in terms of quality of training, and normal quantity of training can be maintained. In such cases, try a few days of adding strides to the middle or end of a daily easy run before jumping back into more typical rep, interval, or threshold training. I have tried to build this return approach into the information provided in table 9.2 on page 174. The process of working your way back to normal training can be particularly difficult if you are training yourself. You may respond to injuries differently from other runners you know, and you should never let someone talk you into normal training if you don't feel up to it.

# Hypertraining

When a setback is the result of overtraining (I hope you never have to experience this firsthand), recovery to normal status can be hastened by being kind to yourself. Don't subject yourself to additional physical or emotional stress. For me, as a coach, the easiest way to detect overtraining is by knowing my athletes, each and every one of them.

Here's how I look for overtraining: When progressing through a season of training, gradual increases in amount and intensity of running are scheduled every few weeks. These increases in training stress should be associated with better performances and should produce no greater subjective stress than did earlier increases to loads and intensities. If training is increased and positive results are not realized within three or four weeks, nor do test workouts go favorably, then I would say it is time to back off or at least make some serious assessments of current training. You are training too hard for the results that are being realized.

I call this "hypertraining," because it corresponds to the definition of hyperventilation so nicely. Hyperventilation means ventilating (breathing) more air than is necessary to do the job at hand. Hypertraining means training harder than is needed to perform at a level that could be attained with less training. When this happens, it is better to train less and still get the same performances.

## Alleviating Hypertraining

My recommendation for someone experiencing hypertraining is the following four-step program. Try each step, in order, until you find one that works.

1. Back off in your training by lowering total mileage, which will decrease the amount of quality work accordingly, per the rules that designate 10% of weekly mileage at threshold pace, 8% at interval pace, and 5% at repetition pace (see chapters 5, 6, and 7, respectively).
2. Cut out all quality training for a week or two and treat yourself as if you were recovering from an injury. At this point you are already stressed out from subpar races or evaluation sessions, so don't do anything that might add to your mental fatigue.
3. Try maintaining your weekly mileage for a couple of weeks, but switch to a different quality emphasis (usually abandon interval training in favor of threshold or repetition training).
4. Give the same program one more try for a couple of weeks without any changes.

Try the options in the order presented, unless experience tells you that a particular approach works best for you. Usually the first step produces positive results within a week or two. I suggest a 20% drop in mileage as a starting point. You may have to cut back even more, particularly if you are on a high-mileage program.

I hope that one of these options, or some variation thereof, will do the job. If none works and you continue to feel poorly, it's time for a thorough medical checkup and probably a prolonged break from training. But don't worry. No matter how long you are away from running, once you get back into it, all cares about the overtraining will be soon forgotten. In fact, make sure that you learned a valuable lesson the first time and that you don't go right back to overtraining. Remember, of all the types of training available to athletes, hypertraining probably is used the most.

# Balance the Scales in Your Favor

I'd like to add one final reminder about training load as it relates to reaching competitive fitness and the likelihood of experiencing a setback due to injury, illness, or a general loss of desire due to hypertraining. Figure 9.1 shows two response curves related to changes in training stress in the form of greater training volume, greater training intensity, or both. The upper curve (curve a) shows how competitive fitness responds to increases in training stress, showing that diminishing returns ensue. Curve b, which is a mirror image of curve a, depicts the possibility of a setback as training stress increases. It shows that the chance of a setback increases in proportion with an increase in training stress.

Note that setbacks are few until a fairly high training load is reached. However, at some critical point, further increases in training are accompanied by a rapidly rising chance of a setback. At what amount of training a setback actually happens among a group of runners varies, and in addition to being associated with both amount and intensity (collectively referred to as "training stress"), a setback is probably also a function of how rapidly you try to increase that stress. What may be intolerable this season may be fine next year. Steady, consistent, thoughtful training is always the answer.

In figure 9.1 you will notice there is an area of training, shown by a shaded box, that represents the ideal training window for any runner. In this window, about 95% of all possible benefits will be realized with a low chance of setbacks. This is where the bulk of training should take place year in and year out. To reach outstanding performances, a runner may have to venture to the right of this window, but only for a few weeks at a time. This will provide the extra seconds of improvement that may spell the difference between making an Olympic team and staying at home, but it also carries with it a greatly increased risk of a setback—you can't stay out there too long.

# Dealing With Setbacks Due to Illness

When we think about setbacks caused by illness rather than injury, colds are probably the most frequent producers of layoffs. Seldom does a cross-country team get through the fall competitive season without the top seven runners coming down with a total of seven colds.

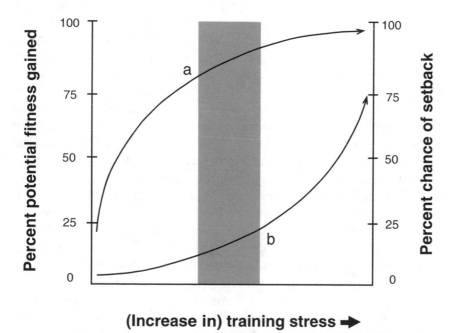

**Figure 9.1**  Comparison of increase in fitness level due to increased training (curve a) to chance of setback due to increased stress from training (curve b).

The types of training least suited for runners suffering from colds and nagging illnesses are intervals and threshold training. I make a point of not including either of these types of stress in an ill runner's schedule. First of all, $\dot{V}O_2max$ (interval) training and threshold workouts represent the kinds of training that require good conditions to produce good results. Runners seldom feel good when they are sick. Second, and more important, stressful exercise of a somewhat prolonged nature may transform a relatively minor illness into something more serious. When athletes are sick they should concentrate on returning to normal health and not try to satisfy the requirements of a rigorous training schedule. Races and demanding workouts should be eliminated for a while.

Just as academics should be the primary focus of high school and college runners, good health must take precedence over training at all levels of athletic endeavor. It's not bad for an athlete in a nonendurance sport to practice some skills during certain illnesses, but endurance athletes can't afford to train as usual when their health is abnormal. However, I have found that steady, easy runs and short repetition sessions, with a heavy emphasis on full recoveries during the rep workout, can usually be performed adequately when an athlete has a nonserious illness. I offer two cautions, though: the athlete should feel able to do the running, and the athlete's doctor should willingly give the okay.

My college runners hate to miss normal training and do everything possible to avoid illness. However, when they are sick, they often find that they get good results from doing a reduced schedule of easy runs and 15–20 × 200 about three seconds faster than current 5K race pace with full recoveries. In fact, sometimes they feel that they are getting a better deal by being sick and backing off the harder training for a while. Mentally, they are good at accepting the alteration in training and are enthusiastic about returning to a normal running schedule.

If an athlete needs to do less training because of an illness, competition must also be cut out at this time. Naturally, if a doctor gives medical clearance, I would permit a runner with a certain illness to compete in a national championship or other very important competition, but it is neither consistent nor fair to let sick runners compete in lesser meets when policy is to avoid demanding training sessions for a period of time. A coach must consider the effect his or her decisions have on the rest of the team; consistency is critical in

# JERRY LAWSON

Jerry Lawson was born in Syracuse, New York. He attended high school in Chittenango, New York and college at Mohawk Valley Community College and Boston University. Jerry took up running at age 15 because he was "cut from basketball and baseball teams." His main running goal, since early in his career, has been to race in the Olympics.

I became aware of Jerry's running abilities when I first started coaching at SUNY Cortland in the 1980s when Jerry was at Mohawk Valley. A few years later Jerry asked me to look over his training log. Upon reviewing it, my first thought was that this guy was another Gerry Lindgren; he was able to handle very large amounts of running. It was a few more years before I actually started offering him my coaching assistance on a regular basis, and a formal coaching relationship began in the mid 1990s.

At one time, Jerry held the American 25K road record, and he currently holds the American loop-course marathon record. Jerry's typical training involves 100- to 120- mile weeks (although stories abound regarding periods of considerably greater mileage, some of which are true). Long intervals are what he feels have been most beneficial to his success.

Jerry is a true marathoner. He is methodical and realistic in approaching his goals; he is not obsessed with achieving them quickly. He realizes that proper development takes time. I have learned from Jerry that physiological characteristics limit what the body can do but that mental determination can increase physiological thresholds.

**Jerry's Bests**   25K: 1:15:34   Half-marathon: 1:01:43
Marathon: 2:09:35

building team morale. Furthermore, replacing one of the team's better, yet ill, runners with a lesser athlete may be the very opportunity this "backup" runner needs to experience a breakthrough in performance.

With serious illnesses, including all those that require a doctor's care or a prescription or that involve a fever, no training should be performed without a doctor's support and knowledge. The same thing is true when an athlete feels badly enough to want time off, despite a lack of any particular symptoms. Again, it is far better to take some time off, even though it may not be absolutely necessary, than it is to train or race when it is inappropriate. To many athletes and coaches, injuries and illnesses seem to last forever, but once they are cleared up things get back to normal quite quickly.

# Planned Breaks in Training

In addition to various setbacks that runners are bound to experience at one time or another over the course of a career, there should also be some planned breaks in training. The best time for a planned break will vary for runners depending on their interests and lifestyles. It also will depend somewhat on the type of training program being followed. For example, some runners don't train very much during the winter, especially if they live in adverse climates and have limited facilities for indoor training. For them, winter is a good time to take a planned break. Other distance runners have little or no interest in cross-country, so the competitive cross-country season may be a good time for a planned break. Many high school and college runners use early summer as their downtime from regular training.

Planning a break is similar to plotting out a season of training. Simply work back from the most important part of the coming season and see where a break best fits in. Don't just take a break because it's the end of a particular season or because friends and teammates are goofing off for a while. Each runner should have his or her own plan. Of course, if your plan is the same as a whole group of other runners, you may all have the same break time. In any case, I recommend a serious break from training at least once per year, and it may even be wise to take other small breaks at different times in the same year.

# How Long Should a Break Last?

The length and timing of a break depends on how hard training has been and how many unplanned setbacks occurred during the past year. If there has been a lengthy setback or two or a few smaller setbacks during the season, it may have provided sufficient physical and mental recovery that a planned break is unnecessary. In this case a runner might be able to go right into the next season without taking a planned break.

In the case of a female runner who is having a baby, the break may last for a year or more, and the same would be true for a runner who wants to devote a significant amount of time to pursuing a career. At the other extreme, a break may last only a few weeks. Sometimes, a couple of two-week breaks fit an annual schedule quite well, but eventually a more prolonged break of four to six weeks will probably be useful.

Many coaches and runners don't want to take time away from running, especially when things are going well, for fear of losing fitness. Such individuals tend to be pessimistic types who figure there will eventually be an unplanned setback that will serve the same purpose. I don't think you should ever plan on unplanned setbacks, because that is a pretty sure way for a serious setback to occur. In any case, don't look at a planned break from training as a setback in your progression toward better times. Look at breaks as important, useful steps toward reaching your long-term goals. Convince yourself that the break is an actual phase of training, a stepping-stone toward better training and superior performances.

# What to Do During a Planned Break

A planned break may include small amounts of running or may be a furlough from running. If it takes place during the winter, the break may consist of fairly extensive cross-country skiing or other sports, depending on interests, climate, and conditions during the break time. It is also okay for the break to involve no special physical activities at all; a break can be an escape from a structured lifestyle.

In the hierarchy of training, breaks rank right up there with threshold runs, intervals, reps, and steady running. All have a function, and when placed in proper sequence, all build on one another. If it makes you feel any better about breaks, add "break training" to the other types of workouts I have described earlier, and then plan a specific program to follow during this phase. It may involve walking two hours a day, reading one hour each day, or visiting friends for six hours on weekends, for example. Often, a training break offers a great opportunity to carry out a strength program or to learn more about stretching and relaxation. However you visualize your break, remember to look at it as a positive part of your overall plan.

# Cross-Training During Downtime

Cross-training refers to the use of nonrunning activities as part of a running program to increase a runner's chances of success. I want to make it clear that I believe the best way to become a better runner is through running training, which follows the principle of specificity of training (principle #2, page 15). However, despite the specificity-of-training principle, I do believe there is a place for cross-training.

While some runners may never need cross-training, some may occasionally find it beneficial; still others might depend on cross-training as part of every week's training plan. Hiking, stretching, weight training, swimming, and cycling all qualify, as does anything else that can benefit a runner's body and mind as he or she becomes better prepared for racing.

While only running can improve running fitness, other activities can help an athlete reduce tension or anxiety in his or her daily life (bowling, table tennis, yoga, and hiking are examples of possible stress-reducing activities). There are also activities that help an athlete ward off or recover from injury; these are the ones most often part of effective cross-training. I include weight training, stretching, swimming, water running, and cross-country skiing in this category.

Some individuals believe that nonrunning activities can do a better job of preparing runners for competition than can a program of only running. I believe that this can be true, but only for those individuals who can spend a small amount of time actually running or for those who consistently suffer from setbacks whenever they try to undertake a fairly high-volume (or high-intensity) running program.

Unfortunately, more running doesn't always keep you injury free, and if cross-training permits harder running training through injury reduction, then these supplemental activities are well worth the effort. Through trial and error and through scientific research, we are always learning more about training, and it may be true that some nonrunning activities will produce future running breakthroughs. I want to make it clear that improvements in running that accompany the use of cross-training are most likely to occur when the cross-training permits an individual to run more intensely, more effectively, or with less physical and emotional stress.

One can argue that it doesn't really matter why you get better, as long as you do so. However, it is important for runners to understand the factors that directly and indirectly affect performance. It is particularly important to realize that because some weight loss or some cross-training leads to an improvement in running performance, it doesn't necessarily follow that more weight loss or more cross-training will result in further improvement. Just as adding greater mileage to your training program doesn't always produce positive results, there are limits regarding how much weight or body fat to lose or how much cross-training you should undertake. The ultimate goal of any coach or competitive runner should be to produce better race results, not to become super lean or to develop a bodybuilder's physique.

## Running Performance Is What Counts

I remember a guy who used to get paid a few hundred dollars a month to coordinate stretching exercises for a couple of elite runners. After 18 months of the program, I asked him how it was going. He said, "We're getting great results." I asked how he was so certain (my scientific mind in operation again). He replied, "These guys are clearly more flexible than they were two years ago, based on some flexibility tests." I believe he quoted a percent improvement, but I can't remember the figure. I guess my thinking was too logical when I asked, "Can they run any faster?" The reply was, "I'm certain they will anytime now, as soon as they get over some injuries they have suffered"—injuries most likely induced by the strenuous stretching program.

The first thing to ask anyone who offers a quick (or not so quick) fix for problems you might encounter is, "Can you provide me with some hard evidence to support your claims?" I learned this fact when working at Athletics West. People were often contacting me to sing the praises of some great training device or powerful pill that they wanted Alberto Salazar or Joan Benoit or Mary Slaney to try out, claiming that use of their product would make good runners out of these people. Why didn't anyone try to make a great runner out of me with their secret devices or potent medications? When I gave the "show me the research" line, the answer was usually, "That's what we want you to do for us." I guess I was supposed to do all the work, using proven running stars, to show that their products won't destroy great athletes.

It's natural to look for a quick fix, particularly if it relates to an injury or illness. However, rather than searching for a quick fix, it's better to involve yourself with something that's proven to be productive and let the overall approach to reaching your goals take care of getting you there. In the case of performing supplemental exercises during a period of nonrunning training, keep in mind that running fitness will deteriorate, at least to some degree, while you are not running. This is not to say the alternative exercises are not beneficial—they certainly help keep most runners' minds straight during times when they can't run. Furthermore, a serious runner who is prevented from running for a while may forget to back off on food consumption a bit, and in this case the supplemental activity can help maintain a good body composition.

If a runner can be reasonable about nutrition and not lose anything psychologically while an injury heals, I think it is fair to say that cross-training during a layoff will prevent some of the fitness decay that would be associated with the same time off in the absense of cross-training.

## Changes in Body Composition

Another way in which cross-training can benefit running is by producing a loss of unnecessary body mass. The extra activity associated with cross-training burns calories, and there is no doubt that the loss of nonessential body fat will result in better race performances, even in the absence of improved fitness. It is hard to tell, however, how much of improved running performance can be traced to a leaner frame rather than the fact that quality training can be carried out more effectively with a slimmer body. I want to emphasize that becoming too lean or overly conscious about body fat can be very detrimental to a quality training program. Losing unneeded body fat is one matter; losing body mass for the sake of weighing less can be counterproductive, and often leads to the downfall of a runner's otherwise bright future.

Although cross-training can give you a break from running, don't depend on it to get you into peak running shape. The only way to "leap" into the new season ready to race is to get out your running shoes and get on the road or trail.

# Returning to Running After a Break

When a break ends and you are ready to start working out seriously again, follow this advice:

1. Refer to tables 9.1 and 9.2 and review the information associated with these tables.

2. Don't race until you have completed at least one phase of training.

3. Refer to chapter 8 to review the procedure used in designing a new or revised program.

4. Long breaks can be associated with substantial changes in body composition (for better or for worse) or may have been accompanied by serious illness, injury, surgery, or pregnancy, so regain normal, healthy strength and body weight

before progressing into quality phases of training (you may have to extend the initial steady run phase of training to accomplish this). Don't let a break cause concern that time has been lost and that training should therefore be accelerated to make up for lost time. Follow appropriate training rules, and previous levels of competitive fitness will return more quickly than expected.

5. Have confidence in what you are doing. You have a sensible plan of training and it will produce excellent results.

## Don't Overdo It

Not all injuries are the same, and the desirable rate of return to normal training may have to be even more gradual. If a doctor tells you how long to spend in recovery, follow that advice and don't try to rush things. My main concern is to avoid too rapid a return to normal training. In a worst-case situation, in an attempt to make up for lost time you train even harder than before the setback and cause further injury. Working extra hard to catch up is never recommended. Remember, the rest from running probably did some good and it shouldn't be viewed as totally negative. The layoff allows for rejuvenation and rebuilding to take place in the runner's entire body, not just in the injured area. In addition, after a layoff, runners often don't expect as much from themselves and go into races feeling relaxed and fresh (the pressure is off). I've noticed that runners often run some outstanding races during the few weeks after they have recovered from an injury. Think, for example, of Joan Benoit Samuelson's 1984 Olympic Trials and Olympic Games victories which occurred just a couple of weeks after she had undergone arthroscopic knee surgery. Her forced break from normal training may have been just what was needed to be victorious in the first women's Olympic marathon. But this is not always the case. Don't push yourself.

## Making Adjustments After Time Off

In an attempt to take some of the guesswork out of return to training following a break or setback, I have designed some tables that can be referred to. But first, keep in mind that there are two basic adjustments that must be made in your training program—one is in intensity of running and the other is in amount.

# Adjusting Intensity

Table 9.1 provides a guide for adjusting intensity of training based on your time away from normal training. Remember how I have presented the idea of using a VDOT value to determine training intensities? Current VDOT drives the speed at which you do each type of training—steady/long runs, marathon-pace runs, threshold runs, intervals, and reps. As you improve your fitness with training, your VDOT improves, as do the various training intensities. The same thing applies when your fitness deteriorates, as invariably occurs with a setback. If you have not engaged in cross-training, multiply the FVDOT–1 value in the table times your pre-setback VDOT to determine your new VDOT. If you have done cross-training while away from running, multiply FVDOT–2 times your pre-setback VDOT.

For example, if two weeks of training have been missed during a setback, table 9.1 indicates that the return-to-training VDOT should be 97.3% of the pre-setback VDOT (multiply the pre-setback VDOT by .973 to get a new training-intensity VDOT). If, during the period of rehabilitation, ideal cross-training was carried out, use an adjustment of .986 instead of .973. Table 9.1 also indicates some extremes. You may notice that with five or fewer days missed, there is no adjustment needed. Once you have missed 72 days you have just about reached the end of possible deterioration. This adjustment (.800) is representative of the fact that optimum training can improve VDOT by about 20% (.200), so it stands to reason that you can't deteriorate more than you could improve in the first place. (This 20% change is not entirely representative of the total deterioration or improvement possible, and I will address this issue later on.)

Since your weight probably will have fluctuated in your time off, an adjustment in VDOT must be made to account for your weight change. Use the following method to figure your adjusted VDOT.

Enter your pre-setback weight in kilograms (kg) in A
(weight in kg = weight in pounds × 0.454)
(A)_____
Enter pre-setback VDOT in B
(B)_____
Multiply A × B to get C
(C)_____
Divide C by current weight in kg to get = D
(D)_____

D is your weight-adjusted VDOT. Apply the appropriate FVDOT value from table 9.1 to D to determine the VDOT on which you should base your comeback training. Once racing resumes, use race times to establish an updated VDOT.

## Adjusting Mileage

Just as table 9.1 addresses the issue of intensity adjustment, table 9.2 provides a guide for adjusting the amount of training (mileage) following a setback. Table 9.2 also provides recommendations and examples for the time spent at reduced amounts of weekly mileage.

In addition to the formula for mileage reduction shown in column 4, I have given the exact time at various reduced loads that would apply for one or more examples in that category. For a category II setback, for example, the first half of the return time is easy running at 50% of the pre-setback weekly mileage. A runner who had been doing 40 miles per week prior to setback, and who missed two weeks of training, would total about 20 miles the first week back (50% of pre-setback weekly mileage) and 30 miles the second week back (75% of original mileage). Both of these return weeks would involve nothing more than steady, easy running. Easy pace would be driven by 97.3% of original VDOT, shown in table 9.1 as .973 for two weeks off.

Another runner who missed six weeks, but who cross-trained diligently, would take 94.4% of original VDOT to determine training intensity (.944 in table 9.1) and would determine load adjustments from category III in table 9.2 on page 174. If this runner was doing 60 miles per week pre-setback, then the first third of the return time (two weeks) would be at 20 miles per week (one-third of 60 is 20) of easy running, which would be followed by two weeks at 30 miles per week (50% load) of easy running. The final two weeks of return would allow for 45 miles per week (75% load) of easy running, plus some strides to start to regain a feeling for moving a little faster than easy pace.

Following whatever time frame, mileages, and intensity that the return formulae dictate, the runner is then free to return to the full pre-setback values and to follow normal procedures for increasing load and intensity as outlined in earlier chapters. I want to reiterate the possible need to revalue VDOT as dictated by changes in weight or body composition.

## Table 9.1 Training Intensity (VDOT) Adjustments for Time Off from Running

| Time off from running | FVDOT–1 | FVDOT–2 |
|---|---|---|
| Up to 5 days | 1.00 | 1.00 |
| 6 days | .997 | .998 |
| 1 wk (7 days) | .994 | .997 |
| 10 days | .985 | .992 |
| 2 wk (14 days) | .973 | .986 |
| 3 wk (21 days) | .952 | .976 |
| 4 wk (28 days) | .931 | .965 |
| 5 wk (35 days) | .910 | .955 |
| 6 wk (42 days) | .889 | .944 |
| 7 wk (49 days) | .868 | .934 |
| 8 wk (56 days) | .847 | .923 |
| 9 wk (63 days) | .826 | .913 |
| 10 wk (70 days) | .805 | .902 |
| 72 days or more* | .800 | .900 |

# Racing After Time Off or Following Illness

Surprisingly, runners often run the best races of their lives immediately after an illness. My wife qualified for the Olympic Trials
marathon in her first attempt at the distance, following several
weeks of illness. Jerry Lawson ran the Chicago Marathon in 2:10
(in 1996) after a cold had curtailed his running for a couple of
weeks leading up to the race. A world record was set in the six-
mile some years ago by a runner who reportedly had cut back his
mileage drastically for several months because of injury. I'm sure

| Table 9.2 | Guide to Amount and Intensity of Training Following a Setback | | | |
|---|---|---|---|---|
| Category | Time off from running Weeks/Days (wk/d) | Time at adjusted load/intensity Weeks/Days (wk/d) | Adjustment made: | Percent pre-setback VDOT |
| I | up to 5 d | up to 5 d | Easy run at 100% pre-setback load | 100% |
| | Example: 5 d | 5 d | 5 d **E** @ 100% | 100% |
| II | 6 - 28 d | 6 - 28 d | First half: **E** @ 50% Second half: **E** @ 75% | per table 9.1 |
| | Example: 6 d | 6 d | 3 d **E** @ 50% load, + 3 d **E** @ 75% | 99.7% |
| | Example: 28 d | 28 d | 14 d **E** @ 50% load, + 14 d **E** @ 75% | 93.1% |
| III | 4 - 8 wk | 4 - 8 wk | First third: **E** @ 33% Second third: **E** @ 50% Final third: **E** @ 75% w/ strides | per table 9.1 |
| | Example: 29d | 29d | 9 d **E** @ 33% + 10 d **E** @ 50% + 10 d **E** @ 75% w/ strides | 93.1% |
| | Example: 8 wk | 8 wk | 18 d **E** @ 33% +19 d **E** @ 50% + 19 d **E** @ 75% w/ strides | 84.7% |
| IV | 8 wk or more | 8 wk or more | 3 wk **E** @ 33%; not greater than 30 miles/wk 3 wk **E** @ 50%; not greater than 40 miles/wk 3 wk **E** @ 70% + strides; not greater than 60 miles/wk 3 wk **E** @ 85% + strides + **R**; not greater than 75 miles/wk 3 wk **E** @ 100% + strides + **T** + **R**; less than 90 miles/wk | per table 9.1 |

*Notes:* In category I, goal load is not to be greater than pre-setback load (once back to normal training, increase distance following the normal rate of increase rules described in chapter 4). Refer to table 9.1 for a detailed list of percent of VDOT to use upon return to running, based on days off. Go to normal training (see phases of training in chapter 8) after at least six weeks of return training. With serious cross-training, reduce VDOT by only half the amount shown in the above table. Adjustments to VDOT may be needed due to weight change, explained on page 171.

everyone has heard such stories, and interestingly, it is not un-common for the runner involved to wonder how much faster they might have run had they not been "held back" in training.

## Adjusting the Phases of Training

A prolonged injury can have a disruptive effect on a well-planned seasonal program. For example, if you have set up a four-phase, 24-week program with an emphasis on intervals during the second 6-week phase, and an injury stops you from training for 2 weeks, how should you adjust the remaining schedule? It is not a big problem if you remember that your program is designed so that you perform the most important things—the type of training that gets you ready for important racing—during the final weeks of training. So, don't sacrifice the final phase of training in an attempt to complete training that you missed due to an injury. Keep as much of the final 6-week block of training intact as possible. Simply cut out portions of the phase that you were in

## JIM RYUN

**Jim Ryun** was born in Wichita, Kansas and got involved in run-ning because he "couldn't do anything else." His initial goal was to make his high school team and earn a letter jacket. He ended up doing much more.

During his years at Kansas Uni-versity, Ryun won five NCAA national titles and broke numer-ous collegiate, national, and world records. I became associ-ated with Jim while doing alti-tude research in Alamosa, Colo-rado in 1967. It was during this research that Jim broke the world records for the mile and the 1500 (with a final 1320 of 2:49 in the latter race). Both races were run within one day of leaving

© Jeff Johnson

altitude, which strongly suggests that races as short as the mile are not negatively affected during an acute re-exposure to sea level following altitude training of as long as four weeks. Ryun made three Olympic teams and won a silver medal at Mexico City. During his peak years of racing, Ryun ran 110 to 120 miles per week, and he credits interval and speed work as being most productive in his racing career.

Jim is currently a United States Congressman from Kansas. I learned from him that there are many important things in life, and as important as sport may be it is only a part of the bigger picture.

**Jim's bests**   880: 1:44.9   1500: 3:33.1   mile: 3:51.1

when the injury occurred, or some of that phase and some of the next-to-last phase. Evaluate what you need most and go with that. Refer to chapter 8 when trying to determine what to keep and what to discard.

# A Final Word

A word of caution about performing other types of exercise during a period of nonrunning. If a runner feels that cardiovascular fitness has been maintained by doing a lot of swimming or water running during an absence from running, this individual runs the risk of overstressing the antigravity muscles, tendons, and ligaments by training too intensely on the resumption of running. These muscles and connective tissues have actually been de-trained during the layoff, even though cardiovascular fitness was maintained in the water. In this case, the good feeling of fitness, caused by the poolwork, can actually increase the risk of injury once running is resumed. Remember, when you return to running after a break or setback, more than just your cardiovascular system has missed the training stress; in fact, the cardiovascular system may bounce back most quickly. The muscles used specifically for running will be undertrained after a layoff, no matter how much cross-training you do, so you must resume your running training cautiously.

# CHAPTER 10

# Utilizing Your Training Environment

*Always trust a positive response;
question any negative ones.*

Factors to be considered under the umbrella of environment are weather (including heat, cold, rain, snow, ice, and wind), altitude, and terrain (footing and hills). With regard to weather and terrain, many runners face nearly all types during a typical training year. Altitude, on the other hand is either available or is not. For some runners altitude may be a fact of life, for others, a never-experienced phenomenon. A small percentage of runners reside at sea level, but spend a specific phase of training at altitude.

My approach will be to discuss each environmental factor in terms of the reactions it produces in the human body. Further, I will talk about how to deal with each environmental factor in training and competition, both on an acute (short-term) basis and as a possible prolonged daily fact of life.

# Terrain

Some runners live in flat areas, while others inhabit hilly terrain. Some runners have only paved streets and paths on which to run; others see only dirt, sand, grass, or rocky trails. Most runners have a nearby running track, be it all-weather or natural material in composition. Some runners have a treadmill at their disposal, which in itself, constitutes another terrain feature that must be dealt with (see the sidebar about treadmills in chapter 7, pages 118 to 121).

Regardless of the type of terrain facing you, it is important to feel that no one has any advantages over you because of where they train, or because of where you train. Certainly, given all the resources possible, an ideal terrain could be concocted for any runner, and chances are that this ideal would vary considerably depending on personal taste.

A hilly terrain may seem downright obnoxious to some runners, but others feel that the constant challenge of hills makes them tougher competitors. So whatever terrain you're working with, find the good things about it. Think of hills as having the ability to make flat races seem easy. Think of flat terrain as allowing for easier speedwork or steadier tempo runs. Think of rough footing as developing greater resistance to injury, not as producing injuries. Smooth footing is the optimum in providing for planned, consistent conditions. In other words, try to take what the terrain has to offer and work with it, not against it.

# Hills

Hilly terrain takes some adjustment for proper threshold training, but once you learn to monitor intensity properly, running speed will vary as you go up and down, and the effort can remain constant—the goal of a tempo run. With hills, a greater variety of workouts can be incorporated into the repetition phase of training—uphills for greater strength and economy, downhills (preferably gradual, grassy slopes rather than steep hard-surfaced ones) for speed and additional economy development. Further, athletes who constantly deal with a hilly terrain will undoubtedly perform well on hilly courses. The old specificity principle (principle #2, page 15) surfaces again.

Hills can offer a nice variation of interval training. By running over a rolling course at a fairly constant pace, the uphills can be used to stress $VO_2$max intensity, while the downhills and flats become the recovery parts of the workout. By selecting different courses, the higher-intensity portion of the workout can be varied from fairly brief periods to longer workbouts of several minutes each.

It is important to seek out some relatively long (at least one minute and up to several minutes), gradually sloping hills for faster downhill runs, in which good speed can be maintained with minimal effort. Of course, the availability of a track also provides the opportunity not only for quality, timed, fast runs but also controlled threshold training.

Possibly the most difficult type of workout to perform in a totally hilly environment is a nice, steady long run. It becomes mentally demanding to hold a constant intensity of effort for a two-hour long run when hills of varying grade and size are constantly confronting you. Holding a steady intensity over hilly terrain can be accomplished by thoughtful use of a heart rate monitor—a specific situation in which such a device is useful.

Still, the challenge is there, and at race time the hilly terrain runners can look around and imagine that they are just a little tougher than the rest of the crowd they see lining up around them.

# Flatlands

For runners who have no hills available, the challenge is to come up with other ways to change the demands of workouts. The advantage these runners have is that no matter what course they design for training or for testing themselves, they can always make legitimate time comparisons in order to monitor fitness. They can more easily have "controlled variety" in their workouts.

Unless they are training for a race that is over a particularly hilly course, I don't think that flat-terrain runners need to be concerned about not having hills available. Flat-terrain residents should think of themselves as "finesse" runners; proper intensity of effort for them is associated with a slightly faster pace than it would be if always going over hills. The result is that a steady fast pace becomes comfortable and is not an unusual occurrence come race time.

Since there is nothing particularly tough about the terrain facing flatlanders, the intensity of the workouts themselves is where these runners learn to be tough. Tempo runs can be well controlled, and by selecting longer workbouts (three to five minutes each) in interval sessions, the constant prolonged demands of racing are closely mimicked.

Where hill runners learn to deal with constant changes in intensity, flatlanders learn to deal with constant, unrelenting intensity without the occasional break afforded by downhills. Of course, a flatlander may have other ways to make a workout demanding, such as using sand, soft grass, or other types of rough footing for some training sessions.

## Variations in Footing

There are those runners whose environment may be mostly slow footing, such as sand, grass, gravel roads, or rocky trails. These runners face the lack of good footing that is conducive to faster training. They become tough to beat when the footing is poor, but not many races are held under these conditions. Residents of slow-footing environments learn to be strength runners and also develop good resistance to many injuries because they are constantly dealing with twisting and turning feet. Residents of cold winter climates also face a poor-footing problem during long periods of snow and ice. Fortunately, snow and ice are temporary obstacles that give way to dry footing the rest of the year.

Because poor footing affects running economy (the amount of energy required to run at any particular speed) by increasing the cost of running, a runner need not go as fast to be stressing the body to the same degree as would be associated with a faster pace on better footing. Here's where learning to read your body becomes important. When a workout calls for a particular relative intensity of effort

Running on uneven terrain requires agility and concentration, but it also provides for an interesting workout.

(as is the case in threshold, marathon-pace, and interval workouts), then the pace can be slower on poor footing and still satisfy the physiological requirements of the workout.

In addition, a runner who is constantly subjected to slow footing may have to use track work more than other runners, particularly for repetitions. If no track is available, then some smooth, fast footing must be sought out so that the mechanics that will be used in races on good footing can be practiced. Nothing can be more frustrating than to be in great shape but to lack the speed to finish well or stay with a pace that is a little too fast, just because conditions prevented quality repetition work.

A more concrete way of identifying proper intensity would be to learn what heart rates correspond to various intensities on a flat, dry course, and let heart rate rather than running speed be the guide on poor footing, just as can be done on undulating terrain. An even better way to monitor threshold intensity is by using a lactate analyzer (rapidly becoming more available to the average runner). Percentages of both maximum heart rate and predetermined blood-lactate values can be used effectively when terrain or weather conditions affect normal running economy.

# Weather

The role that weather can play in distance running, both in races and in training, is amazing. The conditions that some runners face on a day-to-day basis may never be part of another runner's life. Some runners never deal with the heat; others seldom face the cold. In some parts of the world, rain is an almost daily occurrence; in other locales the sun always shines. I tend to think there is a positive side to any weather adversity that may confront you, if you are willing to look for it.

## Wind

Of the variety of adverse weather conditions that runners face, probably the only one that every runner is confronted with at one time or another is wind, and if there is anything that interrupts training or racing more than wind, I have yet to meet it.

I consider myself fortunate to have coached for four years in Oklahoma, where you really learn to respect the wind. Wind is as much a part of running in Oklahoma as is heat in Florida or Arizona. I don't mean to say that other places aren't windy, but the wind in Oklahoma seems unique. I also lived for a year in Hawaii, where wind is a constant companion, but is soft and friendly—most of the time, anyway. In Oklahoma the wind is always on your mind. The story we liked to pass around was about the steel logging chain that we hung on the back porch as a wind gauge. When the chain hung straight down, it meant a storm was coming. If it was at a 45-degree angle, the wind was moderate, and when it was at 90 degrees (horizontal), winds were up for the day.

Under conditions like that you learn to work with the wind, and you learn to avoid it when you can. Avoiding the wind means running early in the morning or in the evening. It also means that a calm period following a storm can be expected, particularly when a storm blows in from a direction opposite from the usual.

Here are some facts about the wind that are important to runners.

• Wind generally moves heat away from the body, enhancing cooling. The exception is when you are running with a steady tailwind that is equal in velocity to your running speed, in which case removal of air surrounding the body is prevented. The result is a loss of heat dissipation and an increase in body temperature. This can be disastrous on a warm day, but advantageous under cold conditions.

• While headwinds can slow you down significantly, a tailwind of equal velocity won't speed you up to the same extent. Unfortunately, as wind velocity increases, the detrimental effects of a headwind increase, and the benefits of a tailwind decrease. With winds up to about 5 miles per hour (2.2 meters per second), the loss against a headwind is marginally greater than the benefits of a tailwind. However, by the time wind velocity is 10 to 15 miles per hour (4.5 to 6.7 meters per second), the headwind increases the energy demand of running about 10% to 17%, but a tailwind lowers energy cost by only about 7% to 9%. (Figure 10.1 shows the effect of wind on the aerobic demands of running.)

• Because of the escalated rate of cooling generated by wind, it is important to be aware of the popularly calculated windchill factor during cold weather activity.

• Running behind another runner (drafting) is increasingly beneficial as wind velocity increases. Sometimes it is best to be directly behind another runner, but at other times running off another runner's shoulder is more effective, both for tactical reasons and because of wind direction. Sometimes it is good to work with a competitor under windy conditions, sharing the duties of breaking the wind. This would be appropriate when both runners are trying for a particular time. When time is not important, then helping another runner becomes an individual decision.

• Because of the cooling or warming effects of headwinds and tailwinds, be careful in setting up workouts under different temperature conditions when not going around a track. For example, on cold days, do harder and faster running against the wind and do slower running with the wind. This way the cooling effect is kept short and is related to harder work, whereas recovery (slower running) can take advantage of the warmer tailwind. On warm days, do the

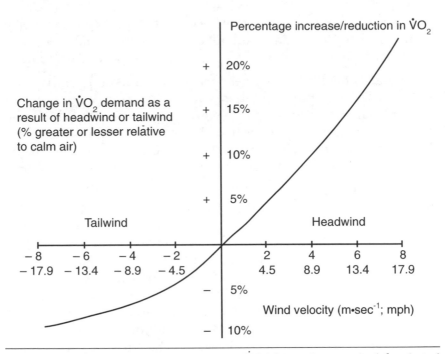

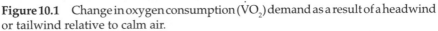

**Figure 10.1**    Change in oxygen consumption ($\dot{V}O_2$) demand as a result of a headwind or tailwind relative to calm air.

opposite—run fast or hard with the wind and run slowly against the cooling wind. This may be opposite of what might be most enjoyable, but it is better to spend more time being warm on a cold day and cool on a warm day than the other way around.

Another example of how to deal with the cooling and warming effects of wind relates to out-and-back steady runs. Start out against the wind on a cold day so that the trip home will be warmer. To run with a tailwind first on a cold day can lead to some really chilly conditions on the return run, particularly if you get sweaty on the way out. The opposite applies to runs in warm weather—go with the tailwind first and return against the cooling wind in order to negate the tendency to overheat later in the run.

# Rain

Rain can be either a pain or a blessing. A cold rain is much worse than snow or cold, dry weather because clothing gets wet and heavy, as do shoes. In fact, a windy day with rain and temperatures in the 30s

(Fahrenheit) can be about as miserable as could ever be asked for. A few degrees cooler and rain becomes snow; clothing stays much drier and the body stays warmer. If rain is combined with colder temperatures, some protection is a must. A garment that repels water yet also breathes is essential. With warmer temperatures, water repellency is of less importance and some synthetics or even light wool can be ideal for an outer garment. Under even warmer conditions, rain may be a blessing, acting to keep the body cool, probably as much from rain clouds blocking the sun as from the direct effect of cool raindrops hitting your skin. A cooling rain can be most welcome to a runner out for a hard or long run in a hot environment. Wearing a cap with a bill that shades or protects the face from rain can also make running in the rain considerably more bearable than if running hatless, when you might have to squint against the raindrops throughout an entire workout or race.

Most runners learn to deal with whatever conditions they face. They learn that in rainy climates, lighter socks or no socks are much better than bulky socks that gain weight with every step. There are many little things that you learn to do in different weather conditions. This is the easy part. The difficult task is to prepare for conditions that are not normal for you. Some tough transitions to make include training in the rainy northwest and flying to a race in Arizona, or training in the lowlands of California and then having to race at altitude in Colorado.

## BENEFITING FROM ADVERSITY

Living under relatively adverse conditions can pay off. If adversity is part of daily training, then it isn't a problem on race day. The trade-off is how negatively these rough training conditions affect daily training or mental attitude, both of which affect performance. I have often felt that a warm-weather resident would have an advantage in high-priority races, where making a team or winning money is at stake. The approach would be to train enough in a warm climate to become acclimatized, then enter important races in which there is a good chance of hot weather. If it turns out to be hot on race day, go for it; if not, consider not running and saving your energy for the next race. In other words, only race under the conditions that give you a decided advantage. The ultimate example of this strategy is to live and train at altitude and only enter altitude races. The drawback, however, is that few runners who aren't altitude residents will venture onto your turf, and as a result you never get to compete with them under your conditions.

# Heat

The exercising human body is far better designed to handle cold than it is to deal with heat. When you exercise, you add internal heat to any heat being imposed by the external environment. Our bodies have a difficult time surviving in an environment that is just a few degrees above normal body temperature, but with the proper clothing we can exercise and perform quite well when the ambient temperature is many degrees below our own body temperature. For a runner, particularly a distance runner, heat is enemy number one. You can dress for the cold, dress for the rain, and you are forced to slow down at altitude, but heat sneaks up on you even if you slow down, which is about all you can do to survive under hot conditions.

The two big problems in heat are an increase in body temperature, which immediately affects performance, and dehydration, which steadily erodes your ability to function. Both increased body temperature and dehydration must be held to a minimum or you just won't be able to continue running.

Normal body temperature is 37 °C (98.6 °F), but exercise, even under cool conditions, can lead to an increase in body temperature by a few degrees. Actually, an increase in body temperature of a degree or two can aid performance (one of the purposes of a warmup), but as body temperature reaches about 39 °C (102 °F), performance begins to suffer, and you definitely start to feel worse. Usually, without consciously knowing it, a runner learns to recognize this limit in training and backs off when increased temperature makes him or her feel bad. In a race, on the other hand, people don't like to back off, which presents a greater likelihood of trouble. This is why heat acclimatization is so important—the body learns to recognize limits and makes some adaptations to allow for optimal performance to be associated with those limits. You can not perform as well in a distance race in the heat as you can in a cooler environment.

As soon as the body starts to heat up, blood is diverted to the skin where cooling (through evaporation of sweat from the skin's surface) takes place. A greater portion of the body's blood volume is at the body's surface to facilitate cooling, leaving less blood available for carrying oxygen to the exercising muscles. In effect, to prevent overheating, the body reduces the amount of blood that is available to enhance performance. It is fortunate that we can't usually override the life preserving functions of the body in favor of the performance enhancing functions. Still, the body can overheat (which is even possible without exercise), and we must learn to adapt.

## Staying Hydrated

Staying properly hydrated (having an adequate amount of water in the body) is a necessity. When fluid levels drop, the cooling mechanisms are affected and temperature goes even higher. Keep in mind that you can overheat without being dehydrated, and dehydration can take place in the absence of overheating. A negative side of lowering your carbohydrate intake, as some runners do during the depletion phase of a "carbohydrate depletion/loading" regimen, is that body fluid levels go down when carbohydrate intake is reduced, and the individual can actually become dehydrated, even in the absence of a noticeable amount of sweating.

Dehydration can also happen because of a lack of attention to fluid intake. When loss of fluid causes body weight to drop 3% to 5%, adverse effects on performance will occur. Certainly, people have had greater fluid losses, but they are getting into dangerous territory when they lose more than about 5% of body weight in fluid. For runners who perspire a great deal, it is important to monitor body weight closely.

The perceived desire for fluid replacement does not keep up with the body's needs and it is easy to get behind in replenishing lost fluids. Failure to replace enough fluids becomes a particular problem in dry climates. It becomes even more of a problem at altitude where it seldom seems that you are sweating because sweat evaporates as fast as it is produced and water doesn't drip off the body as it does under more humid conditions.

It is important to understand the effects of humidity. Remember, the skin is cooled (which allows circulating blood to also be cooled) as a result of moisture evaporating from the surface of the body. Evaporation rate is a function of relative humidity; when humidity is low, the evaporation rate increases and the skin is an effective site for cooling the blood. On the other hand, when humidity is high, evaporation and cooling can slow to a standstill. No wonder you feel

Adequate preparations are made for hydration needs at the 1997 Chicago Marathon. Make sure you are just as well prepared when temperatures rise.

miserable on a warm, muggy day. The warm weather heats your body, exercise produces more body heat, and high humidity prevents cooling. If the sun is not blocked by clouds, things become even worse. Add to this the possibility that you are running with a tailwind, which further hampers cooling, and you will feel even worse and your chances of overheating will increase even more.

When it comes to fighting the effects of heat and dehydration, there can be considerable variations in how different runners respond to the situation. In a study involving heat acclimatized runners, we found that under identical conditions, some runners perspire twice as much as others, even though body composition, weight, and running speeds are identical. During a 25K race, two of our subjects ran within a few seconds of the same time and both consumed exactly 1 liter (about 2.2 pounds) of fluid during the race. One of them lost water at the rate of 200 ml per kilometer of running, while the other lost water at a rate of 100 ml per kilometer. The net effect was a 4-liter loss for one runner (5.6% of his body weight) and a 1.5-liter loss for the other runner (a 2.1% drop in body weight). Clearly, the one runner was on the edge of serious dehydration, while the other could probably have gone on to full marathon distance without much difficulty.

## Test Your Own Fluid Loss

The way in which you as an individual react to running under various environmental conditions is something that is not too difficult to check through prerun and postrun weigh-ins. Without any clothes on, weigh yourself before and after training runs of different durations, intensities, and heat and humidity conditions. If 30 minutes of running under a specific set of environmental conditions results in a 1-pound weight loss, you can figure what will happen after an hour or more under similar conditions. You can also go a step further and learn to consume fluids at various rates and frequencies to counteract the fluid loss that you experience.

## Drinking on the Run

Runners tend to have a particular amount of fluid they feel comfortable consuming at any given time. If runners are given two opportunities for fluid intake during a race, they will take in about half as much fluid as they would if given four opportunities to drink. Good hydration is closely related to the number of opportunities available for drinking, which makes the situation more difficult for the average (relatively slower) distance runner. When you realize that net fluid loss is a function of fluid intake and time spent running (more than distance run), and slower runners take longer to reach each fluid station, it becomes a bigger problem to care for the masses than for the elite.

Our research showed that in the absence of required amounts of intake at fluid stations, some runners drink very little (we had a runner who consistently drank less than 100 ml in each 25K race that he ran), while others manage to gulp down a great deal (one runner took in 2000 ml in a 25K race). The only way to properly replace lost body fluids is to be aware of your own needs under various conditions. If you can't influence race directors to provide more fluid stations along their race courses, then you must learn to ingest more when you do get the opportunity to drink. This certainly is something that can be improved with practice.

## Heat Acclimatization

The body does acclimatize to heat after a couple of weeks of training in warm conditions, but it is important to learn when to train under these conditions. Early morning is the coolest time of day, but also usually the most humid. Evening, after the sun goes down, is the least humid, but hotter than morning. For runners who train twice a day, there is no good choice other than early and late in the day. When training for an important race that is likely to be run under hot conditions, then some training and even competition experiences must take place under those conditions and at the appropriate time of day.

If you attend a warm race and are not used to the conditions, you must adjust your pace, just as you would at altitude. Table 10.1 gives an idea of how much slower you might expect to race when conditions are above 20 °C (69 °F). Shorter races would not be affected quite as much, so I am only presenting figures for races in excess of two hours, but you could estimate, for instance, that a 35-minute 10K run in 90° weather could be slowed by over a minute. As with a race at altitude, it's best to calculate what you can reasonably do, race at that pace for about two-thirds of the distance, and then, if feeling good, increase the pace a bit.

When training in warm weather, learn how to minimize the effects of the heat by dressing appropriately. The general rule is to wear as little clothing as possible, and what you do wear should fit loosely. Porous materials tend not to stick to your skin, and therefore allow the movement of heat away from the body. As mentioned in regard to rain, wearing a cap with a sun-protecting bill may help, but a cap often makes the head much hotter. Make sure that whatever you wear allows air to flow freely to and from the parts of the body being covered.

# Running in the Cold

It is easier to dress for various degrees of cold than for the heat, because wearing layers of clothes works very well. It is not wise to wear one

## Table 10.1   The Estimated Effect of Heat on Race Duration

| Temperature | Race Duration (hours:minutes) | | | |
|---|---|---|---|---|
| (°C/°F) | 2:10 | 2:30 | 3:00 | 4:00 |
| 21/70 | +2 min | +2.5 min | +3 min | +4 min |
| 27/81 | +4 min | +4.5 min | +5.5 min | +7.5 min |
| 32/90 | +6 min | +7 min | +8.5 min | +11.5 min |
| 38/100 | +8 min | +10 min | +12.5 min | +17.5 min |

heavy garment that may feel nice when you start your run, but gets too hot later and can't be shed because of insufficient clothing under it. Learn to know what is necessary for runs under a variety of temperatures and wind conditions. A windbreaker that is needed when running into a cold wind can be taken off and tied around the waist on the way home when a tailwind provides a warmer surrounding blanket of air. Hats and mittens (mittens are much better than gloves when it is really cold) are other items that are nice to wear early in a run and can be taken off later if you get too warm.

The chest discomfort sometimes experienced on cold days is not normally a sign of damage due to cold air. The human body has an excellent internal air heating system, which rapidly heats inhaled air to prevent freezing of lung tissue. However, cold air is often very dry and the drying effect of air moving rapidly in and out of the air passages can irritate the linings of the throat and lungs. The damage is usually not serious. For those who worry about breathing hard during cold weather races, consider cross-country skiers who race in very cold conditions and seldom have problems with the cold air.

Naturally, it is important to keep as much skin as possible covered in freezing temperatures. The first parts to suffer are usually the hands and ears. When racing in very cold conditions it is a good idea to warm up in one set of clothes, and then change to dry racing clothes just before the race (find a warm place to make the change, if possible). After a hard workout or race in the cold, add a layer of clothing for the cool-down, and then shower or go where it is warm to stretch and relax.

When there is ice or snow on the ground it can be dangerous to run, depending on the temperature. When it is really cold, packed snow and even smooth ice are not bad, but things get worse when it is warm enough to produce a little water on the surface, or when conditions get slushy. Spikes can be worn in cross country races or even when training under some snowy conditions. When using spikes in snow, try some nonstick cooking substance or spray-on oil on the bottom of your shoes to prevent snow buildup around the spikes. Of course, slick footing is more risky during downhill stretches and on turns, so take shorter, more flat-footed steps under these conditions.

# Altitude

The two areas of running research in which I have done the most work are related to running economy and altitude training and racing. There are many publications in a variety of journals that address the altitude issue, but I will try to summarize the more important aspects of altitude as it relates to distance running.

Altitude affects distance running by lowering the amount of oxygen that can be delivered to the running muscles, which is the result of the blood's reduced saturation of oxygen. As stated in chapter 2, hemoglobin is the substance in red blood cells that combines with oxygen; it acts as the carrier of oxygen from the capillaries in the lungs, through the left side of the heart, and then to the rest of the body. The amount of oxygen that is carried by the blood—through its association with hemoglobin—is a function of the partial pressure of oxygen in the blood, which reflects the pressure in the lungs and in the atmosphere.

Since atmospheric pressure gets lower as altitude gets higher, the effects of higher altitudes are a lower pressure of oxygen in the blood and a diminished oxygen–hemoglobin association. That is, less oxygen is carried by the all-important hemoglobin. The percentage of oxygen in the air does not change with changes in altitude, but the pressure does change, which means there is a lower partial pressure of oxygen available to drive it into association with hemoglobin. The higher the altitude, the greater the problem.

© Richard C. Etchberger

Running in winter can be exhilarating, but make sure you are properly dressed.

Actually, because of the characteristics of the relationship between oxygen pressure and hemoglobin association and dissociation (that is, how easily oxygen is freed from hemoglobin in order to enter the exercising muscles), the effect of lowered air pressure (high altitude) and oxygen saturation of the blood is not a linear one. The effect of altitude on endurance performance starts at an altitude of about 1000 meters (around 3000 feet). For practical purposes, I would consider the altitudes from about 1000 to 2500 meters (3280 to 8202 feet) to be moderate; these are the altitudes most frequently encountered by runners. These are also the altitudes at which training produces good acclimatization. I prefer the 2000- to 2500-meter (6562- to 8202-foot) range for reaping the benefits of altitude training.

## Negative Effects of Altitude

Being at altitude has a direct negative effect on distance running performance. You can't run as fast at altitude (for races of 1500 meters and longer) as you can at sea level. This applies to both sea-level residents and to those who live at altitude.

## Improving Performance at Altitude

Training at altitude improves performance at altitude. The body acclimatizes to a certain degree, but not to the extent that performances will be just as good at altitude as at sea level.

## The Effects of Altitude on $\dot{V}O_2Max$

As you go up in altitude, the atmospheric pressure gets lower, and the lower the atmospheric pressure, the lower the pressure of oxygen. Since oxygen pressure is what determines how much oxygen will be carried by the hemoglobin in the blood, the result is that a given amount of hemoglobin carries less oxygen to the exercising muscles at altitude. This resulting drop in oxygen delivery also lowers your $\dot{V}O_2$max at altitude. However, altitude does not affect performance as much as it affects $\dot{V}O_2$max. This is because economy improves at altitude due to the decreased air resistance encountered in the less dense altitude air. Further, aerobic capacity ($\dot{V}O_2$max) does not represent the only available energy source, and anaerobic power is not negatively affected by being at altitude.

## The Ongoing Benefits of Training at Altitude

Improvements in performance that may be realized as a result of altitude training are not temporary in nature, provided training back at sea level is adequate to maintain the fitness achieved at altitude. What I am saying is that altitude training often allows for—or stimulates—a better fitness level in an athlete, just as does serious training anywhere. The fitness level achieved through altitude training may be better than that previously reached at sea level, but not necessarily better than could be reached with continued sea-level workouts.

Altitude training seems to permit runners to more quickly reach their potential, an attainable potential that just wasn't being realized through sea-level training. Some runners experience a breakthrough as the result of increases in weekly mileage or through a more structured interval or threshold program. Altitude training can have the same effect on some runners; a significant breakthrough can come on the heels of time spent training at altitude. I have observed many breakthroughs following altitude training, and seldom have the athletes involved had any trouble maintaining their newfound success, even if they return to sea level for entire seasons, or years, of performance.

## Individual Reactions to Altitude

Not all endurance runners react the same way to altitude. Some benefit little while others have significant breakthroughs. Again, it's best to compare altitude training to other types of training. Not everyone responds well to 100-mile weeks. Likewise, not everyone benefits from training at altitude. The reasons for this are undoubtedly numerous and may involve both physical and mental factors. The success, or lack thereof, of altitude training is most certainly a function of how you train at altitude and the confidence you have in your program or coach.

## Altitude Acclimatization

There are two kinds of acclimatization that take place with altitude training: the body makes some physiological adjustments within a month or two that result in better altitude performance; and, there is a certain degree of competitive acclimatization that takes place as a result of racing at altitude—you learn how to race under the stress of altitude. The net result of these two acclimatizations is that on returning to altitude, even after months or years spent at sea level, overall performance will not be so adversely affected the second time around. This is primarily because the competitive acclimatization pretty much stays with you. You have remembered how to race at altitude even though your body is a little out of tune physiologically. You can train as hard and as much at altitude as you did at sea level.

It is not uncommon for athletes to travel to altitude for a few weeks of altitude training, and either to take it too easy at first (hoping to ease into the new environment gradually) or to increase the training load and intensity in order to make the most of the time spent at altitude. Actually, there is no need to follow either approach. The proper way to go about it is to simply press on with training as usual—normal loads and intensities (absolute and relative intensities are addressed below).

If your normal training program calls for 70 miles of running per week, there is no reason to vary from that, unless it is time for a change anyway. If your current program calls for 3.0 miles of reps and 5.0 miles of intervals once each week, these amounts are also appropriate at altitude, with the adjustments outlined below. There is no problem keeping up a 17-mile long run at altitude, if that's been a normal long run for you. Please keep in mind that I am talking about training at moderate altitude, not tackling a 12,000-foot mountain as a training site.

# Making Training Adjustments at Altitude

Running intensity can be identified in absolute terms or in relative terms. A relative intensity is expressed in relation to an individual's $\dot{V}O_2$max. For example, I have recommended running at 86% to 88% of $\dot{V}O_2$max for threshold training. On the other hand, an absolute intensity is a specific running velocity (pace), such as six minutes per mile.

When you train at altitude for races at sea level, some training must be geared to sea-level race paces, or absolute intensity. This principle applies to reps, which are primarily related to race intensity, not to $\dot{V}O_2$max. This means that reps run at altitude would be run at the same speed as they would be at sea level. However, intervals and threshold training (including cruise intervals and tempo runs) will actually be slower at altitude than at sea level to accommodate the lower VDOT value that dictates training intensities at altitude. Remember, however, that the loss in VDOT is not as great as the loss in $\dot{V}O_2$max because of a gain in economy at altitude. In effect, at an altitude of 2000 meters (6500 feet), $\dot{V}O_2$max is diminished by about 12%, but performance is only about 6% worse (as is VDOT) because of improved economy. Most people would perform about 10 to 20 seconds per mile slower at this altitude, compared to recent sea-level times. Figure 10.2 shows how various altitudes affect training and race performances, depending on performances at sea-level.

Naturally, as any individual acclimatizes to altitude, his or her altitude $\dot{V}O_2$max and VDOT increase, becoming a greater percentage of the former sea-level values. All in all, there is no need to plan adjustments in training intensities. They will pretty much occur as you become acclimatized.

One way of monitoring the relative intensity of workouts is to be aware of breathing patterns. If you can handle threshold runs comfortably at sea level with a 2-2 breathing rhythm (see "Breathing Rhythms" in chapter 5), then use this same rhythm and associated subjective feelings for altitude threshold training.

The same applies to intervals. By shooting for the same subjective ratings during this type of training, you can be pretty accurate in adjusting intensities to remain the same at altitude, relative to your new lower $\dot{V}O_2$max. Insofar as training effect goes, the slower training speeds for intervals and threshold runs at altitude will be as effective as the faster relative speeds at sea level.

Repetition workouts may have to change if altitude training is geared toward upcoming sea-level races. To maintain desired speed, economy, and sense of pace, normal **R** intensity (speed) must be retained at all costs. This may mean taking longer recoveries during an **R** workout, or it may mean using shorter **R** workbouts (300s instead of 400s, for example). Also keep the usual total amount of reps. To carry out 3.0 miles of reps, for example, which might normally be accomplished by doing $12 \times 400$, the 400s could be replaced by $16 \times 300$. Both sessions produce the same amount of work at the desired pace.

When altitude training is geared toward an altitude race, then **R** pace can be adjusted to coincide with the demands of the anticipated altitude race pace. Usually though, altitude residents venture to sea level for a fair number of races, and for this reason their training should incorporate sea-level performance **R** intensities.

The body usually goes through a fairly predictable reaction to going to altitude. The first day at altitude is the best time to race, unless you have a week or more of acclimatization time available to you. Somewhere around the third to fifth day at altitude, newcomers feel their worst. But with normal training, performances are usually better by the end of the first week. From that point on, confidence and acclimatization improve and workouts and races go much better.

It is also important to take in more than normal amounts of fluids at altitude, where the effects of dry air on body fluids are deceiving.

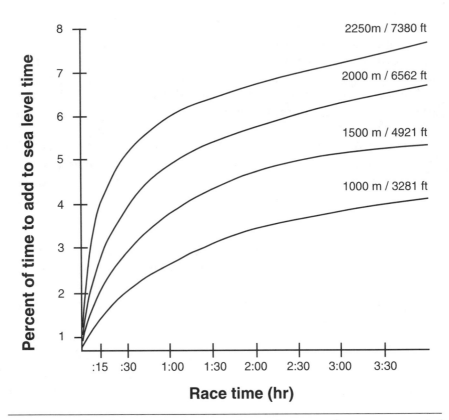

**Figure 10.2**   The effects of altitude on running performance, shown as a percent of sea-level time to add to running time for races of different durations at various altitudes for acclimatized runners. Nonacclimatized runners may expect to add up to double those amounts.

Adapted from Daniels, J. 1975. *Track and Field Quarterly Review* 75(4):38-9.

Furthermore, some altitude newcomers always feel sleepy, yet find it difficult to sleep. Naps are beneficial, and early morning runs are easier to carry out at altitude than at sea level.

It is normal to increase your ventilation at altitude, an adjustment that carries over to sea level for a few days. Some runners find it somewhat frightening to hear themselves breathing so hard the first few days back at sea level, but if you ignore how it sounds, performance will be fine. Consume a well-balanced diet with adequate iron-rich foods, or use supplements, if necessary. This will allow the body to take advantage of its desire to build more red blood cells at altitude.

I have always found altitude training to be enjoyable. I'm sure that where you go and with whom is an important aspect of altitude training; certainly being happy is an important part of performing well, be it at altitude or at sea level. Runners who make substantial alterations to their lifestyles, especially to their social or financial circumstances, just to train at altitude, often end up not doing well because of the psychological stresses involved.  You're better off training at sea level if the shift to altitude is going to wear you down mentally.

In the final analysis, how you approach adversity goes a long way in how that adversity will affect your running. I think of altitude as a good environment, and it has yet to let me down.

# A Final Word

I wouldn't bother changing your habits in the last days before a race. For instance, wearing racing shoes once during the week before a race, or traveling to a track once or twice in the final week before a competition would probably cause more damage than good. Remember, the body needs time to react to new stresses; if you can't give it time (a few weeks at least), it's better to wait and make the race your first experience with new conditions.

At a national meet on a hilly course, my team ran particularly well compared with the other teams from our region. One of the coaches said to me, "You sure must have worked on hills this week. We did, too, but I guess we didn't work at it enough." In fact, they most likely did too much of a new thing. My team avoided hills totally the week before the race. More than likely, we felt worse than the other teams the next few days after the race, but the important thing was that we felt strong on the hills during the race.

There is absolutely no reason to create a new concern for your team or yourself by changing training at the very last minute. In many cases, it is better to hold steady with what you are doing and simply do your best on race day.

# Part III

# Racing

# CHAPTER 11

# Preparing for Competition

*Run with your head the first two-thirds of the race
and with your heart the final third.*

To many people who run, competition is the last thing on their minds. These runners enjoy the many good things they feel and receive from regular running. Some of these noncompetitors become very knowledgeable about training and racing, but do not want to be competitive themselves. All of this seems perfectly legitimate, in my opinion. Just as millions of people read about one topic or another without becoming actively involved in what they are studying, there are many people who want to read about running, training, and competing without ever taking a competitive step themselves.

There is a lot to be learned about training and competing in regard to sports in general, simply by reading about training and competing in running. Certainly, a great deal of my knowledge about training and about athletic competition comes from learning about the body in general and about how athletes in other sports prepare themselves mentally, physically, and competitively.

I write this chapter on competition primarily for runners who want to test themselves against others, against the clock, or against their own expectations. I also present this material in hopes that competitors in other sports or that noncompetitive runners may learn a little more about competing. I address such issues as what races to run and how often to run. I also describe final race preparation, including prerace meals, what to wear, prerace warm-ups, and predicting your time (even for races you have never run before). Finally, I provide some suggestions about race tactics and what to think about when running a race.

# Why Compete?

The idea of competition is to compete. I'm sure that someone has said this before, but it needs restating in order to get into the proper frame of mind. Competition is a special part of the sport of running. It's fine to plan some competitions as part of an overall training program, but each competition is important and must be taken seriously. The purpose of competing is to achieve a specific goal or performance. You should know why you are running each race, just as you should know the purpose of every workout that you complete. Improving your ability to hold a fast pace, sticking with a group of tough competitors for a prolonged period, helping to build confidence in your kick, learning patience, and aiding the development of a particular physiological or mental attribute that is beneficial to your long-term development as a runner are all examples of why races are run. Of course there are the more obvious reasons: to win a championship, to qualify for a championship, or to win an award of some kind.

# Defining Your Competitive Goals

The goal of competition doesn't have to be to see how fast you can race a particular distance, although that is often the case. Another goal may be to try a new tactic in a competitive setting. For example, you might be the type of runner who goes out too fast in the early part of a race and ends up paying the price later. Your goal for an upcoming competition may be to set a more cautious early pace. You may strive for as even a pace as possible, or you may attempt to run negative splits (run progressively faster throughout the race).

Maybe your goal for the race is to stay with a particular competitor or particular pace as long as you can, or to a certain stage of the race. This can be a useful goal, in terms of helping a developing runner overcome the fear of certain competitors or a particular pace. For example, you may decide to run to at least the two-mile mark of a 5K race with a teammate or competitor whose pace is well known but who has always been faster than you. Such a goal provides a greater opportunity for success than does a goal of beating this person to the finish line. An equally valid goal may be to go out more cautiously than usual and to run the last part of the race faster than your competitors, after conceding to them a better first mile. This helps you to realize that you can run the bulk of the race at their pace.

There are many possibilities for race goals, and it is a good idea to select goals that will further your confidence in your ability to compete. It is discouraging to always fail, when actually you are trying to achieve an unrealistic race goal. It is also not difficult to set yourself up (or to set up an athlete you are coaching) for failure in a race.

Even the current world record holders will continuously fail if their prerace goals are to better their world records. There were many "failures" along the road to breaking the 4-minute barrier in the mile run, just as women have had numerous "failures" at breaking 2 hours and 20 minutes in the marathon. Certainly there are many marathoners whose goal to break 3 hours is not achieved. The same thing happens in the game of golf, where the goal for thousands of weekend golfers is to break 100. I often wonder how success rates might vary if the goal were to run with good technique or to make each iron shot a smooth and artful effort, rather than to worry about the final outcome.

Just as the idea of competing is to achieve a specific goal or performance, the idea behind goal setting is to establish a goal that has a decent chance of being attained. It is unrealistic for everyone entered in a cross-country race or road race to have first place as a goal, but the chance of team victory is enhanced if each runner on the team achieves his or her own realistic goal for that particular race.

It is a perfectly valid goal for an aspiring, inexperienced runner to enter a long race or a marathon with the main goal being to test his or her ability to consume fluids at a certain rate. Fluid consumption can make or break a marathoner, so learning to take in fluids at an adequate rate is a crucial part of ultimately achieving a good time in a marathon.

I don't want to leave anyone with the impression that you must set goals that will be achieved all of the time. Losing can sometimes be more valuable than winning, and setting tough goals for races can mean not reaching your goals now and then. If you make an honest evaluation of why you failed on these occasions, you may benefit even more than if you had achieved your goal.

Strength comes from the confidence of winning and from learning to accept and evaluate losses. Sometimes it takes an overenthusiastic approach to a race to really test yourself and to find out just where your current limits are. So, take a positive attitude toward victory and toward defeat, but also try to tip the scales a little so there are more personal wins than losses.

# What Race Should You Run?

Most competitive runners, particularly those involved with school teams, are faced with three important questions.

1. Which race should I run?
2. When is the right time to run races of different lengths?
3. How often should I race a particular distance?

When you are involved in a season full of races, it is a good idea to vary your race distance, but also to repeat the same distance often enough to let yourself use what you learn in one race for improvement the next time around. This works better for shorter races (up to

© Victah Sailer

Setting goals can help you to overcome many of the obstacles that get in the way of your development as a runner.

about 5K) than it does in longer ones—obviously, you don't run several marathons a few weeks apart in order to benefit from what you learned in the first one. The recovery time and preparation required for a hard marathon dictate that a couple of marathons in one year are adequate for anyone who races them seriously.

## Plan Ahead

It is important to have a plan in setting up races. For example, someone who is planning to race a 10K at the end of the season may want to be in good enough shape to run a qualifying time early in the season. Once the qualifying time is achieved, the runner can then concentrate on training and running shorter races for the bulk of the season before returning to another 10K. There is a panicky feeling when, late in the season, you find yourself not yet qualified for the championship event for which you are peaking.

One plan used by many runners is to race longer and shorter than their favorite distance early in the season, and then run several races at the preferred distance toward the end of the season. There are a couple of reasons for racing over and under a specific distance. First, underdistance racing helps running economy and also gives a runner confidence in being able to handle the race pace of the longer race. Racing 5Ks helps make 10K pace feel easier, and 1500s make 3K and 5K races feel mechanically more comfortable. If your running mechanics don't feel fairly manageable, a race usually seems longer than it really is. On the other hand, overdistance racing can also help you, because the important (shorter) race can be viewed as going by more quickly, and you are therefore more willing to endure the greater race intensity associated with the shorter race.

## Factors to Consider When Choosing Races

Whether to choose shorter or longer races as tune-up events depends on the individual, the conditions of the race, and the competition. You may need an ego boost, and you might be able to win or set a personal record (PR) by racing a particular distance (a shorter distance, for example), whereas going longer may put you in a tougher field of competitors or in a race where your PR is currently out of reach.

It may be unusually warm or windy, and a longer race would present too many problems to achieve success. Adverse conditions, even though not ideal as far as time is concerned, may present the perfect ego boost if the conditions are to your liking or strengths. A good "mudder" on a wet, sloppy cross-country course may profit considerably against some very good runners who don't do well under those conditions. The same can hold true for an altitude runner or a good heat runner going against competitors who may be great but who are not ready for the specific race conditions they are facing on that day.

When conditions don't dictate much, as is usually the case indoors, then the competitors and the race distance are the two factors of most importance. You may want tough competition for a particular race, so you pick the race with the best field of competitors. If the level of competition is irrelevant, then you pick the race distance that will best help you in your preparation for later in the season when performance is more important.

All things being equal, I normally favor shorter-distance tune-up races, but there are always exceptions. A particular runner may be stronger over longer distances and the benefits of success in a longer race may outweigh the benefits of the fast-paced tune-up afforded by the shorter race.

## How Often Should You Race the Same Distance?

Some runners like to vary race distances every meet; others stay with the same distance several meets in a row. I usually suggest racing the same distance a couple of times in a row, so that learning can take place more effectively. Especially for beginners, there is usually something to be learned from a race, and it is nice to turn right around and repeat the same distance in the next meet. Naturally, a 10K, because of its longer distance, is not something you want to repeat often, but early in the season it may not be bad to run a couple of 10Ks fairly close together. In the case of shorter races, it's usually best to repeat the same race a few times, then leave that race for a while before returning to it again later on. An understanding coach is particularly valuable in helping determine race distances and frequency.

# How Many Races Should You Do in a Season?

How often to race is of major concern to most coaches and runners. Again, there are individual considerations. Many novice runners benefit by racing often; they learn to race and improve performance by doing just that. The veterans don't need as much race experience in order to feel comfortable racing. The better runners like to have confidence that they are ready for their best performance, and this can come from specific workouts, races, or a combination of the two.

Runners who are part of a school or college team usually have a fuller race schedule than do club runners, so school runners must select races that complement their progress toward end-of-the-season championships.

Fit races into your training schedule. For runners who have control of, or confidence in, their coach's selection of races, the important thing to keep in mind is how each race complements the season's overall program. Back to the all-important question that requires an answer: Why am I doing this race (or this workout)? What is it doing for me?

Setting out your racing schedule early in the season will help keep you on track to be at your best in your most important races.

# Race Preparation

I have talked about race selection; it's now time to discuss prepara-tion for a race. There are some differences between preparing for midseason races and end-of-season championships.

First, let's deal with the similarities between these two types of races. You must have a plan for any race, yet be able to alter your plan if the situation so dictates (due to weather or the tactics of other competitors, for example).

## Sleep

Sleep is an important consideration for any race, and the simplest approach here is to be consistent. Get into a sleep routine in training and stick with it as closely as possible. Try to avoid a situation where short nights of sleep are compensated for by long nights. If you are routinely well rested, a short night's sleep on the night before a race will have no impact on performance. Several nights of poor rest may ruin a performance, but a single night will hardly ever have a detrimental effect.

# Meals

Consistency is the key. Paying attention to good nutrition for a few days before a race may help a little, but will never make up for weeks of inadequate nutrition. Another important consideration is eating before competition. Like warm-ups and race tactics, when and what to eat is an individual matter, but should be based on sound principles.

Some people have lots of problems running with any food in their stomachs; others can do well eating shortly before a race or strenuous workout. I once saw a guy at the Indoor Nationals consume a hot dog and a soft drink just 30 minutes before his second race of the meet (the two-mile run). When asked about the last-minute food consumption, he casually replied, "I run with my legs, not with my stomach." He went on to win the race.

In contrast to this approach was a runner I used to coach who wasn't able to eat anything within eight hours of a race or he would lose it all, either during or following the race. Another runner, whom I did not coach, told me that his stomach had been uncomfortable for two days prior to a 10K road race he had entered, and that he had eaten absolutely nothing for the 36 hours leading up to the race—in which he set a PR. Because of his unexpected success, from that day on, he always fasted for 36 hours before he ran a race of any distance.

What's best is whatever works well for you. I would suggest as a starting point, however, that little or no food be consumed for three to four hours prior to any race. Leading up to that time period, food consisting of carbohydrates usually works best. Bread, bagels, pancakes, rice, and pasta are all foods that most runners tolerate pretty well on race day or leading up to race day. Some runners like some protein and even some fat, as in eggs, pastries, and meat, but this type of food is usually consumed a little farther ahead of race time than if the food is carbohydrates. Moderation is a good rule to follow. "Practice" is another good word. Try various foods prior to hard training sessions and races of lesser importance, and then use whatever works best in more important competitions.

Water is an excellent fluid to take with prerace meals, because it is quickly absorbed. But many modern-day sports drinks also have ideal rates of absorption. It's best to avoid large amounts of foods that are sweet, because more fluid will be retained in the stomach to aid in dilution of the sugars, leading to a feeling of being bloated. Do most of your drinking four to eight hours prior to race time, and try to stay well hydrated right up to race time, but not to the extent that going to the toilet becomes a nuisance.

It is also a good idea to get in the habit of drinking and eating some carbohydrates within 30 to 60 minutes following training sessions. This speeds up the replenishment of depleted glycogen stores, a desirable process following long races. The longer the race or training session, the more important this postexercise practice becomes.

# Shoes

Contrary to popular belief, it is not necessarily true that the lighter the shoe, the more economical will be the running. This is because the effectiveness of running shoes is a function of both shoe weight and design, not just one factor or the other. The situation is further complicated by individual running style. Stride length and rate play a role in running economy, as does the way each runner's feet strike the ground. Some runners use less energy with one type of foot plant, while others do best with a different technique. It is a case of individual makeup interacting with various combinations of stride rate, stride length, shoe type, and foot strike, in addition to the surface over which you are running. There is no right way that suits everyone. Just as different coaches and runners relate differently, so do different techniques suit various runners in different ways.

The materials used in various parts of shoe midsoles and the composition and design of outsoles also affect running economy. Plus, the surface over which the athlete is running becomes a factor. A very light shoe with poor cushioning may be a relatively "costly" shoe, especially for a rear-foot runner (a runner whose feet first strike the ground with their heels, or rear of the foot). This would be particularly true on a hard surface, such as a road.

## Barefoot Running

Barefoot running produces poor economy for most runners on a hard road (or treadmill) but may be the most economical way to go on a forgiving synthetic track. Barefoot running on the proper surface would probably produce the best race times. This is because the lightest possible footwear is being used and the cushioning characteristics of the track surface eliminate the need for any midsole between the runner's foot and the ground.

Of course, there are potential problems with barefoot running, but the facts remain that what is on the feet, and the surface on which the feet are landing and from which they are pushing off, are important factors in running economy. This last statement deserves attention for another reason, and that is the importance of training in racing shoes.

## Training and Racing Shoes

I am convinced that some training should be done in racing shoes, for two reasons:

1. Each type of shoe has its own economy characteristics and to take full advantage of these characteristics you must do some actual training in the shoes.
2. Each type of shoe has its own mechanical characteristics, and it can be disastrous never to train under the conditions that will be facing you in a race.

It is hard to document how many injuries have resulted from wearing "new" shoes in a race, shoes that fit and function differently from those used in practice. To never wear racing shoes in practice is like never training at race pace. It's always risky to let the conditions of a race be completely foreign to you, and that includes wearing shoes whose effects on your economy and your feet are unpredictable.

## Spikes and Orthotics

Runners are often concerned about whether to wear orthotics during races, and some runners question the value of wearing spikes in longer track races. I have performed research regarding both of these issues and have found that with good traction (which is a function of the running surface and shoe outsole material), spikes are no more economical than racing flats, provided shoe weight and cushioning characteristics don't differ. In other words, putting spikes on the bottom of shoes doesn't necessarily help in longer races, such as 5000 and 10,000 meters. Of course, on slippery footing, as is often the case in cross-country races, spikes are usually advantageous.

The problem, of course, is to find flats that fit like spikes and have the same biomechanical characteristics in terms of resiliency and shock absorbency. Since there is no real advantage or disadvantage from an energy demand standpoint (in longer races), it makes sense that the athlete would select what is most comfortable and that which provides the most confidence. On a flat indoor track, the argument could be made that it is better not to wear spikes so that the rotation that takes place on the sharp turns is between the shoe and the track rather than between the foot and the shoe, or within the ankle itself.

Runners are often concerned about wearing orthotics during races. Since a function of these devices is to provide the runner with better mechanics, the increased cost of carrying the extra weight should be counteracted by the decreased cost of running with better mechanics. On the average, this seems to be the case. However, under racing conditions, some people are more economical with their orthotics, while others see their economy worsen when orthotics are used. Naturally, there are different kinds of orthotics, and racing shoes may require a different pair than training shoes. If you feel better racing without orthotics, I would suggest asking the doctor who provided them if racing without them would be of any consequence. If it is okay to race without the orthotics, be certain to do some training in your racing shoes without orthotics before the actual race.

## Clothing

In regard to clothing and performance, I suggest wearing the least amount of clothes necessary to maintain comfort. Being overdressed typically leads to dehydration and overheating, and can even cause you to become chilled under certain conditions. The latter case is likely if you are running in cold weather at a hard pace and then must slow down, or if you are running in cold weather with a tailwind and must turn into a headwind. In both situations the moisture on and around your body can become a chilling or even a freezing layer of coolant.

In general, increased weight or increased restriction of clothing increases the cost of running. However, flexible tights do not affect economy, according to some extensive tests that I have conducted in the lab. Further, we found no difference in cost of running whether stirrups at the bottom of tights were or were not used. Since the weight and restrictiveness of modern materials do not affect economy, one could argue that under the right conditions they could actually improve economy. If the tights allow the runner to be more relaxed and comfortable during the act of running, they might indeed lower the cost of running.

I should point out that with the great variety of tights available, one sort or another could affect running economy negatively. It's best to use the lightest, least restrictive pair that adequately warm the legs under the given conditions. It may even take more than one pair or more than one style to meet all conditions.

# Focus on the Task and Monitor the Response

When you perform a quality workout, say a set of 1000-meter intervals, you repeat a given task at a specific intensity with a certain amount of rest. You expect a particular sense of discomfort and satisfaction. If you have been following a good running program, you can expect that this workout will be as fast as ever but with less discomfort and a quicker recovery.

Similarly, midseason races give you a chance to see where you are in terms of race fitness. You may plan a particular pace to see how that affects you, or you may see how fast you can go in an all-out attempt. In any case, you will have some plan in mind, and you will then follow that plan and analyze the result.

Dress according to the conditions in which you will be competing. Wearing light-weight clothing will help this group of racers to avoid overheating and dehydration.

In a championship race, on the other hand (barring setbacks along the way), you have every reason to believe that this will be your best race of the season, or maybe even of your life, so far. You have done the training and resting necessary for success. The important difference is rest. For a championship race, or series of races, you are in a mode of final-quality training designed to let your body take advantage of all the stress that it has been through during the season. This is a time to reflect on the many great training sessions you have completed, the successful races you have run, and the joy associated with a good, hard-run race. Take advantage of it!

# Tapering

As described in chapter 8, I believe in phases of training, each designed to prepare you for what comes next. In keeping with this philosophy, the final-quality phase of training prior to an important race must include those things that best prepare you for the race. When applicable, this is the time to get in the proper time zone, in the proper environmental conditions, and into training that allows for maintenance of earned race attributes. It is also the time for optimal performance and sharpening of qualities needed for a successful race. Although this tapering period generally lasts six weeks, I feel that anywhere from three to eight weeks is fine.

The shorter the taper phase, the less opportunity for any final sharpening races, which vary in importance among individuals based on race distance, past experience, and length of season, for example. Normally, you will decrease mileage in this phase (depending on how high it has been), and the total amount of quality work. This is where sticking with percentages of weekly mileage as a guide to amount of quality running is very helpful. It is a time to minimize overall stress and still maintain good quality, which is accomplished by less work. This is not a time to put the body under new stresses, which could cause uncertain results.

It is tempting during a period of lesser mileage to want to do everything faster than usual, but this is not the best strategy. Chances are that most runners would be happy with a 1% or 2% improvement in performance over what has already been accomplished (a 1% improvement is about two to three seconds in a 1500-meter or mile race and about one to two and a half minutes in a marathon time). Naturally, the slower your race times are, the greater the time drop that is associated with a 1% change.

# Race-Day Routine

On occasion, attention to some matters may have to take place a day or more ahead of a race, and it's always wise to get ready for each race well ahead of time. Have all possible pairs of shoes (and lengths of spikes, if used) packed and ready for each competition. Have a competition kit or bag that is always ready well before departing for a race. This kit should have shoes, uniforms, spare clothing (including appropriate clothing for a postrace awards ceremony), and something to drink and eat. Do not forget any food or fluids to be used before and during the race itself. Depending on the weather and location of the competition, other items may also be required, such as soap, a towel, a padlock for a locker, and a stopwatch. Take whatever you think you might need.

Probably the most important items are racing shoes and any required uniforms, which you should have in your carry-on bag if flying to a competition. Consider an additional uniform in the event the first one doesn't fit properly or gets wet or sweaty before the start of the race (it's usually best to put on your competition uniform after completing your warm-up). Marathoners who are allowed to provide their own fluids must consider water bottles, marking pens for their bottles, the specific drinks to be used, and placement of the drinks on the course.

In cross-country racing, some runners prefer particular kinds of shoes or lengths of spikes. Always have both racing spikes and flats for cross-country races. Rapidly changing course conditions can alter the type of footwear that is appropriate for a particular course.

I well remember a young runner who, when he took off his warm-up suit just before a cross-country race, realized he had no shorts on. Another time I watched a runner take his shorts off along with his warm-up pants just as he was getting ready to take the baton for his (anchor) leg of a sprint relay. A teammate handed him his shorts, but it was too late, so he ran with his shorts in one hand and the baton in the other, right through the finish line and out of the stadium. He won the race, but I never did hear if he was disqualified for not wearing a proper uniform during his leg of the relay.

## Morning Runs

Before discussing the common prerace warm-up, let me encourage the practice of a morning run on the day of a race. This is usually a run of about 20 to 30 minutes, performed sometime in the morning before a midday or afternoon race. During cross-country season, when races are typically run before noon, this easy run is performed early enough that it can still be followed by a light meal. The advantages of such a practice are that it gets runners up and going (rather than sleeping late or just sitting around worrying about their race) and it allows for a refreshing shower and a light meal well ahead of the race.

## Final Race Preparation

During the last hour or so before a race, have a routine to follow, regardless of the importance of the race. This helps in two ways. First, a good warm-up and mental attitude prepare you for competing at your best. Second, if you have a good routine to follow in less important races, then you can concentrate on the same routine before more important competitions, when many runners get nervous and don't know what to do when the chips are down.

Try to avoid as part of a prerace preparation anything that cannot be easily adhered to, things that I call warm-up or race superstitions. As the old adage goes, it's bad luck to be superstitious; I wholeheartedly agree. I remember a high school runner who had a great race while wearing a particular T-shirt under his racing singlet, a rubber band around his wrist, and a penny in his shoe. From then on, he felt that he wasn't ready to race well without all three of these good-luck charms in place. In fact, the penny had to be given to him by his mother just prior to the start of the race. I don't know how long he followed this ritual, but I do know that it went on into college. He must have been a little uncomfortable wearing two shirts on really hot days.

To break a runner from relying on good-luck charms, I try to set up a certain success situation and then find a way to hide the runner's "secret victory socks." If you can be victorious once in the absence of a good-luck item, chances of future success without it are greatly improved. The day will come when you forget or lose your good-luck charm, and you just have to hope that it isn't at the Olympic Trials.

## Warming Up

Just as you experiment with different types of training, you should try out different prerace warm-ups. One approach is to think about some good, quality training sessions you have had and how you felt at different stages of those workouts. Recall a workout that involved repeating some 800s, 1000s, or 1200s, with a designated recovery between each bout of the workout. How did you feel during various repeated runs? Was the first one the easiest? The second, or the third? Sometimes it is even the last one that feels best (probably because it is the last one).

The term "warm-up" is actually misleading, becasue warming up the muscles is only part of the process. In fact, "pre-race preparation" may better describe what a runner goes through during the 30 minutes to one hour prior to the race itself. This is a time to prepare ourself both physically and mentally for the task ahead. Following are some characteristics of a pre-race "warm-up" that warrant attention.

## Try a Harder Warm-Up

In a series of repeated runs, often you will find a second or third run to be more comfortable than the first or the first couple. Think about this. If this applies to you, then maybe you should consider this when warming up for a race. In other words, don't be afraid to put in some pretty solid running not too long before the start of a competitive effort.

Many of the successful distance runners I have coached will end their warm-up with a 1000- or 1200-meter run at about threshold pace. Others prefer a couple of repeated 400s at about interval pace with two minutes of recovery between them. In either case, this tune-up works quite well if the somewhat demanding part of the warm-up is completed 15 to 20 minutes prior to the race. I have seen cases in which such a warm-up ended 30 minutes before race time and yet the race went very well. This is good to remember in the event that a race doesn't start as scheduled.

## Experiment With New Approaches

To try a demanding, prolonged run as part of a prerace warm-up often takes a little courage, but don't wait until your most important race of the year to try it out. Give it a fair trial in some less important races, and if it's successful, use it with confidence when it really counts.

The same principle of trying a particular prerace warm-up for lesser races applies to every type of warm-up. Always practice a new method in training and in meets of lesser importance so that you will know what works best for you. Coaches, as well as runners, should realize and cater to the fact that each athlete performs best with his or her own warm-up and race strategies.

Proper physical and mental preparation will allow you to run your best when it counts.

## Cater to Individual Differences

Not everyone performs the same in a particular race situation. This is sometimes difficult to deal with when warming up for a cross-country race, where everyone will race at the same time. Many coaches like to have the whole team warm up at the same time and same pace. This can look nice and encourage team cohesiveness in race preparation, but it may not be the best approach for the individuals on the team. It is better for all of the team members to race well— even if it means individual variation in warm-up strategies—than to look great warming up together and then to have a few subpar race efforts.

Some members of a team may be seasoned veterans, who train 70 to 80 miles per week, while others are gifted newcomers who have yet to experience a 40-mile week. Often, the higher-mileage runner is accustomed to a longer warm-up and knows that a few miles of running prior to a race won't be unduly fatiguing. On the other hand, a beginner may find that a mile of easy running and some quality minutes work best, and that trying to do what the veterans do puts him or her in a fatigued state of mind going into the race.

In general, the same principles apply to warming up as to racing and training. If you're a coach, accommodate individual differences, and, to encourage team spirit, spend some time explaining the reasons why different strategies work best for different people.

## Characteristics of Effective Warm-Ups

Following are some general characteristics of effective warm-ups.

1. Muscular activity (involving the muscles that will do the running) enhances performance through a slight elevation of muscle temperature. However, more than a degree or two of increase in muscle temperature can lead to a worse performance, especially if the weather is very warm or humid and the race is long (more than one mile).

In warm conditions, wearing warm-ups is not a good idea. One of a distance runner's greatest enemies is heat, and there is no need to accelerate body heating by overdressing prior to a race. If the weather is warm enough to feel comfortable sitting around without a warm-up suit on, then it's too warm to wear one during a warm-up routine. If during a rest period between warm-up and race time you feel that you will cool down without some extra clothing, then put on your warm-up suit.

## WARM-UPS FOR YOU TO TRY

Following are some prerace warm-ups that you can experiment with at different times to determine which works best for various races and environmental conditions. You may use some of these to prepare for quality training sessions as well.

It is important to plan the total warm-up time carefully, with the critical factor being when the warm-up session will end relative to the start of the race. The idea behind a warm-up is, at least in part, to elevate the temperature of the exercising muscles, so have adequate clothing available for maintaining warmth between the end of the warm-up and the start of the race (or training session). If a race gets delayed after the warm-up has been terminated, add a few more strides or some more easy running until a short time before the race.

# Easy Running

This warm-up involves only easy running, with the possibility of adding on a few strides and some stretching at the end. The amount of running can vary greatly, from as little as 5 to 10 minutes to several miles. Complete the warm-up 5 to 10 minutes before the start of the race. Any stretching that is done should be following at least some, if not all, of the running. Easy running warm-ups are applicable before very long races, where race intensity is not particularly fast; before a second or third race in a track meet in which the runner is competing in more than one event; and for runners who have not been training very long or hard for the race in question.

# Easy Running Plus Strides or Light Repetitions

This is a variation of the easy running warm-up, the difference being that either during or following the easy run portion of the warm-up, you engage in a series of strides (usually from 3 or 4 to as many as 10 or 12). Strides are relatively fast runs lasting about 20 seconds each, but could be as short as 10 seconds or as long as 40 seconds each. Stride speed is about the pace you would race 1500 meters or 1 mile. Fast strides might also be incorporated into this warm-up for additional speed. Fast strides are close to 800-meter race pace and are used as part of a warm-up for shorter races in which the starting pace must be fast. It is important to understand that strides and even fast strides are not sprints but are comfortably fast runs that are controlled and performed with light, quick leg turnover, rather than long, powerful strides. Take 20 to 60 seconds of recovery between strides. The recovery can be either walking or easy running, as seems appropriate. Try to have completed all of the strides about 10 minutes prior to race time. Some runners prefer doing their strides in racing shoes; others use their training flats and change to racing shoes during their final minutes of recovery and stretching, just before the race starts.

# Easy–Hard–Easy Running

With this warm-up, start off with one or two miles of easy running, some stretching, a few strides, and then a solid 3- to 4-minute run at about threshold pace. There should be about 15 to 20 minutes of relaxation time after the threshold run prior to the start of the race itself. During the final relaxation period you should do some easy running, typically to get yourself over to the area of the start in time to make final preparations.

A variation of the single 3- to 4-minute run would be two 2- to 3-minute threshold runs, which would end 15 to 20 minutes prior to race time. This warm-up may seem demanding, and is somewhat intimidating, but if you reflect back on some training sessions composed of several long intervals or cruise intervals, you might remember that you typically start feeling better after the first, second, or even third workout of the session. This warm-up is worth trying in a couple of low-key races before using it in an important competition. I have gone so far as to have my runners include in their warm-up a full 1200 meters (over the first segment of a cross-country course, for example) at race pace with good success.

## Race Pace Running

The race pace warm-up often works best for shorter and medium-distance races, when you want to get a feel for the pace at which you would like to start the race. Following some easy running, stretching, and strides, run 200 or 400 meters a couple of times at the pace that you want to run the first 400 meters of the race. Usually it is better to run 2 × 400 meters or 2 to 3 × 200 meters (or a couple of 200s followed by a 400) than it is to run a single one of these runs. Take a full recovery between runs. During the race pace warm-up, try to imagine being in the race with people around you, and imagine how easy and comfortable the pace will be once the race begins. Fall into a normal 2-2 breathing pattern at the start of the warm-up, and be wearing racing shoes and racing uniform (weather permitting) in order to mimic race conditions as closely as possible. Time the warm-up so that you have about 10 minutes of full recovery before the start of the race.

## Accelerations

This is similar to the easy run plus strides warm-up, except that this warm-up involves a brief easy run followed by a series of strides of increasing velocity. In this warm-up, the strides make up the bulk of the prerace preparation, so it is important to pay attention to how they are going. For instance, run each stride over the same stretch of ground and note the time that you take to perform each stride. Without making a conscious effort to lengthen your stride or to speed up, let each stride be a little faster than the previous one. This usually happens automatically, and it is nice to see yourself getting faster and faster with no additional effort as the warm-up progresses.

A variation of the timed strides is to count 30 or 40 right-foot steps as you do the strides and see how far this number of steps takes you. Count the same number of right footfalls for each stride, and notice that you are going farther each time as you loosen up and warm up, and as you fall into a good running rhythm. Once you have started to repeat the same number of steps (or to run the same time) for the same distance, you can figure the warm-up is complete.

Usually it takes about five or six strides to feel ready, but on occasion you might need 10 or more minutes of striding to get the feeling you want. Always take a good recovery after each stride so that you feel as rested for the new stride as you did for the previous one. Allow about 10 minutes after the last stride for making final race preparations. Since you are not running a particular distance in a particular time, it is not imperative that you are wearing racing shoes during this warm-up. However, if you want to get a true feel for the opening pace of the race, you may want to throw in a timed run in racing shoes. An acceleration warm-up often works well for people who are entered in more than one event in a meet, and for runners who regularly include a set of strides in their daily training schedule.

Be aware that warm-ups that include fast short runs as the major part of the warm-up (or the final part of the warm-up) can lead to going out faster than desired in the race, unless race pace coincides with the final stride pace.

2. Stretching following the bulk of warm-up activity prepares the body for efficient movement and offers additional time to mentally prepare for the race. Try to avoid doing more stretching than is usual during regular training, since this will likely produce some muscle soreness in subsequent days. This is particularly undesirable if an athlete does more than the usual amount of stretching during preparation for a preliminary race, which can result in unwanted muscle soreness just in time for the finals, which might be contested a day or two later.

3. Quality running, such as some quick strides or more prolonged threshold- or interval-intensity running prepares the body for the

task ahead. Not only does the runner get a feeling for race pace, but fuel sources are made readily available and physiological systems are prepared for higher-intensity operation. It is desirable to stimulate carbohydrate metabolism (as compared to fat oxidation) for most race distances, and higher-intensity running accomplishes this. An exception for many people may be warming up for a marathon race, where race pace uses a combination of fat and carbohydrate for fuel, and carbohydrate sparing is a desirable goal. The reason for avoiding a higher-intensity warm-up for long races is that the faster you run, the more your body selects carbohydrate for fuel, and you want to save as much of your available carbohydrate as possible for the race itself. Some easy running and stretching is usually adequate for long races.

4. Mental preparation is a desirable part of a warm-up routine. This is an area of prerace preparation in which vast individual differences can occur. I've had athletes who want me to be talking to them almost constantly during the final minutes before a race; others would just as soon not even make eye contact for over an hour prior to a race. Actually, I'd prefer the latter approach for my athletes, because it indicates that they can make their final preparation without me; then when the day comes that I am not with them, they will fare just as well on their own.

Some runners need to avoid thinking about their race, while others seem to thrive on almost constant visualization of how the race will proceed from start to finish. Whatever time is afforded for mental preparation should be fit into the overall prerace routine, so that it does not detract from other equally important aspects of preparing for the race (such as having racing shoes on in time, race number pinned in place, proper racing uniform on, and physical warm-up completed).

If you find it beneficial to go through some last-minute mental preparation, make a point of reviewing only positive thoughts. Do not think of mistakes of past races, advantages opponents may have had in previous encounters, or how awful you felt at the four-mile mark of your last 10K race. Visualize how you will perform, how you will adjust to any midrace surprises, how you will just let your legs carry you over the ground, as if some outside force is picking up each leg for you as you float along (or roll along) over the ground. Have a plan for the race and include a flexibility factor that allows you to change your plan if so dictated by the situation once the race begins.

Try to go into every race with confidence that you can achieve a particular performance but with a certain amount of anxiety about how well you might really be able to do. Great performances come at the most unexpected times and seldom come when they are intensely pre-planned.

Remember during your prerace preparation that a race is a serious yet enjoyable expression of your ability to do something that you very much look forward to doing. The preparation for a championship race varies mainly in the groundwork preceding a less important race and in the training leading up to race day. Midseason races are important tests of where you are during various stages of training; championship races are a test of how fast you have become as the result of a season of training. You typically rest for a midseason race as you would for an important workout, whereas you give championship races special attention during the final-quality phase of training.

# The Moment of Truth

A race is an individual's expression of his or her ability to perform in a particular setting. It may be against time, or it may be against an opponent, with time being irrelevant. In either case, the runner is out there alone calling on all the ability given to him or her by parents; all the energy provided through weeks, months, or years of training; and all the mental toughness and motivation afforded by previous competitions, supportive coaches, and teammates. The goal of all this is to achieve some predesignated time or place. The best that can happen is that prerace expectations are exceeded; the worst is that performance is not up to expectations. Look for a lesson that each particular race offers, and log that experience in a positive way. With a negative result, remember the race in terms of how the race could have been run differently for a more desirable outcome. With a positive result, remember how it felt and how various aspects of the race were run.

It is usually better to finish a race saying, "I probably could have run a little faster if I had been up a little farther in the early stages," rather than, "I wonder how much better I would have run if I hadn't gone out so fast and died." Most mistakes in a race are made in the first two minutes, perhaps in the very first minute. Going out too slowly during the first minute or two of a race will not necessarily cause the rest of the race to be too slow. However, going out too quickly can produce a pace that is too slow for the rest of the race. Going out 10 seconds too fast in the first 400 meters of a 5K race can lead to losing a few seconds in each 400 thereafter. So, you may gain 10 seconds and lose 30, for a net loss of 20 seconds. On the other hand, giving away 5 seconds in the first 400 of a 5K will probably produce no loss the rest of the way. In this case, you lose a total of 5 seconds, and you will undoubtedly find yourself passing many people during the middle and later stages of the race—and it is much more enjoyable to be the passer than the "passee."

Some runners are good front runners and thrive on being in the lead; others do better staying behind the leader and letting others set the pace. In either case, the majority of runners are better off running even-intensity races and settling down somewhere in the pack of leaders, if that is a reasonable possibility. I prefer to use the term "even-intensity" rather than "even-paced," in reference to what I consider the best approach to most distance races. Conditions such as wind, footing, and hills can alter a pace, even when the effort or intensity is constant. Changing the intensity of effort is costly, while changing pace may not be if it is due to external factors, such as those just mentioned. On a track, particularly an indoor track where wind never plays a role, pace and intensity often become one and the same.

# Relax!

If you realize that you have gone out faster than anticipated, don't slow down abruptly, just relax, concentrate on the task at hand and let the pace slow down on its own. The exception is in a marathon or other long race when you need to make adjustments as soon as the problem is realized.

## Listen to Your Breathing

If you can't hold a 2-2 rhythm during the first two-thirds of the race, your early pace is probably too fast.

## Stitches

If you feel a stitch (a stabbing pain in the abdomen) coming on, make a conscious effort to take slower, deeper breaths (3-3 is usually a

# PENNY WERTHNER

**Penny Werthner** was the first world-class runner whom I had the privilege of coaching, and it couldn't have been a better introduction to that caliber of athlete. Penny was born in Ottawa, Ontario, Canada, on the day after Americans celebrate their independence. She started running at age 12 because, in her words, she "liked to run and then liked that feeling of success, of getting better, of accomplishing something." Penny continued to run in high school, at McMaster University in Hamilton, Ontario, and then with the Harriers Club in Ottawa. It was at this time that Penny finally achieved her major goal in running, to make her National Team.

Werthner was relatively successful as a young 800 runner, but was disappointed with not qualifying for the Canadian Olympic Team headed for Munich in 1972. It was in 1973 that I (working as a consultant to Sport Canada) became acquainted with and began to coach Penny. During the summer, I was able to spend time in Canada working directly with her. The rest of the year, we conversed by phone and mail. But our work together paid off. Penny won multiple Canadian national championships in the 800 and 1500, and at one time held the world record for the indoor 1000. She was the top-ranked Canadian in the 800, 1500, and 3000 in 1978. She was also a member of the Canadian Olympic Team in 1976 and 1980, qualifying for the 1500. During her best years, she ran 50 to 60 miles per week and felt that track intervals were the most important aspect of her training. Penny stopped competing at age 31. According to her, it was "time to move on."

"Despite my hard work, my dedication, and perhaps some talent," Penny relates, "there is no doubt in my mind that without the expertise of Jack, I would not have achieved the success that I did." Penny and I were the ideal combination of a coach and athlete. We trusted each other, respected each other and would go to any length to prove that we knew what we were doing. The same things hold today. I learned from Penny that the pursuit of excellence in athletics is a small endeavor compared to the need to pursue excellence in everyday life.

**Penny's Bests**   800: 2:01.5      1500: 4:08      3000: 9:00

helpful pattern). Rapid, shallow breathing often aggravates a side stitch. Usually stitches on the right side are most troublesome.

## Concentrate on Your Own Actions

Concentrate on what you are doing, rather than what is going on around you. I have had some Olympic runners tell me that if they hear lap times, they know they aren't adequately focused on the task at hand. For young runners, there is a lot to be learned from getting splits at various stages of a race, but a well-trained veteran should be able to feel how the race is going. Naturally, when a particular time is the goal of a race, splits may be a necessity and other aspects of the race can be ignored (including competitors in some cases).

## Don't Be Distracted by Discomfort

When discomfort occurs, don't shift your thoughts to how much of the race is remaining. Concentrate on what you are doing and on being as relaxed as possible. Before a long race (particularly cross-country races), I remind my runners that if they find themselves feeling lousy as they run alongside a group of other runners, they should realize that those around them must be feeling at least as terrible or they would be ahead of my runners.

## When Struggling . . . Speed Up!

A race tactic that began as a joke, but which has merit, is one that I came up with when I was coaching in South America in the 1960s. One of my runners was a young mountain boy who was running a tough 5K race after having won a good 1500-meter race earlier in the day. About seven or eight laps into the 5K he was 20 seconds behind the leaders, and as he ran by me he asked if he could drop out. The next time he ran by, I told him that if he would run ahead and catch the leaders, then he could drop out. He took me at my word, and over the next two and a half laps, he did catch the leaders, but instead of dropping out he ran with them and then outkicked them for the win.

Another way of looking at a race is to stay with your competitors until you can't stay with them any longer, then pass them. It's worth a try. Often in a long race, the unvarying pace gets you down and you simply need a change. However, most people don't consider a change to a faster pace; they only think of a slower one. Always try a pace increase before deciding to let the pace drop; you may find that you feel better.

## Take It One Step at a Time

When things get really tough in a race, you might have to think about running just one lap at a time, or just to a particular place on a cross-country or road course. I once had a young runner set a 30-second PR in a two-mile race during which I had encouraged him by saying, "Just work on this next lap." After the race I asked him if that advice had helped and his reply was that one lap at a time was too much to think about: "All I could think about was the next step." If that's what it takes, then that's what needs to be done.

## Never Sell Yourself Short

If things keep going better than expected in a race, it's probably time to realize that you are better than you thought you were. Enjoy the fact that everything is clicking. There is no need to slow down just to satisfy some preconceived idea of how fast the pace should be. Usually a runner will know in the first few minutes of a race how things are going to go, so use that early assessment to make feasible adjustments.

## Two-Thirds Tactic

In distance races, a good tactic is to be in your desired finishing position two-thirds of the way into the race. Arrive at that point as if

© Beth Schneider

Competing can show you how far you are able to push yourself. Although you should never endanger your health and well-being, if you have trained properly, don't hold back when it counts!

it were the finish. Not many races change drastically (aside from a few position changes brought about by a kick) during the final third of a race. If you are not with the lead pack in a mile race by the 1200-meter mark, things aren't in your favor for being with the leaders at the finish. In a 10K, working your way up to a desired place of finish by the four-mile mark is a sound tactic, but waiting much longer will make your job a much tougher one.

The same thing applies to reaching a time goal. Try for an even or negative-split race two-thirds or three-quarters of the way through the race, with the idea of being on pace at that point. Being on pace for the first 400 meters of a 5K race is nothing, and being much ahead of pace may spell disaster. Often a runner will say, "I was right on pace at the mile (of a two-mile race, for example), but I couldn't hold the pace the second mile." Actually, the runner was out in 70 seconds for the first 400 meters, then ran 76-, 77-, and 77-second 400s to arrive at the mile mark at 5:00 (just what he or she wanted for the first mile). But the pace was not a 5:00 pace at the mile; it was 5:08 pace, based on the two 77-second laps. The runner would be likely to run the second mile in over 5:00, if that was the pace going into the second mile.

Maybe the right way to think about pace is to think in terms of speed per 200 or 400 meters (or per kilometer or mile in longer races). Don't think of arriving at distance markers in a certain time, a practice that can lead to disappointing results. If, for example, your goal is to run 3200 meters in 12:00 on an indoor track, then the appropriate pace is 45 seconds per 200 meters or 90 seconds per 400 meters. If the first 200 is 43, forget that lap and try for the desired 45 on the next lap. If a lap goes slower than 45, make an immediate adjustment to get back on pace. On the other hand, if 44- or 43-second laps come without undue stress, just relax and let each lap take care of itself, trying for 45 but accepting a faster pace if it comes easily.

## Avoid Obstacles

Make an effort to avoid traffic and confrontations during a race. It can be costly to be pushing and shoving other runners, and having to run around other runners during a race. If you like to start out conservatively, then do just that; start at an easy pace and most of the jostling will be in front of you. By the time you have settled into your pace and are ready to move past all the runners who chose to fight each other in the first couple minutes, they will be in no mood to resist you.

On the track, once you are comfortable running at your desired pace, do your best not to lose that rhythm, even if it means moving outside other runners around the curve. It's more costly to slow down and drop behind a runner around the curve, and then have to accelerate on the straight, than it is to maintain pace and move out a little. Running to the outside of another runner around the curve actually means you are going faster than your competition, and once you reach the straight your momentum will carry you by without the need to accelerate.

## Avoid the Wind

Headwinds are extremely costly, and tailwinds never make up for what is lost going against the same wind. When you are racing at 6:00-mile pace (3:45 per kilometer), you are creating a headwind of 10 miles per hour (mph), or 16 kilometers per hour, even if there is no wind blowing. Remember, the maximum allowable tailwind for a sprint or horizontal jump is 2.0 meters per second, less than half of the headwind created by running in calm air at 6:00 pace. Imagine the effort required to run against a 15 mph headwind, which is created in calm air when running at 4:00 pace.

With this in mind, it is easy to understand how damaging an additional wind of 10 or 15 mph can be. The fact is, the energy required to run a 6:00 mile against a fairly strong headwind (about 15 mph) is the same amount of energy as required to run at 5:00 pace in calm air. A headwind means a slower pace and any runner who fails to heed this fact is asking for disaster somewhere during a race.

The same thing applies to leading or following in a distance race. Drafting off another runner can reduce the cost of the task a great deal. Unless you are considerably better than any of your opponents, trying to lead a 10K race all the way is almost certain to produce disappointment.

# Dropping Out

Some runners, and probably even some coaches, feel that dropping out of a race is an absolute no-no. I agree that it is not a great idea, particularly if dropping out is associated with not wanting to keep going when it starts to hurt. However, there are some legitimate times when abandoning a race is acceptable. One is when an injury has been sustained, and continuing to race may cause complications or additional injury. Another legitimate time is when an illness or existing health problem, such as exercise-induced asthma, turns a race into a struggle for survival.

I have known people to run through a bad stitch to avoid dropping out of a race, only to aggravate the stitch to such a degree that training is curtailed for several weeks or even months. It's better to abandon the race than to put your future health in jeopardy.

A note to those who might consider dropping out of a cross-country race—never assume anything. A runner who is struggling along as the sixth runner on a team, well back in the pack and feeling pretty dejected and worthless to the team, may decide to drop out. The runner often justifies this by saying, "I'm not scoring in our top five, so my place won't affect the scoring anyway." Moments after the runner drops out, one of the top five runners on the same team steps into a hole and is forced out of the race by injury. Not having the sixth runner as a backup becomes a major factor in the team scoring, and if there is no seventh runner, the team is completely out of the team race.

Feeling sorry for yourself is not a good reason to drop out of a race. On the other hand, avoiding a major setback that could occur if you continue in a race can be a legitimate reason to stop running.

# A Final Word

Racing is the ultimate expression of a runner's ability, training, and motivation. A race should be thought out, prepared for, and performed with determined intensity. Results of every race should be analyzed and used to adjust the training for and the tactics used in future competitions.

# CHAPTER 12

# 1500- to 3000-Meter Racing

© Ken Lee

*Whether you view a race as a day off from training or as a test, treat every race seriously and with respect.*

In keeping with my approach toward the physiological demands of training and racing distance events, I feel that it is appropriate to plan training sessions based on the duration of time to be raced rather than on the distance to be raced. For example, an elite runner concentrating on racing the 5000-meter distance is training for a race that will last about 13 to 15 minutes, the same duration of time a less gifted or beginner runner might spend racing 3000 meters and not much beyond the time spent racing a 1-mile distance for some runners. You should gear your training toward racing for a particular duration of time, such as 4 minutes, 15 minutes, 30 minutes, or a few hours, as opposed to a particular distance.

Add to the time and distance dilemma the fact that some individuals have different physiological (and psychological) makeups than others, and it is no wonder that a particular coach's training system works well for one athlete and not so well for another. One of the greatest mistakes we can make in training beginner runners is to throw them into a program currently used by a successful star athlete. In this case, we are forcing one runner to fit someone else's mold. It can be confusing enough to say different individuals need different training programs; to further cloud the issue by saying that all milers should train the same because the race distance is the same can often result in disappointment.

I will present some ideas and sample training phases and workouts, based on a 24-week season, that are geared toward preparing runners to race durations of time that rely heavily on both aerobic and anaerobic energy sources. I call these races "intense–distance events" or "speed–distance events," and they are typically those that will cover 1500 meters to 2 miles in distance.

Included in this chapter is a full 24-week training table that you can use if you are planning to train and race 1500 to 3000 meters. What I feel I do best is to identify the types of training and training intensities that meet the needs of different body systems. I also suggest some logical order of training that will suit most people, but the best mix of ingredients is an individual matter that can be identified and finalized only through numerous seasons of training. Hang onto the positives and set aside the negatives (but don't be too quick to discard the negatives altogether). If you don't have 24 weeks for your season, refer to chapter 8 for suggestions.

# Approaching 1500- to 3000- Meter Training

The approach to these races is to learn to get out well but with as little effort as needed to stay with the pace you want. This is followed by a conscious effort to increase the pace during the middle portion of the race and eventually to shift into an even faster, more anaerobic finish.

To accomplish this, you need to train for speed, economy, and for aerobic power. These races are won with speed, but a high aerobic capacity allows for some control in the middle of the race and provides a strong base and recovery system that provides for optimal anaerobic training. There is a definite need for steady, comfortable distance runs, for demanding intervals, and for a variety of repetition-type workouts. Threshold training becomes an extension of easy runs and allows for light quality training that can be mixed with reduced amounts of faster runs.

You must learn to run fast and still be in control of your mechanics; run fast and not strain; run fast and still feel there is another gear when needed. This is where having a high aerobic capacity pays off. It means saving anaerobic reserves for the final gear, rather than having to call on them to maintain the intensity of the midrace pace.

There is no doubt that some runners in the speed–distance events rely more on endurance than do others, and this is where being able to read your reactions to various types of training (or having a coach who can do that for you) really pays off. This is also why it takes years to develop your full potential. Some seasons are spent developing one aspect of your talent, while other seasons are spent realizing the approaches that aren't right for you. Each individual must experiment to find the proper mix of training ingredients.

# Phase I Training

In a four-phase program, Phase I—weeks 1-6 in a 24-week program—is set aside for foundation work and injury prevention, for building up to the point of being able to take on more formal quality training. For the first three weeks of Phase I, do only steady, easy running. Runners with a good background who have maintained a

## 1500 to 3000 Meters

| Week | Day 1 | Day 2 | Day 3 | Day 4 | Day 5 | Day 6 | Day 7 |
|---|---|---|---|---|---|---|---|
| 1 - 3 | E | E | E | E | E | E | E |
| 4 - 6 | L | E strides | E strides | E | E | E strides | E strides |
| 7 | L strides | R-1 | E | I-1 | E | E strides | Ti |
| 8 | L strides | E | R-2 | E strides | E | E strides | T |
| 9 | L strides | R-1 | E | I-1 | E | E strides | Ti |
| 10 | L strides | E | R-2 | E strides | E | E strides | T |
| 11 | L strides | R-1 | E | I-2 | E | E strides | Ti |
| 12 | L strides | E | R-2 | E strides | E | E strides | T |
| 13 | L strides | I-1 | E | T* | E | E strides | R or Race* |
| 14 | L strides | E | I-1 | T* | E | E strides | R or Race* |

1500 to 3000 Meters

| Week | Day 1 | Day 2 | Day 3 | Day 4 | Day 5 | Day 6 | Day 7 |
|------|-------|-------|-------|-------|-------|-------|-------|
| 15 | L<br>strides | I-1 | E | T* | E | E<br>strides | R or<br>Race* |
| 16 | L<br>strides | E | I-1 | T* | E | E<br>strides | R or<br>Race* |
| 17 | L<br>strides | I-1 | E | T* | E | E<br>strides | R or<br>Race * |
| 18 | L<br>strides | E | I-1 | T* | E | E<br>strides | R or<br>Race* |
| 19 | E/L<br>strides | R-1 | E<br>strides | T* | E | E | Race or<br>Mix |
| 20 | E/L<br>strides | E | R-2 | T* | E | E | Race or<br>Mix |
| 21 | E/L<br>strides | R-1 | T* | E<br>strides | E | E | Race or<br>Mix |
| 22 | E/L<br>strides | E | R-2 | E<br>strides | E | E | Race or<br>Mix |
| 23 | E/L<br>strides | R-1 | E<br>strides | T* | E | E | Race or<br>Mix |
| 24 | E/L<br>strides | E | T* | E<br>strides | E | E | Race or<br>Mix |

(see next page for key)

## Workout Description

| | |
|---|---|
| **E** | Comfortable running with good light turnover and rhythmic breathing. Amount of running is flexible—do enough to reach week's goal. Can be one or two runs (during heavier weeks) or can be no run if more rest is necessary. |
| **E/L** | Easy run; may or may not be as long as usual Day 1 |
| **L** | Up to 25% of week's total mileage |
| **Strides** | **Weeks 1-12:** 5-6×20- to 30-second runs at comfortably-fast pace using light quick turnover (do not sprint these) <br> **Weeks 13-24:** On L days, 5-10×20-30 seconds in middle or at end of run |
| **T** | 20-minute steady tempo run at **T**-pace, plus the possible addition of 4×200s. |
| **Ti** | Repeat 1000s at **T**-pace with 1-minute rests up to 8% of week's mileage, plus the possible addition of 4 × 200s |
| **T*** | **Weeks 13-18:** Sets of 2×1000 or 2×1-mile **T** + 4×200 **R,** up to 8% of week's mileage <br> **Weeks 19-24:** 3×1000 or 1-mile **T** with 2-minute rests, plus 4-8×200 **R** with full recoveries |
| **I-1** | **Weeks 7-12:** Sets of 3-minute hard runs at **I**-pace with 1 minute easy, up to 8% of week's total mileage <br> **Weeks 13-18:** Sets of 1000s, 1200s, or miles at **I**-pace, up to 8% of week's mileage, or 3-6×5 minutes hard running with 5 minutes easy to recover (for bad conditions) |
| **I-2** | Sets of 2 minutes hard + 1 minute easy + 1 minute hard + 30 seconds easy + 30 seconds hard + 30 seconds easy, up to 8% of week's total mileage |
| **R** | Sets of 1×800 + 2×400 + 4×200 all at **R**-pace with full recoveries, up to 5% of week's mileage |
| **R-1** | **Weeks 7-12:** Sets of 2×200 + 1×400 at **R**-pace, up to 5% of week's mileage (may be hills) <br> **Weeks 19-24:** 3×800 increasing speed with first a little slower than current 1500 race pace, next at 1500 pace, and finally 2-3 seconds faster, plus 4×200 at 800 race pace |
| **R-2** | **Weeks 7-12:** Sets of 2×200 + 1×800 at **R**-pace, up to 5% of week's mileage (may be hills) <br> **Weeks 19-24:** 2 or 3 sets 1×800 + 1×400 + 2×200, not over 4% of week's mileage |

## Workout Description

| Mix | Sets of $2\times200$ **R** + $1\times1000$ or 1-mile **T**+ 4 $\times$ 200 **R**, up to 6% of week's mileage |
|---|---|
| Race* | Add some of above **R** session, or at least some rep 200s, after race |

*Note:* 1) Start with a reasonable amount of running and follow mileage rules when increasing total distance; 2) Days of the week can be arranged in any order. I usually identify Day 1 as Sunday; 3) I have shown alternate weeks with back-to-back quality days, as opposed to alternate days of quality. Try both approaches to see which one works best for you.

reasonably good level of fitness may run twice a day. However, if you are returning from a period of no running, single runs should be limited to about 30 minutes each. Also, review the information presented in chapter 9 on returning to running after a planned time off.

After the first three weeks of steady running, add five or six strides to each of the daily easy runs, four days each week. Also, starting with week four, you can increase your mileage and add a long run once a week. Be sure to follow mileage rules when increasing your distance, though: Increase weekly mileage up to 10 miles per week, but only every third week.

# Phase II Training

In Phase II, or weeks 7-12, some quality running is added to the program and mileage may still be increasing, depending on the time and desire of the individual. It is a good idea to record at the top of the program weekly mileage and the types of training being emphasized.

Beginning with Phase II, a VDOT value should be used in setting training intensities. When no recent races have been run, a current race performance can be estimated to establish an initial VDOT. Or, use an adjusted VDOT determined from tables 9.1 and 9.2. A final possibility would be to use an early **T** run to estimate a starting VDOT. In any case determine VDOT training intensities by using table 3.2.

# BOB WILLIAMS

**Bob Williams** was born in Eugene, Oregon, the "Track Capital of the United States," and got into the spirit of running at the early age of 10. His involvement in running in high school came about, according to him, because there was "no high school baseball program." After high school, Bob went on to be a successful member of the University of Oregon track and field team. Along with coaching, he continues to run for the Oregon Track Club. His initial goal as a runner was to make a U.S. Olympic Team and to race in Europe.

I became involved with Bob during the summer leading up to the Mexico City Olympics when the top distance runners in the country were together for altitude training outside South Lake Tahoe, California. During his peak competitive days, Bob typically ran 65 to 70 miles per week and felt that hill training and long, race-specific intervals were the key to his success. Bob ran the steeplechase, an event in which he earned All-American honors and was Pac-8 Conference Champion. He was also listed in 1973 in the *Guinness Book of World Records* for completing the fastest round of 18 holes of golf.

Bob is a real lover of running and has always found success as an athlete and coach because of his devotion to the fun side of the sport. Bob taught me that 1) it is very important for every distance runner to do long runs at marathon pace and 2) you should always keep running fun.

**Bob's Best**     Mile: 4:07.6     Steeplechase: 8:41.1

# Phase III Training

Typically, Phase III—weeks 13-18—is the toughest phase of any training program. The first phases have prepared the body for what is ahead, and the runner is now fit enough to enter some races, which will help to identify a current VDOT.

Some runners in a school situation find themselves facing a midweek race as well as a race the following Saturday. If you have a race on Tuesday, consider Tuesday and Wednesday as two midweek quality days, with the possibility of some additional light interval training worked in following the Tuesday race. Of course, the training session scheduled for Tuesday must be adjusted or eliminated altogether in favor of the race. Wednesday's session remains as scheduled. With a Wednesday race, follow a Monday–Wednesday quality-day schedule, perhaps adding some light interval training after Wednesday's race. With no midweek race, use Monday and Wednesday as the two early-week quality days.

Saturdays are set aside for a solid **R** session. If you have a Saturday race on the schedule, it may be possible to add a reduced version of the **R** session after the race (possibly one set); at least some 200s can be run as part of a postrace cool-down. If you have no races during this phase, just follow the training sessions as outlined. Total mileage should not go up during this phase; the training itself is demanding enough without introducing an additional stress of more mileage.

# Phase IV Training

Weeks 19-24 make up the final-quality phase of the intense–distance program and should be set up to take advantage of your strengths and previous training and racing experiences. The key components of this phase should be adequate rest and recovery from workouts; quality training, but of limited volume; well-chosen races; and possibly a drop in overall weekly mileage. The toughest physical work is behind you and improved performances will come as a result of what has already been done. Don't increase training stress during this phase. Just do quality workouts with minimal effort and put your energy into high-quality races.

Those **R** sessions will pay off when you're in an all-out sprint for the finish line!

It is still fine to get in two quality days prior to a Saturday race, but if the race is a particularly important one (a qualifier for a championship or a championship race itself) limit quality training to one, usually Tuesday, session. In the six-week plan, I have provided four approaches to arranging quality days leading up to a Saturday race:

1. Monday–Wednesday quality days, which is the standard approach

2. Tuesday–Wednesday quality days, which allow a slightly longer recovery from a previous weekend's race

3. Monday–Tuesday quality days, which provide an additional easy day before a Saturday race; when the previous week's work requires little recovery

4. Tuesday as the only quality day, when the coming race is of particular importance

Follow Sunday runs with a few light and quick 200s. Easy-day 200s should never be sprints; 800-meter race pace is the fastest they need to be, and always with adequate recoveries to feel good for the next run.

In the final two weeks prior to a major competition, you can follow a special two-week taper session. This would include six 200-meter reps on Sundays (following an easy run), a "**mix**" workout or a "**T***" workout on Tuesdays (as described at the bottom of the Phase IV schedule) and four 200-meter reps on Wednesdays. On the other days, just do easy runs. If there is not a race on the first Saturday, run another "**mix**" session on that day.

# A Final Word

A good rule to follow regarding special races is not to do anything special. An important race is not the time to experiment with a new warm-up or race tactic. However, there may be times when your competition throws something new at you and you must respond. You must be flexible and willing to take some chances when the chips are down. But these chances must be within reason, based on your experience and your knowledge of the competition. For example, a 5:00 miler doesn't chance going with a 4:30 miler, but a 4:50 pace may be within reason if he or she feels good about how recent training and racing have been going.

With a cautious first lap, I have always felt that the second 400 meters of a 1500-meter or mile race is the most important part of the race if you are trying for a fast time, because you are still fresh enough to make any necessary adjustments, and the third 400 is usually the same pace as the second 400. My advice is to float through the first minute of the race, make a conscious effort to pick up the pace after the first minute, and be ready to kick at any time during the final minute of the race.

# CHAPTER 13

# 5- to 15- Kilometer Racing

© Victah Sailer

*The biggest mistakes you can make
in a race are in the first minute.*

I have referred to the shorter distance events as intense, and that they are. When you get into the medium-long events, the term "intense" most often gives way to just plain "hard." Racing the 5K through 15K distances can be cruel, and is usually fatiguing in many senses of the word. To prepare for these distances, you must train your aerobic capacity and lactate threshold to their maximum capabilities. This means solid foundation work, a strong emphasis on interval training, and enough time spent on repetitions and threshold runs that speeds close to your aerobic capacity become pleasant—or acceptable, at worst.

In the category of medium distances, in terms of time spent racing, about 11 or 12 minutes is the lower limit, and races that take about one hour constitute the upper limit. Race distances range, therefore, from 5000 meters for better runners, or 3000 meters for less developed athletes, to the half-marathon for elite runners, and at least 10,000 meters for slower competitive runners.

The sample training program that I present in this chapter is set up for a 24-week season and is geared for preparing you to race distances that are demanding both in intensity and duration. Because of the combined intensity and duration of these races, I have presented a good deal of back-to-back quality training days. This schedule should provide a solid base for enduring both the physical and mental demands of racing any medium-distance event. You can lengthen or shorten the schedule based on your time constraints by following the suggestions presented in chapter 8.

Each of the three categories of distance races that I address in chapters 12, 13, and 14 has its own way of attempting to make the runner's life stressful. With the intense, shorter-distance events presented in chapter 12, the stress comes primarily from a steadily increasing rise in blood-lactate concentration that challenges your ability to fight off the urge to give in to its unmerciful attack on your running muscles.

In the case of the medium-distance races, the enemy is total body fatigue. It's often hard to pinpoint the exact spot of discomfort (probably because it is everywhere, but nowhere in particular). During these races, the degree of discomfort doesn't always get progressively worse throughout the race, and your job is to learn to deal with a consistent feeling of overall stress.

In setting up a season of training for medium-distance races, adequate time must be spent on developing a powerful aerobic system, but this does not mean that there is no place for repetition training. On the contrary, reps lead not only to speed development but also to improvements in running economy, which in turn helps raise the lactate threshold to a faster running pace. In a sense, reps make any given running speed more acceptable for longer periods of time. The secret to a good training program for medium-distance events is to come up with the right combinations of when to do the various types of training and how much to do.

# Phase I Training

Phase I training—weeks 1-6 in a 24-week program—is the same for runners preparing for any race distance, at least regarding the type of running you need to do. The shorter-distance specialists may not get in as much mileage as those who are gearing up to race the medium- or longer-distance events, but all runners need to take it pretty easy in terms of intensity. Phase I is for easy running, stretching, strengthening exercises, and for getting back into the habit of regular, daily training.

As for the shorter-distance runners, I prescribe nothing but steady, easy running for the first three weeks of Phase I for medium-distance specialists; weeks four through six can have a longer run and some strides thrown into the weekly plan. Remember, you shouldn't increase mileage more often than every third week and a long (L) run shouldn't be longer than 25% of the week's total mileage.

# Phase II Training

The early-quality Phase II (weeks 7-12) program for runners keying on medium-distance events is a time for adjusting to quality running. Repetition (R) workouts are important because they will allow an adjustment to faster running. But with full recoveries between quality runs in a workout, reps feel relatively comfortable, while they work on good, light, and quick leg turnover. Increase weekly mileage up to 10 miles per week, but only every third week.

Threshold (T) runs are introduced, immediately following days of reps, and nonstructured interval (I) sessions are added at the end of each week. An occasional low-key race could be run in place of a weekend interval session.

## 5 to 15 Kilometers

| Week | Day 1 | Day 2 | Day 3 | Day 4 | Day 5 | Day 6 | Day 7 |
|------|-------|-------|-------|-------|-------|-------|-------|
| 1 - 3 | E | E | E | E | E | E | E |
| 4 - 6 | L | E strides | E strides | E | E | E strides | E strides |
| 7 | L strides | E | R-1 | Ti* | E | E | I-1 |
| 8 | L strides | E | E strides | R-2 | E | E | I-1 |
| 9 | L strides | E | R-1 | Ti* | E | E | I-2 strides |
| 10 | L strides | E | E strides | R-2 | E | E | I-1 |
| 11 | L strides | E | R-1 | Ti* | E | E | I-2 strides |
| 12 | L strides | E | E strides | R-2 | E | E | I-1 |
| 13 | L strides | E | I-1 | T* | E | E | I or Race |
| 14 | L strides | E | I-1 | Ti* | E | E | I or Race |

| Week | Day 1 | Day 2 | Day 3 | Day 4 | Day 5 | Day 6 | Day 7 |
|------|-------|-------|-------|-------|-------|-------|-------|
| 15 | L<br>strides | E | I-1 | T* | E | E | I or<br>Race |
| 16 | L<br>strides | E | I-1 | Ti* | E | E | I or<br>Race |
| 17 | L<br>strides | E | I-1 | T* | E | E | I or<br>Race |
| 18 | L<br>strides | E | I-1 | Ti* | E | E | I or<br>Race |
| 19 | L<br>strides | E | T* | Mix | E | E | Race or<br>I-1 |
| 20 | L<br>strides | E | Ti* | Mix | E | E | Race or<br>I-2 |
| 21 | L<br>strides | E | T* | E | E | E | Race or<br>I-1 |
| 22 | L<br>strides | E | Ti* | Mix or<br>E | E | E | Race or<br>Mix |
| 23 | L<br>strides | E | T* | Mix or<br>E | E | E | Race or<br>Mix |
| 24 | L<br>strides | E | Ti* | E | E | E | Race |

(see next page for key)

## Workout Description

| E | Comfortable running with good light turnover and rhythmic breathing. Amount of running is flexible—do enough to reach week's goal. Can be one or two runs or no run if you feel you need complete rest. |
|---|---|
| L | **Weeks 1-6:** Up to 25% of week's total mileage<br>**Weeks 7-12:** Up to 25% of week's mileage or 15 miles (whichever is less), plus some strides in middle or at end of the run<br>**Weeks 13-18:** Up to 25% week's mileage or 2 hr (whichever is less)<br>**Weeks 19-24:** Should diminish in distance to 20% of week's mileage + 4 strides |
| Strides | **Weeks 1-12:** 5-6×20- to 30-second runs at comfortably-fast pace using light quick turnover (do not sprint these)<br>**Weeks I3-18:** 5-6×20 to 30-second runs with 1-minute rests at about mile race pace |
| T* | Steady 20-minute tempo run at **T**-pace, plus 4×200 **R** |
| Ti* | **Weeks 7-12:** Sets of repeated miles at **T**-pace with 1-min rests, up to 8% of week's total mileage or 10 km (whichever is less)<br>**Weeks 13-18:** Repeated runs of 1 mile to 15 minutes each at **T**-pace with 1-minute rests, up to 10% of week's mileage or 8 miles (whichever is less), plus 4 strides<br>**Weeks 19-24:** Repeated 1000s, 1200s, or miles at **T**-pace with 2-minute rests, up to 8% of week's mileage or 10 km (whichever is less) |
| I | Perform either **I-1** or **I-2** + 4-6×200 **R,** up to 6% of week's mileage or 8 km (whichever is less) |
| I-1 | **Weeks 7-12:** Sets of 2 minutes hard + 1 minute easy + 1 minute hard + 30 seconds easy + 30 seconds hard + 30 seconds easy, up to 8% of week's mileage or 10 km (whichever is less)<br>**Weeks I3-18:** Repeated 1000s, 1200s, or miles to suit ability (4-5 minutes per run) with 3- to 4-minute jog recoveries, up to 8% of week's total mileage or 10 km (whichever is less)<br>**Weeks 19-24:** Sets of 2 minutes hard + 1 minute easy + 1 minute hard + 30 seconds easy + 30 seconds hard + 30 seconds easy, up to 6% or 5 km (whichever is less), plus 4×200 **R** |
| I-2 | **Weeks 7-12:** Sets of 4-min hard, 3-min easy up to 8% of week's mileage or 10,000 meters.<br>**Weeks 19-24:** Sets of 3-min hard, 2-min easy up to 6% of week's mileage, plus 4×200 **R**. |

## Workout Description

| R-1 | Sets of 2×200 + 1×400 at **R**-pace, up to 5% of week's mileage (may be hills) |
|-----|-------------------------------------------------------------------------------|
| R-2 | **Weeks 7-12:** Repeat 400s at **R**-pace, up to 5% of week's mileage (may be hills) <br> **Weeks 19-24:** 2 or 3 sets of 1×800 + 1×400 + 2×200, not over 4% of week's mileage |
| Mix | 2-4×1000 to 1-mile **T** + 2×1000-1200 **I** + 4×200 **R,** or 3-4×1000 **T** + 6×200 **R** + 2-mile acceleration: Each 400 should be 5 seconds faster than previous, with final 400 at about 3-km pace |

*Note:* 1) Start with a reasonable amount of running and follow mileage rules when increasing total distance; 2) Days of the week can be arranged in any order. I usually identify Day 1 as Sunday; 3) All **R** workouts are to be done with full recoveries between all runs in the workout.

# Phase III Training

Weeks 13-18, Phase III is the most stressful phase of a medium-distance runner's program. It is possible to increase weekly mileage slightly (every third week), but mileage is not the main stress during this phase. The main emphasis is on long intervals (**I** training). Also, either a few races or additional nonstructured intervals are added on weekends. The other type of quality training that receives a fair bit of emphasis during this Phase III is threshold (**T**) training, both the steady, tempo type and longer sets of cruise intervals (**Ti**). Keep in mind that races that last from 12 to 40 minutes produce most of the same benefits reaped from a good interval session, so occasional races of this duration can replace the late-week interval sessions that are planned for nonrace weeks.

If a demanding race is run on a weekend, then the next week's quality workouts should follow the Tuesday–Wednesday format. Without a weekend race, you could go with Monday and Wednesday quality days the following week. I have indicated a Tuesday–Wednesday format, which is good for school runners who are required to race on a Tuesday or Thursday (often the case during cross-country season). If this is the schedule you are forced to follow, try to count race day as an interval session, and get in the threshold session on a

Running with your team or with a group of friends of the same level of conditioning and ability will make long runs a very enjoyable experience.

nonrace day. You can always run a few two-minute intervals around a cross-country course after the race, if you need additional quality.

Remember, easy (**E**) days can be anything from more than one run on that day to not running at all, if a rest is warranted. The important thing about **E** days is that the intensity of running is comfortable; they are used to maintain the desired weekly mileage totals. Adding a few strides to the middle—or the end—of easy runs is another option that you could explore.

# Phase IV Training

Phase IV—weeks 19-24—is the final phase of the season's program and should be viewed as a high-performance phase. Clearly, the toughest days should be races, not training sessions. The long runs become a little less long and the quality sessions become a little less strenuous. The highly-structured long-interval workouts that were of primary concern during Phase III are dropped completely. However, some less structured intervals are included during weeks when no races are scheduled, and shorter bits of intervals are tacked onto some workouts that feature a variety of training stresses.

As is true of any final phase of training, this is not a time for experimentation; familiar types of training that produce good quality with limited stress are of utmost importance. Total weekly mileage will probably drop somewhat, particularly for those runners who have reached high weekly totals. Usually, runners who have been running more than 50 miles per week will benefit from cutting back by about 20%, but those who have not reached the 50-mile total can usually stay at their current load and do just fine. It is an individual matter; some elite runners can maintain high mileage levels and still produce top performances in races.

During weeks of less important races, it is okay to get in two moderate quality days prior to the race day, but when races are more important one early-week quality day is sufficient. I advise you to allow one easy recovery day for each 3000 meters of distance raced, and this may dictate whether more than one quality day can be included in a week of training. It is also best to allow three or four easy days before a championship race.

When doing two quality days prior to a Saturday race, Tuesday and Wednesday may be best if the previous Saturday was also a race day, but Monday–Wednesday works well if there was no race the previous week. Either Monday-only or Tuesday-only quality days are advisable before a championship race. If dropping one of two quality workouts indicated on the training plan, keep the one that provides the best feelings for you at this time of the season.

# A Final Word

The races that I have dealt with in this chapter are probably the most popular distances for runners beyond their school years. These races last long enough that you can get into a nice pace for the bulk of the race, yet are short enough that the intensity of effort is not particularly enjoyable. That so many runners compete in these races is testimony to the dedication that runners exhibit in their chosen sport. These races definitely cater to the quote I presented at the beginning of this chapter, and usually turn out well if you abide by my quote at the start of chapter 11, which I will restate here in an expanded version: "Run with your head during the first two-thirds of a medium-distance race, with the goal of arriving at that point where you want to be positioned for the finishing drive; race the rest of the way with your heart."

# CHAPTER 14

# Half-Marathon and Marathon Racing

*No one is unbeatable.*

What separates longer distance races from shorter distances is that the bulk of a longer race is performed below the individual's lactate threshold. This means several things.

- The runner is not going to accumulate very much blood lactic acid. Accumulation is limited to brief stages of the race (such as, perhaps, the early and the final minutes of the race), unless the duration of the race has taken its toll on the supply of carbohydrate fuel and has thus reduced the body's ability to produce lactic acid.

- The runner will not normally suffer from local muscular stress, as is often experienced in a 5K or 10K race, for example.

- Ventilation is relatively comfortable throughout the race.

- If heart rate is monitored it will not be at a max value, as it will be in shorter races.

In addition, longer races most certainly place a considerable demand on carbohydrate fuel supply, body temperature mechanisms, and maintenance of adequate body fluids, all of which can affect race performance. Fatigue comes in a more subtle way than in shorter races, and it is sometimes difficult to accept that while racing at relatively comfortable intensities, the urge to slow down can still raise its ugly head.

It is not valid to say that training for all distance races beyond 15K requires the same training schedule, and I would vary my approach based on the specific event in question. It is difficult to prescribe a generalized training program that is designed specifically for the half-marathon, because the elite runners will race this distance in about one hour (the same time that many slower runners take when racing a 10K) and slower runners will spend as much time racing as does an elite runner in completing a full marathon. In fact, I don't plan to present a half-marathon schedule. Instead I propose that elite runners would be well served to basically train for a 10K and be willing to hang in there for an hour in the race. Intervals and threshold training will do an ideal job for preparing for just such a race. In fact, a one-hour race could be considered as the ultimate test of lactate threshold—the intensity that can be maintained for just about one hour.

On the other hand, for runners who are out there racing a half-marathon for a couple hours, many stresses are the same as those faced in a marathon—heat and dehydration, to mention a couple

—and following a marathon schedule may be the best way to go. Just think of yourself as an elite marathoner and prepare accordingly. One- to two-hour runs, threshold runs followed by some one-hour steady efforts, and a solid phase of some intervals will do a good job of preparing you for a two-hour race. As is true for the fastest half-marathoners, the slower runners need to spend time maximizing their lactate threshold, on top of a solid interval background.

A relatively nice thing about the half-marathon is that the amount of work done is within the body's ability to perform primarily on carbohydrates as fuel. The associated danger with this is that the intensity of effort needed for a half-marathon can put you over your lactate threshold, forcing you to unexpectedly drop off your pace. The half-marathon therefore has the potential to be enjoyable or very demanding.

However, the full marathon distance seems to attract the most attention, and for this reason the training plans I present in this chapter are aimed at the marathon distance. Because of the seemingly unlimited number of approaches to preparing for a marathon (and there are many valid approaches, because of the variety of reasons people run marathons), I will provide you with three somewhat different 24-week schedules from which to choose or adapt your own program. I have identified these as Plan A, Plan B, and Plan C. All three will have the same Phase I, which you can stay with for as little or as long a period of time as you feel necessary to bring you up to the demands of your chosen Phase II plan. Then I will present Phases II, III, and IV for Plan A, followed by these three phases for Plan B, and finally for Plan C.

The "A" plan is for people who like a typical marathon approach. It is designed to cater to any amount of mileage because you pick the highest ("peak") mileage that you plan to hit over the course of the program, and determine each week's mileage from there. This plan does not contain a formal repetition phase and includes typical marathon-specific training throughout all three quality phases (II, III, and IV).

Plan B suggests some specific mileage guidelines, which could be adjusted up or down depending on individual backgrounds and commitments. This plan includes some quality longer sessions throughout, but also goes through formal repetition and interval sessions. Plan B is probably the one you would choose if not planning many races during the overall program.

# JOAN BENOIT SAMUELSON

**Joan Benoit Samuelson** was born in Portland, Maine, and began her competitive running career at age 15 while attending high school. She continued to run at Bowdoin College in Maine and also for North Carolina State, which she attended during her junior year. After college, she spent several years running for Athletics West, Nike's elite-athlete club.

I first became associated with Joan when she was working as one of my lab assistants at Nike's Sport Research Lab in Exeter, New Hampshire. She not only helped test other runners, she also served as a subject herself. She has the distinction of recording the highest $VO_2max$ of any female I have ever tested.

Internationally and nationally, Joan is probably best known for winning the first ever Olympic Marathon for women at Los Angeles in 1984. But she had already proven her tenacity, winning numerous top-level marathons and other road races.

When running at her peak, Joan typically ran 80 to 100 miles per week. Her confidence and strength came from running hard over a variety of distances, often on the road. She has held world records for the marathon and half-marathon and currently holds the American marathon record. She was also an NCAA and American champion in the 10,000.

Joan is a tenacious competitor who has the ability to run at the very edge of her ability without being deterred by discomfort. I learned from her that 1) consistency and 2) performance in training can be used to let you know just how fit and fast you currently are, even in the absence of a recent high-quality race performance.

**Joan's Bests**   10,000: 31:43      Half-marathon: 1:08
Marathon: 2:21:21

Plan C also suggests some specific mileage guidelines, which can be adjusted up or down to meet individual desires and needs. The "C" plan also includes formal repetition and interval training , and is nice for runners who want to race other distances during the season, but who intend to run a full marathon at the end of the program. In addition, Plan C requires a final 2-week taper (in addition to what is presented in Phase IV), so allow 20 weeks, not just 18, for the final three phases of a Plan C schedule. I suggest following the final 2-week taper as shown in either Plan A or Plan B.

I realize that for runners who enjoy running marathons for the pure thrill of being part of a long race and the feeling associated with being physically fit, it is possible to set up a training program that is designed strictly to help a runner successfully cover the distance. Such a program can be quite simple in design and may involve nothing more than steady runs of various distances. In fact, that approach combined with picking out a few specific workouts from one of the programs I present in this chapter may add some special challenges. Eventually, however, most runners want to see how much better they can run, and this requires setting up a training program that helps develop a variety of body systems. This means some training similar to that included in a medium-distance program, but with a greater emphasis on threshold runs, marathon-pace runs, and threshold runs combined with steady, long runs.

Training for longer races must emphasize making the best of available fuel sources, development of a strong aerobic profile, the ability to replace diminishing body fluids, and the ability to maintain an optimal body temperature. Also important is the need for a well-planned taper leading up to a long-distance race. A runner doesn't run so many long races as short ones over a year's time, and a mistake in a long race seems to have more far-reaching effects than it would in a shorter race.

# Predicting Performances

It is useful to have a reliable predicting table (table 3.1 is invaluable in this regard) available to you when training for marathons, particularly if it has been a while since you ran one (if indeed you have run one before). By looking up a recent time for a more familiar race distance (10K, for example), you can do a good job of predicting how fast you can expect to run a marathon (or almost any other race

Predicting marathon time based on previous races can give you splits to shoot for throughout the race.

distance, for that matter). Naturally, a performance in a longer race (20K or half-marathon) is a better predictor of marathon ability than is a shorter race, such as a 5K. However, this is not necessarily the case, because you may have performed more 5K races recently, and under a variety of conditions, than longer races. In this case the information provided by your 5K times may be more valid, and a better predictor of current fitness under conditions that are anticipated for the upcoming marathon.

I offer a word of caution about predicting times. When a table equates times, indicating that a 19:57 5K equals a 3:10:49 marathon, for example (see table 3.1), this doesn't necessarily mean that by breaking 20:00 in a 5K you will run a sub-3:11 marathon. What it means is that these two performances are equal, and that with reasonable mileage and marathon training under your belt, you could expect to run a 3:11 marathon if you recently ran a 20:00 5K under conditions and terrain similar to the marathon.

Keep in mind that certain people may never achieve some of the predicted times, no matter how hard they train. Some individuals are physiologically designed to race better over shorter distances, while others are better at longer races. Actually, runners at lower levels of performance—those not aspiring to being Olympians or national champions—probably will have an easier time reaching times predicted over a variety of distances than will the elite competitors, because the elite have found their absolute best event through years of dedicated training and racing experiences.

# Phase I Training for Plans A, B, and C

The first phase of a program geared toward a marathon or other longer-distance race can often last longer than the usually recommended six weeks. This is because some marathoners want to spend a long period of time building up mileage before launching into quality training. If it hasn't been long since serious training was performed, then six weeks is adequate for Phase I, but if moving into marathon training for the first time or if returning to marathon training after a long layoff, you may want to spend as much as two or three months just running and building up mileage to a point where you feel that you have a solid base.

Regardless of the duration of this first phase of training, the emphasis is on getting comfortable with steady, easy running and with some runs of an hour or more. It is also a good idea to add some strides to the program after three or four weeks of steady, easy runs so that moving into quality workouts won't be a great shock to the body. Remember, add mileage to the overall program not more often than every third week. When you do increase mileage, don't add more than 10 miles to the previous weekly total. It is very important when building up to a long-distance race that you progress gradually and thoughtfully; avoiding injury is of great importance. You are usually preparing for a race that is several months down the road, and an interruption for an injury is the last thing you need.

If you manage to get beyond about 50 miles per week, it is a good idea to start running twice a day most days of the week, rather than increasing the single daily runs to longer and longer distances. Twoa-days take more time out of your day, but they are also less stressful. Still, you will eventually get into some regular long (L) runs that will provide as much continuous stress as you will need in any given week. Phase I is set up for two 3-week blocks, but they could just as easily be 4-week blocks or even longer if you have lots of time before the marathon you are shooting for.

Before going into the second, third, and fourth phases of a program set up for racing longer distances, I want to make a couple of clarifying comments. First, I will show all phases of training for Plan A before going on to Plans B and C. The final 2-week period of Phase IV in Plans A and B is a "taper" that should be added to the end of Phase IV in Plan C. Plan C involves 20 weeks of training rather than the 18 weeks shown. Make sure that you plot out your total training season carefully.

Second, if you want to allow more than 18 (or 20) weeks for the last three phases of training, you can extend by a week or more any of the three phases by repeating any of the weeks in the appropriate phase that was particularly appealing to you. I don't recommend repeating two demanding weeks back-to-back.

# Plan A

Following is the 24-week training table and a full explanation of Phases II-IV for Plan A. I recommend reading through every program before choosing the one that suits you best.

## Plan A Phase II Training

It is during Phase II of a long-distance program that you prepare the body for the most strenuous Phase III training that is ahead. This means adding some quality sessions to the previous steady, easy runs that made up the bulk of Phase I training.

Some runners like to include hill running in their marathon build-up, and this is the phase where that fits best. However, you will also notice that formal repetition training is not introduced into the "A" program; strides are the fastest running that you will do. This means that any hill training will have to be accomplished as part of interval sessions or incorporated into some of the longer runs. Or, you could add some short, steep, but slow treadmill hill sessions (say, 10 one-minute runs with one-minute rests) into any week of Phase II or III training, even on an easy (E) day of training. It is useful to include some hill running throughout your training season if the marathon course that you will be running is hilly. Even downhill running can be beneficial if the course you will race over has long downhills on it.

Always be careful to work gradually into downhill training, to avoid imposing too much landing shock on your feet, legs, hips, and back.

## Plan A Phase III Training

As is true with all of my training programs, Phase III is the most demanding. This is because of an increase in mileage, longer threshold workouts, and more demanding marathon-pace (**MP**) workouts and long runs that involve some threshold-pace running (**TLT**).

Many runners have opportunities to run a variety of shorter (medium-distance) races, and fitting these into the training scheme is important. The general rule is to allow three **E** days of running prior to any race, and at least three **E** days following a race before taking on another quality-training session. In addition, I suggest not running more than two races during this 6-week phase.

When you do have a race, you should drop one of the scheduled training sessions for that week. In Plan A, you can do this either by dropping the Day 1 quality session or by dropping the midweek session and replacing it with the Day 1 session that was scheduled at the time of the race. Avoid dropping the **MP** runs, unless a scheduled race is a half-marathon, in which case you can just go through the race at marathon pace, thus accomplishing two things at once. Of course, if the race is an important (all-out) effort, then the training session will just have to be sacrificed.

## Plan A Phase IV Training

Phase IV is the final-quality phase and should be less stressful than the previous phase of training. As you progress through Phase IV you should feel stronger and start looking forward to your upcoming long race. You may begin thinking that you are not training hard enough or that you are starting to get out of shape. This is often the feeling you get when you have been doing demanding workouts at interval pace or demanding mixtures of threshold and long runs. Actually, people following Plan A will be continuing with training similar to the training that they did in the previous phase, but they should be feeling better primarily because they get more accustomed to the type of training they are doing, and mileage is coming down.

## Marathon, Program A

| Week | Day 1 | Day 2 | Day 3 | Day 4 | Day 5 | Day 6 | Day 7 |
|------|-------|-------|-------|-------|-------|-------|-------|
| **1 - 3** | E | E | E | E | E | E | E |
| **4 - 6** | L | E<br>strides | E<br>strides | E | E | E<br>strides | E<br>strides |
| **7**<br>.80P | L | E<br>strides | E | E | I-2 | E<br>strides | E |
| **8**<br>.80P | T-1 | E<br>strides | E | I-2 | E<br>strides | E | E |
| **9**<br>.70P | TL-1 | E | E | E<br>strides | I-1 | E | E<br>strides |
| **10**<br>.90P | L | E<br>strides | E | I-1 | E<br>strides | E | E |
| **11**<br>.90P | TL-2 | E | E<br>strides | I-3 | E | E | L |
| **12**<br>.70P | E<br>strides | T-2 | E | E<br>strides | I-1 | E | E |
| **13**<br>1.00P | L | E<br>strides | E | Ti-1 | E<br>strides | E | E |
| **14**<br>.90P | TLT-1 | E<br>strides | E | E | Ti-2<br>strides | E | E |

Adapted from Daniels, J. August 1996. "One size fits all." *Runner's World* 31(8):54-55.

Marathon, Program A

| Week | Day 1 | Day 2 | Day 3 | Day 4 | Day 5 | Day 6 | Day 7 |
|---|---|---|---|---|---|---|---|
| **15** .80P | MP-1 | E strides | E | E | Ti-3 strides | E | E |
| **16** 1.00P | L | E strides | E | T* | E strides | E | E |
| **17** .90P | TLT-2 | E strides | E | E | Ti-4 strides | E | E |
| **18** .70P | MP | E strides | E | E | Ti-1 strides | E | E |
| **19** 1.00P | L-1 | E | E | E | T-1 | E | E |
| **20** .80P | TLT | E | E | E | T* | E | E |
| **21** .70P | L-1 | E | E | T-2 | E | E | E |
| **22** .70P | MP | E | E | E | Ti-1 | E | E |
| **23** .60P | TL | E-1 | E-2 | E-2 | Ti-2 | E-3 | E-3 |
| **24** | L-2 | E-4 | T-3 | E-4 | E-2 | E-5 | E-5 Race Tomorrow |

(see next page for key)

## Workout Description

| E | Comfortable running with good light turnover and rhythmic breathing. Amount of running is flexible—do enough to reach week's goal. Can be one or two runs or no run if you feel you need complete rest. |
|---|---|
| E-1 | 14% of week's total mileage |
| E-2 | 10-12% of week's total mileage |
| E-3 | 10-15% of week's total mileage |
| E-4 | 16% of week's total mileage |
| E-5 | 20- to 30-minute easy run (may take one day off if travel to race interrupts) |
| L | **Weeks 1-6:** Up to 25% of week's total mileage<br>**Weeks 7-18:** Up to 25% of week's mileage or 2 1/2 hours (whichever is less) |
| L-1 | Lesser of 22 miles or 2 1/2 hours |
| L-2 | Lesser of 15 miles or 2 hours |
| Strides | 5-6×20- to 30-second runs at comfortably-fast pace (do not sprint these) |
| MP | Lesser of 15 miles or 2 hours at **MP** (projected marathon race pace) |
| MP-1 | Lesser of 12 miles or 1 2/3 hours at **MP** |
| T* | **Weeks 13-18:** 20-minute **T**, 10-minute jog, 20-minute **T**<br>**Weeks 19-24:** 1-hour **E**, 6×5- to 6-minute **T**, 15-minute **E** |
| T-1 | **Weeks 7-18:** Steady 20-minute tempo run at current **T**-pace, followed by 5 or 6 strides<br>**Weeks 19-24:** 20-minute **E** and 15-20 minute **T**, all done twice |
| T-2 | **Weeks 7-18:** 6 sets of 5- to 6-minute runs at **T**-pace with 1-minute rests<br>**Weeks 19-24:** 35- to 40-minute **E** and 15- to 20-minute **T** done twice |
| T-3 | 4×4-minute **T** with full recoveries |
| Ti-1 | **Weeks 13-24:** 4×10- to 12-minute **T** with 2-minute recoveries |
| Ti-2 | **Weeks 13-24:** 4×5- to 6-minute **T** with 1-minute recoveries + 5 minutes rest + 3×5- to 6-minute **T** with 1-minute rests<br>**Weeks 19-24:** 3×10- to 12-minute **T** with 2-minute rests |

## Workout Description

| | |
|---|---|
| **Ti-3** | 15- to 20-minute **T** + 3 minutes rest + 15- to 20-minute **T** + 3 minutes rest + 10- to 12-minute **T** |
| **Ti-4** | 8×5- to 6-minute **T** with 30-second rests |
| **TL** | 2×10- to 15-minute **T** + 5-7 miles **E** |
| **TL-1** | 5×5- to 6-minute **T** with 1-minute rests + 1-hour easy run |
| **TL-2** | 2×10- to 12-minute **T** with 2-minute rests + 1-hour easy run |
| **TLT** | 4×5- to 6-minute **T** with 1-minute rests + lesser of 10 miles or 80-minute **E** + 4×5- to 6-minute **T** with 1-minute rests |
| **TLT-1** | 4×5- to 6-minute **T** with 1-minute rests + 1-hour **E** + 15- to 20-minute steady **T**-pace |
| **TLT-2** | 2×10- to 12-minute **T** with 2-minute rests + lesser of 10 miles or 80-minute **E** + 15- to 20-minute **T** |
| **I-1** | Sets of 1000s, 1200s, or miles at **I**-pace with 3- to 5-minute easy runs to recover, up to 8% of week's mileage or 10 km (whichever is less) |
| **I-2** | Sets of 4 minutes hard + 3 minutes easy, up to 8% of week's mileage or 10 km (whichever is less). *Note:* The word "hard" in **I** workouts means about 5 km race pace, not faster |
| **I-3** | Sets of 5 minutes hard + 3-5 minutes easy, up to 8% of week's mileage or 10 km |

*Note:*   1) The P value under each numbered week of training refers to the amount of mileage for that coming week. A peak amount of weekly mileage for the season must first be established. The decimal portion of that peak is then set for the week in question. For example, if 120 miles will be the greatest (peak) mileage for any week this season, then .90P = .90×120 = 108 miles for that week. 2) Start with a reasonable amount of running and follow mileage rules when increasing total distance; 3) Days of the week can be arranged in any order. I usually identify Day 1 as Sunday.

There is still time for one or two competitions during this phase, but choose them carefully. You may want to enter a marathon race and complete only part of it, as you perform one of your **MP** training sessions. If you enter a race that you don't plan to complete, still enter officially and be considerate of the officials and the other runners, who will be going on after you have stopped.

## Marathon, Program B

| Week | Day 1 | Day 2 | Day 3 | Day 4 | Day 5 | Day 6 | Day 7 |
|---|---|---|---|---|---|---|---|
| **1 - 3** | E | E | E | E | E | E | E |
| **4 - 6** | L | E<br>strides | E<br>strides | E | E | E<br>strides | E<br>strides |
| **7**<br>60 mi. | L | E | E<br>strides | R-1 | E | E<br>strides | E<br>strides |
| **8**<br>60 mi. | TLT-1<br>strides | E | E<br>strides | R-2 | E | E<br>strides | Ti-1 |
| **9**<br>70 mi. | L | E | E<br>strides | R-3 | E | E<br>strides | E<br>strides |
| **10**<br>70 mi. | MP | E | E | E<br>strides | R-4 | E<br>strides | E<br>strides |
| **11**<br>70 mi. | TLT-2 | E | E<br>strides | R-5 | E | E<br>strides | Ti-2 |
| **12**<br>80 mi. | L | E | E<br>strides | R-1 | E | E<br>strides | E<br>strides |
| **13**<br>80 mi. | TLT-1 | E<br>strides | E | I-1 | E<br>strides | E | E |
| **14**<br>80 mi. | MP | E | E | E<br>strides | I-2 | E | E<br>strides |

Adapted from Daniels, J. August 1996. "One size fits all." *Runner's World* 31(8):54-55.

| Week | Day 1 | Day 2 | Day 3 | Day 4 | Day 5 | Day 6 | Day 7 |
|------|-------|-------|-------|-------|-------|-------|-------|
| **15**<br>90 mi. | L | E<br>strides | E | I-3 | E<br>strides | E | E |
| **16**<br>80 mi. | TLT-2 | E<br>strides | E | E<br>strides | I-4 | E | E |
| **17**<br>90 mi. | L | E<br>strides | E | I-3 | E<br>strides | E | E |
| **18**<br>80 mi. | MP | E | E | E<br>strides | I-3 | E | E<br>strides |
| **19**<br>80 mi. | TL | E | E | Ti-1 | E | E | E |
| **20**<br>80 mi. | TLT | E | E | E | T-1 | E | E |
| **21**<br>70-80 mi. | L-1 | E | E | Ti-2 | E | E | E |
| **22**<br>60-70 mi. | MP | E | E | E | T-2 | E | E |
| **23**<br>60 mi. | TL | E | E | E | Ti-2 | E | E |
| **24** | L-2 | E-1 | Ti-3 | E-1 | E-2 | E-3 | E-3<br>Race Tomorrow |

(see next page for key)

## Workout Description

| E | Comfortable running with good light turnover and rhythmic breathing. Amount of running is flexible—do enough to reach week's goal. Can be one of two runs or no run if you feel you need complete rest. |
|---|---|
| E-1 | Lesser of 8-mile or 1-hour **E** |
| E-2 | 5-mile **E** |
| E-3 | 2- to 3-mile **E;** may take one day completely off if travel to race takes too much time out of schedule |
| L | **Weeks 1-12:** Up to 25% of week's total mileage or 2 1/2 hours (whichever is less) <br> **Weeks 13-18:** Up to 20 miles or 2 1/2 hours (whichever is less) |
| L-1 | Lesser of 22 miles or 2 1/2 hours at **E**-pace |
| L-2 | Lesser of 15 miles or 1 3/4 hours **E**-pace |
| Strides | 5-6×20- to 30-second runs at comfortably-fast pace using quick, light turnover with 1-minute rests (don't sprint these) |
| MP | **Weeks 7-12:** Lesser of 10 miles or 1 hour at projected marathon race pace (**MP**) <br> **Weeks 13-18:** Lesser of 12-13 miles or 1 1/2 hours <br> **Weeks 19-24:** Lesser of 15 miles or 2 hours at **MP** |
| T-1 | 20-minute **T** + 10-minute **E** + 20-minute **T** |
| T-2 | 20-minute **T** with 5-minute rest + 2×10- to 12-minute **T** with 2-minute rests |
| Ti-1 | **Weeks 7-12:** 6×1-mile **T** with 1-minute rest <br> **Weeks 19-24:** 10×800 to 1000 at **T**-pace with 30-second rests |
| Ti-2 | **Weeks 7-12:** 3×2-miles **T** with 2-minute rests <br> **Weeks 19-24:** 4×10- to 12-minute **T** with 2-minute rests |
| Ti-3 | 4×1000 to 1200 **T** with full recoveries |
| TL | 3×2-mile **T** + lesser of 10 miles or 1 1/2 hours at **E**-pace |
| TLT | 20-minute **T** + 1-hour **E** + 20-minute **T** |
| TLT-1 | **Weeks 7-12:** 4-5×1000 **T** with 1-minute rests + 1-hour **E** + 3×1000 **T** with 1-minute rests <br> **Weeks 13-18:** 2×10-minute **T** with 2-minute rests + 1-hour **E** + 10-minute **T** |

*(continued)*

## Workout Description

| | |
|---|---|
| TLT-2 | **Weeks 7-12:** 2-3×1-mile **T** with 1-minute rests + 1-hour **E** + 2×1-mile with 1-minute rests<br>**Weeks 13-18:** 3-mile **T** + 1-hour **E** + 3×1-mile **T** with 1-minute rests |
| I-1 | 6×1000 to 1200 **I** with 4-minute easy runs for recovery |
| I-2 | 4×1000 to 1-mile **I** with 5-minute easy runs for recovery |
| I-3 | 5×1000 to 1-mile **I** with 5-minute easy runs for recovery |
| I-4 | 7×4-minutes (1000-1200 m) at **I**-pace with 4-minute easy runs for recovery |
| R-1 | 5 to 6 sets of 2×200 + 1×400 at **R**-pace with full recoveries |
| R-2 | 6×400 **R** + 6-10×200 **R** with full recoveries |
| R-3 | 6×200 **R** + 6-8×400 **R** with full recoveries |
| R-4 | 16-20×200 **R** with full recoveries |
| R-5 | 8-10×400 **R** with full recoveries |

***Note:*** Suggested weekly mileages are indicated for each week. Greater (or lesser) amounts could be used according to individual capabilities.

Probably the best approach to adding a race to the schedule is to drop your scheduled **T** workout in favor of the race. This may mean moving a longer Day 1 session to midweek (to replace the dropped **T** session). Always remember to give yourself three easy days prior to any race and three or more days of easy running following a race.

Be attentive to the final two weeks of this Phase IV schedule; if you follow the taper carefully, you should have a satisfying race.

# Plan B

Plan B includes more short-duration quality workouts than Plan A, so choose this plan if few races will be incorporated into your season. You can also choose Plan B if you like the more traditional approach of Plan A but get a psychological boost from including reps and intervals in your program.

## Marathon, Program C

| Week | Day 1 | Day 2 | Day 3 | Day 4 | Day 5 | Day 6 | Day 7 |
|---|---|---|---|---|---|---|---|
| **1 - 3** | E | E | E | E | E | E | E |
| **4 - 6** | L | E strides | E strides | E | E | E strides | E strides |
| **7** <br> 50-60 mi. | L | E strides | E | Ti-1 | E strides | E | R-1 |
| **8** <br> 50-60 mi. | E strides | E | T | E strides | E | R-2 | E strides |
| **9** <br> 50-60 mi. | L | E strides | E | Ti-2 | E strides | E | R-3 |
| **10** <br> 60-65 mi. | E strides | E | Ti-3 | E strides | E | R-1 | E strides |
| **11** <br> 60-65 mi. | L | E strides | E | T | E strides | E | R-4 |
| **12** <br> 60-65 mi. | E strides | E | Ti-4 | E strides | E | R-5 | E strides |
| **13** <br> 60-65 mi | L | E | I-1 | E | E | E strides | T strides |
| **14** <br> 60-65 mi. | E | E strides | I-2 | E | E | Ti-1 strides | E |

Adapted from Daniels, J. August 1996. "One size fits all." *Runner's World* 31(8):54-55.

| Week | Day 1 | Day 2 | Day 3 | Day 4 | Day 5 | Day 6 | Day 7 |
|------|-------|-------|-------|-------|-------|-------|-------|
| **15**<br>60-65 mi. | L | E | I-3 | E<br>strides | E | E | T<br>strides |
| **16**<br>65-70 mi. | E | E<br>strides | I-1 | E | E | Ti-2<br>strides | E |
| **17**<br>65-70 mi. | L | E | I-4 | E<br>strides | E | E<br>strides | Ti-2 |
| **18**<br>65-70 mi. | E | E<br>strides | I-1 | E | E | Ti-3<br>strides | E |
| **19**<br>70 mi. | TLT-1 | E | E | E | Ti-1 | E | E |
| **20**<br>70 mi. | MP-1 | E | E | E | T | E | E |
| **21**<br>70 mi. | TLT-2 | E | E | E | Ti-2 | E | E |
| **22**<br>70 mi. | MP-1 | E | E | E | Ti-3 | E | E |
| **23**<br>65-70 mi. | TLT-3 | E | E | E | T | E | E |
| **24**<br>60 mi. | MP-2 | E | E | E | T* | E | E |

(see next page for key)

## Workout Description

| | |
|---|---|
| **E** | Comfortable running with good light turnover and rhythmic breathing. Amount of running is flexible—do enough to reach week's goal. Can be one or two runs or no run if you feel you need complete rest. |
| **L** | **Weeks 1-13:** Up to 25% of week's mileage or 2 1/2 hours (whichever is less)<br>**Weeks 13-18:** Lesser of 17 miles or 2 1/2 hours easy |
| **Strides** | 5-6×20- to 30-second runs at comfortably-fast pace using quick, light turnover (don't sprint these) |
| **MP-1** | Lesser of 13 miles or 2 hours at projected marathon pace (**MP**) |
| **MP-2** | Lesser of 15 miles or 2 1/2 hours at **MP** |
| **T** | Steady 20-minute tempo run at **T**-pace |
| **T\*** | Steady 20-minute tempo run + 10-minute **E** + 20-minute tempo run. *Note:* After completing program, it is advisable to follow the final 2 weeks of taper shown for the last 2 weeks of either Plan A or Plan B. |
| **T-3** | 6×1-mile **T** with 1-minute rests |
| **Ti-1** | **Weeks 7-12:** 4×1-mile **T** with 1-minute rests<br>**Weeks 13-18:** 4×1-mile **T** with 1-minute rests + 3×1000 **T** with 1-minute rests<br>**Weeks 19-24:** 2×2000 to 2 miles at **T**-pace with 2-minute rests + 3×1-mile **T** with 1-minute rests |
| **Ti-2** | **Weeks 7-12:** 6×1000 **T** with 1-minute rests<br>**Weeks 13-18:** 3×2-mile **T** with 2-minute rests<br>**Weeks 19-24:** 3×2000 to 2 miles **T** with 2-minute rests |
| **Ti-3** | **Weeks 7-12:** 5×1-mile **T** with 1-minute rests<br>**Weeks 13-18:** 6×1-mile **T** with 1-minute rests<br>**Weeks 19-24:** 7×1000 to 1 mile **T**-pace with 1-minute rests |
| **Ti-4** | 8×1000 **T** with 1-minute rests |
| **TLT- 1** | 4×1000 to 1 mile at **T**-pace with 1-minute rests + 1-hour **E** + 2×1000 to 1 mile at **T**-pace with 1-minute rests |
| **TLT-2** | 2×1-mile **T** with 1-minute rests + 1-hour **E** + 2×1-mile **T** with 1-minute rests |
| **TLT-3** | 4×1000 to 1 mile at **T**-pace with 1-minute rests + 1-hour **E** + 4×1000 to 1 mile at **T**-pace with 1-minute rests |
| **I-1** | 6×1000 to 1200 **I** with 4-minute easy runs for recovery |

*(continued)*

## Workout Description

| | |
|---|---|
| I-2 | 4×1200 to 1-mile at I-pace with 5-minute easy runs for recovery |
| I-3 | 8×800 to 1000 I with 3-minute easy runs for recovery |
| I-4 | 5×1200 to 1 mile at I-pace with 5-minute easy runs to recover |
| R-1 | 8-10×400 R with full recoveries |
| R-2 | 4×200 R + 4×400 R + 6×200 R all with full recoveries |
| R-3 | 4×400 R + 10×200 R with full recoveries |
| R-4 | 20×200 R with full recoveries |
| R-5 | 10×200 R + 5×400 R with full recoveries |

**Note:** Suggested weekly mileages are indicated for each week. Greater (or lesser) amounts could be used according to individual capabilities.

# Plan B Phase II training

This program differs from Plan A in that Phase II is a formal repetition phase, which also includes an introduction to **MP** running and **TLT** sessions. It is not easy to include races during this six weeks and still get in the desired components of the program. Of course, **TLT** and **MP** runs can be performed during a long race, but heed a couple of warnings. Don't just hop into a formal race without entering officially and wearing your assigned number (officials and other runners do not appreciate this). Also, make sure that you carry out the assigned workout; don't let yourself get carried away by racing; remember the purpose of the training session.

# Plan B Phase III Training

This phase of Plan B is the most demanding, because it gets into a weekly session of interval training, and mileage increases. Phase III is a good time to start two-a-days if you can afford the time, because they reduce the overall stress that your body is subjected to during single, longer sessions.

Phase III of Plan B is the best one in which to include some medium-distance races. I have indicated that racing 5K, 10K, and similar distances provides similar benefits as those reaped from interval training. Well, this is an opportunity to replace an interval session with a good medium-distance race. To make this possible, you can drop the **I** session from race week and juggle the days of training so that you can fit in the Day 1 session on a different day. Make every effort to keep the **TLT** and **MP** sessions, even if they become part of a race.

## Plan B Phase IV Training

You will undoubtedly enter this phase of training looking forward to some reduction in stress, and that is exactly what you will get. There are still some demanding Day 1 sessions, but the other quality session each week is of **T**-intensity and should leave you feeling better and better as the weeks go by. Be advised that a feeling of greater strength is not a sign to try setting records in workout sessions. Accept any improvements in how you feel as a sign that the training you have been doing is starting to pay off. Be very selective in racing during this phase; it is not a time to let your enthusiasm be dampened by racing over a tough course or in rough weather conditions where your chances of a poor performance increase. A race in the 10K to 20K range can be good (at least 3 weeks prior to the "big" race), and if you do race, it's probably best to drop that week's scheduled **T** session and juggle the other quality day around to where it fits in best.

# Plan C

If you are planning on running races of varying distances throughout the season but will end the program with a marathon, then Plan C is for you. This is a nice plan to follow if you want to get into some consistent training, probably run some races and watch yourself steadily progress in how comfortable you can feel as a runner. Please be sure to do the two-week taper period to let your body adjust to the change in race intensity.

## Plan C Phase II Training

Plan C differs from the other two training plans I have outlined for marathon preparation in that it could easily pass for a medium-distance program during Phase II, in which **R** and **T** sessions are part of each week, with **L** runs added every other week. Mileage is not

Doing a two-week taper at the end of your training program will bring you up to your race day fresh and ready to perform at your peak.

high, but can be adjusted for those who want more. The **R** sessions introduce relatively low-stress quality (although some or all of the **R** sessions could be hill workouts of equal duration), but set you up for the more demanding Phase III training ahead. A race of 5K or less could be run in place of an **R** session; drop a **T** workout for any race longer than 5K and run the race as a threshold effort.

## Plan C Phase III Training

It is important to get in all the **L** runs scheduled for this phase because they are your main link to the demands of the upcoming marathon race. However, the most demanding part of Phase III is the **I** sessions. A positive way of approaching 6 weeks of interval training is to imagine the improvements in work capacity (aerobic power) that you are achieving with each **I** session.

For some runners, the best part of interval training is getting to the end of a phase of it; if it works, then use that approach yourself. Of course, you can replace one of these demanding **I** sessions with a solid 5K or 10K race, but don't start racing every week just to eliminate interval training from the program. A couple of races (in place of an **I** session, with other quality workouts rescheduled to fit) is a good approach to this phase of training.

# Plan C Phase IV Training

Phase IV of Plan C is a 6-week phase that must be followed by a 2-week taper phase before running your goal race for the season. If you cannot heed my earlier warning relative to the need for an additional two weeks of taper training, then, by all means, drop the final two weeks of this schedule and go directly to the two-week taper outlined in Phase IV of Plans A and B.

It would be a good idea, particularly for first-time marathoners, to enter a half-marathon or marathon race when you are scheduled for an **MP** workout. This will give you a feeling for running amongst a big group of people, will help you realize that there are many runners who are no better than you, and will usually make the planned workout go more easily. It is also a good opportunity to practice drinking in a race situation. Make sure you officially enter any races you participate in and treat them seriously, even if only to try out some things for experience.

# A Final Word

Resist the urge to race too early in a long event, such as a marathon. Allow your competitive spirit to surface only after you have fully evaluated the competition, the conditions of the course, the weather, and, most of all, your body's readiness to compete.

Marathon runners may have a greater justification for dropping out of a race, compared to runners of shorter distances, because the demands of continuing a fruitless race can result in a long recovery time before another race can be run. There are usually only a few reasons to finish a marathon: to finish a distance never before attempted, to qualify for a team or championship, to win a prize or money, to set a new personal best time, and to keep alive a string of race completions.

If you are at the 18-mile mark of a marathon race and you are not in a position to win anything or to qualify for anything, you have done this event before, and your time at this point in the race is well behind what you had planned to do, it seems counterproductive to go on, unless it is a matter of pride associated with never quitting a race, or unless your ride home isn't expecting to meet you for another hour or so. It is not particularly easy to recover from a marathon (although not as difficult as some would make you believe, either), and if things are going poorly and if you plan to run other marathons in the near future, then it's best to "let discretion be the better part of valor." Naturally, continuing a race with a bad pain somewhere in your body, when overheated, or when dehydrated is never a good idea.

By committing yourself to a well-designed training plan, and with proper nutrition and rest, you will be amazed at how enjoyable (at least, rewarding) a marathon, or similar long-distance race, can be. In fact, running, just for the fun of it, is a great activity. I hope that running gives you the enjoyment and satisfaction in life that it has given me.

# Index